More praise for *Best Friends, Worst Enemies*

"Fascinating . . . parents will treasure this book. . . . The authors present touching, sometimes tragic, anecdotes on everything from the typical childhood cruelties of bullies, teasing, and clique formation to the tight bonds of true friendship."

—*Booklist*

"Thompson's unique and deep understanding of why friendship is a crucial aspect of healthy development makes this groundbreaking book a 'best friend' and 'must-read' for every parent, teacher and counselor."

—ROBIE H. HARRIS
Author of *It's Perfectly Normal*

"This book is a gem, and we badly need a gem of a book on this topic. Now, at last, we have a book that brings parents, teachers, and all of us who are concerned about children the knowledge we need on this both heart-wrenching and confusing topic. Warmly written, this book draws upon extensive research, but presents its findings simply and directly. The book is both practical and moving, both research-based and filled with stories, both up-to-date and rooted in old-fashioned wisdom, both informative and exciting. This is an enormously helpful book, which you will really enjoy reading!"

—EDWARD M. HALLOWELL, M.D.
Author of *Driven to Distraction*, *Connect*, and *Human Moments*

Please turn the page for more reviews. . . .

Best Friends, Worst Enemies

UNDERSTANDING THE SOCIAL LIVES OF CHILDREN

Michael Thompson, Ph.D.
and
Catherine O'Neill Grace
with Lawrence J. Cohen, Ph.D.

BALLANTINE BOOKS
NEW YORK

A Ballantine Book
Published by The Random House Publishing Group

Published in the United States by Ballantine Books,
an imprint of The Random House Publishing Group, a division
of Random House, Inc., New York, and simultaneously in Canada
by Random House of Canada Limited, Toronto.

The names of many of the children in this book have been changed to protect their privacy. The real names of some children have been used with their families' permission.

www.ballantinebooks.com

Library of Congress Control Number: 2002091643

ISBN 0-345-44289-X

Front cover photo © John Bildbura/Photonica
Back cover photo © Ed Bock/The Stock Market

Manufactured in the United States of America

First Hardcover Edition: September 2001

First Trade Paperback Edition: August 2002

9

For my children, Joanna and Will, and their wonderful friends.
—Michael

For my husband, Don Grace, and for irreplaceable women friends.
You know who you are!
—Catherine

For my wife, Anne Fabiny, our daughter, Emma,
and my first friend, Dave.
—Larry

Contents

Preface

Some years ago, when my children were twelve and eight years old, our family returned from a two-week vacation—a good and fun trip. We had barely made it through the kitchen door before my son, Will, headed for the phone to call his friend Mitchell and my daughter, Joanna, disappeared into my wife's home office to grab the other phone line so that she could call her friend Miranda. I remember that Theresa and I looked at each other and one of us said, "Well, the *family* vacation is over." Our children were desperate to be in touch with their friends.

This is a book about the importance of children's social lives, the inevitable tendency of kids to torment and reject their peers, and the redemptive power of friendship. Every teacher and every parent watches children's relationships played out in front of them every day. We see the isolated child standing off to the side; we hear our own children gossip viciously in the car; we see how much our children miss their friends. We are able to call up memories, both joyful and excruciatingly painful, from our own childhood relationships. But our memories are not always a good guide to what we should be doing for our own children. Indeed, our social scars from middle school often lead us to worry when we shouldn't, hesitate when we should intervene, and fixate on our children's painful reports when they are, in fact, growing, coping, and adapting in the best possible way.

Very few grown-ups fully understand what is actually going on when children hurt one another's feelings, when they tease and betray each other. Are kids just "mean"? Why is it so hard to stop children from excluding one another? Why is it so hard for some children to make friends? What makes other kids so popular? Why is it that some children thrive with a friend or two and don't seem to care about popularity, while for others it is a matter of life and death?

I hope that by the time you finish this book, you will have the answers to these and many other perplexing questions. Developmental and clinical psychologists have researched the social lives of children in depth. There is an important body of scientific literature on the subject that has never, to my knowledge, been made available to the public in a comprehensive, reader-friendly form. I have been baffled that there have been no good popular books written about the complexities of children's friendships, social groups, and social cruelty. In addition, I think that the media's focus on the bully and bullying has oversimplified the issue and confused the public. The classic bully scenario is only a tiny part of what goes on among children. Similarly, the media's attention to "cool" kids does not illuminate what goes on with most children.

Best Friends, Worst Enemies is my attempt to take you inside the complex social worlds of children that researchers such as Willard Hartup, John Coie, and Kenneth Dodge have studied. On this journey, my clinical knowledge and my classroom observations—as well as my experiences as a parent—will guide you into the lives of children. The map I will employ to prevent us from getting lost in these complicated interactions has been drawn from the work of distinguished social scientists. We will travel the superhighways of popularity and the back roads of intimate friendship. We will begin at my daughter's birthday party, seeing the tensions among twelve-year-old girls from the point of view of a parent. We will then go out into day care centers and schools and observe children leaving their mothers, playing with their toddler buddies, trying to find friends, and loving one another with great loyalty. We will talk to members of cliques in middle school and end up in high schools, where classmates haze one another cruelly—and forge lifelong, intimate friendships. I trust that *Best Friends, Worst Enemies* will illuminate the sometimes invisible forces that drive children's groups.

Best Friends, Worst Enemies also aims to provide teachers and parents with practical strategies for dealing with difficult social conflicts among kids. The last two chapters of the book will offer educators and parents concrete suggestions for creating more harmonious school environments and for supporting children's friendships at home and in the neighborhood. If you are a teacher, you should be able to read this book and know if you have an unusually cruel or dangerous situation in your classroom or if a rejected child needs a serious intervention. If you are a parent, you should be able to finish this book and know the answer to the question that most parents ask every day: "Is my child okay?" This book should tell you whether your child is doing okay socially or whether he or she is at risk and needs additional support.

Before we embark on this journey, there are a couple of introductions I need to make. First, I need to explain the point of view of this book. It is written through my eyes and experience as a child psychologist, school consultant, *and* parent. I couldn't keep the parent part of myself out of this book; I'll tell you why below. Second, I need to explain why this book doesn't emerge primarily from my work with children in therapy, as did my earlier books on the psychology of boys.

Third, I need to introduce the "we" behind the "I" voice that is used throughout the book, because *Best Friends, Worst Enemies* is the result of a collaborative effort of three people. We have chosen to write in the "I" voice, through the lens of my training and experience, because it is clearer for the reader. But my two collaborators, Catherine O'Neill Grace and Lawrence J. Cohen, have been instrumental at every stage in the creation of this book. All three of us possess extensive but very different experience with students in classrooms and with our own children. Finally, I want to introduce you to some of the children who will appear and reappear through *Best Friends, Worst Enemies* because they have been our best teachers.

Child Psychologist, Consultant, and Parent

This book is written, as I said, from the point of view of my three identities—child psychologist, school consultant, and parent. I was trained to be a child psychologist, to do play therapy with small children and talk therapy with older kids and adults. I also was trained to conduct family meetings with children and parents together—and that's what I have done very happily for more than two decades. Over the past ten years, however, I have moved steadily out of the quiet and relative safety of my office into the rough-and-tumble world of psychological consultation in schools. The halls and classrooms of school buildings have provided an opportunity to see children at work—struggling to develop skills, meeting adult demands, avoiding some schoolwork, loving their friends, hating their enemies, and ultimately trying to feel good about themselves.

There are many wonderful moments in a school day, but schools are not sweet places. Any given school day can be ferociously painful for a child, as intense an emotional experience as anything one hears described in a therapist's office. Over the years, my work in schools evolved and I began to conduct workshops for teachers to help them understand the psychological forces swirling around them, which they cannot often stop to ponder during the fast-paced school year. I became a teacher of teachers. And then, as schools began to take more responsibility for educating parents, I was increasingly asked to address issues that concern them as well. Since 1990 I have run workshops for parents and teachers on twenty-two topics, including childhood depression, eating disorders, parent-teacher communication, and the emotional lives of boys. I am perhaps best known for my work on the psychology of boys, contained in two books: *Raising Cain: Protecting the Emotional Life of Boys*, which I coauthored with Dan Kindlon, Ph.D., and *Speaking of Boys: Answers to the Most Asked Questions About Raising Sons*. But I have also had an abiding interest in friendship, popularity, and social cruelty in children's lives and have conducted parent-teacher workshops on these issues for years. In fact, issues about children's friendships are closest to my heart. Parents have shown me that these are the issues in children's lives that they least understand. No speech that I give draws a bigger audience. No topic produces such agonized questions from both parents and teachers. No problem baffles veteran teachers in the way that a poisonous class dynamic does. And no teacher suffers more visibly than one who must witness the daily humiliation of a rejected child and not know how to stop it.

It would have been impossible for me to write this book *just* from the point of view of a psychologist or *just* from the point of view of a parent. Those two experiences have absolutely complemented one another. As a psychologist, I have seen rejected children in therapy and have worked with school administrators to try to help them. As a parent, I have watched my children make friends, lose friends, say dumb things, and miss social cues that were obvious to me. I have also seen my own kids discover solutions to social problems that never would have occurred to me.

Social Cruelty Is Out in the Open

Best Friends, Worst Enemies describes the ongoing drama of psychological pain and creativity in childhood. Some of the stories in this book are tragic; a couple of them end with the death of a child. Despite these tragedies, this book is not about mental illness nor, for the most part, is it about children who need to be in therapy. Arguably, more children should receive psychotherapy for social problems. Rejected children do suffer terribly. Certainly, helping excluded children is a major part of what guidance counselors do in elementary schools. However, the loneliness that children feel is not typically a complaint that brings children into a psychologist's private office.

Why not? Because there is a certain amount of social cruelty that we all live through without needing help. A woman was telling me that her daughter suffered some stinging experiences in school that she cannot forget. "She's thirty," said the mother, "and she still talks about them." The daughter was hurt. Those stings shaped her life, and yet she did not necessarily need treatment for what happened to her. The ongoing paradox is that some children experience intense pain and grow from it, while other kids are crushed by their peers.

For me the interesting thing about children's social lives is that the psychotherapy office doesn't offer the best vantage point from which to view the action. Unlike the hidden traumas of childhood, such as incest or physical abuse, when peers are tormenting a child the torture most often takes place out in the open, where almost everyone can see. The social phenomena that I describe in *Best Friends, Worst Enemies* are right under everyone's nose. Let us say, for example, that a girl has been devastated by the teasing she experiences at a middle school dance. The comments made by boys were hideously painful for her, and everyone witnessed her humiliation. Her classmates overheard the remark "ugly dog," and though the adult chaperones couldn't hear the comments, they understood the nature of the drama. What happens the day after the dance? The victim of that teasing will want to forget the incident as quickly as possible. She is highly unlikely to seek counseling for what happened to her. She might never make it to a counselor's office, though she cries herself to sleep for three nights and carries an enduring sense of shame for the rest of her seventh grade year.

This one example illustrates how my profession does not give me a special window on the social realms in which children live. To write this book I had to rely on a wide variety of my professional and life experiences, not on my work with children in therapy.

The *Best Friends, Worst Enemies* Team

I knew that I could not write this book alone. First, I wanted the help of a woman, because my experience and the research suggest that the texture of girls' friendships is different from that of boys' friendships. In this area my gender was a limiting factor—and the fact that I am the father of a daughter could broaden my experience only to a certain extent. I turned to Catherine O'Neill Grace for help. Catherine had been my editor at *Independent School* magazine for many years.

Catherine grew up in a Foreign Service family, so she and her parents and older brother bounced around the world a good deal as she was growing up. This meant befriending and then saying good-bye to a series of friends during her elementary school years. "The advantage of a childhood like that is that you learn to meet new situations with confidence and interest," Catherine says. "But underneath there's a lot of anxiety. You walk into a new school wondering, 'Do I know the social rules? Are my clothes okay? Will they think I'm cool?' I used to study the social customs of my peers like an anthropologist deep in the Amazon."

Throughout this book, even though it is written in the "I" voice, you will benefit from Catherine's personal experiences, her intuition about children, and her years as a middle school and high school English teacher. Though she isn't teaching teenagers at present, she lives among them on the campus of Chapel Hill-Chauncy Hall, a day and boarding school in Waltham, Massachusetts, where her husband, Don, is head of school.

My other coauthor, Lawrence J. Cohen, is a psychologist and the author of a magical book about the play between children and their parents entitled *Playful Parenting*. Larry is a gifted therapist and writer in his own right and has helped enormously with the research for this book.

Of the three of us, Larry is the shyest. When he was in high school in New Orleans, he was accepted, but he always felt like an outsider.

"Watching movies and reading novels, you get the idea that they are all written by outsiders getting revenge on the popular kids. But you don't have to be rejected to feel like an outsider," says Larry. "I was accepted, but like most people I had experiences that made me feel like an outsider. I was also shy. It was drama club that allowed me to be more visible. The breakthrough for my shyness was *Arsenic and Old Lace*, when I played Dr. Einstein, and later when I appeared in an Elaine May play called *Adaptation*. The nonjudgmental camaraderie of the drama kids was important to me."

For the record, and because I have revealed something about Catherine and Larry's social struggles, I must confess that I was often physically timid and frightened in middle school. When it came to team sports, it was difficult for me to be in the popular group. I have vivid memories of the seventh grade athletes, some of them my friends, who seemed to me to have a lock on cool, because they played baseball well. I hated the sports hierarchy and envied the physical ease of other guys. In contrast to them, I was a constant—and almost certainly annoying—talker. I was always trying to please, always trying to entertain, always feeling that I was just outside the inner circle.

Children Were Our Best Teachers

Over the course of two years Larry, Catherine, and I interviewed more than eighty children, teenagers, parents, and teachers. We gathered material not only from these formal interviews but also from my school consultation work, Larry's clinical work and his work on committees at his daughter's elementary school, and Catherine's experiences as a classroom teacher and member of a boarding-school community. I ran workshops on the subject of classroom cruelty with hundred of teachers and conducted assemblies with several thousand middle school students, inviting questions, discussion, and stories from participants at each event.

We relied on our families as well. Larry's daughter, Emma, age ten, and my two children, Will, ten, and Joanna, sixteen, conducted an unplanned course in the vicissitudes of friendship for us. Each day they lived out social pleasures and group tensions, and we watched intently. I hope we weren't too intrusive; we certainly learned a lot from them. At times Joanna would appear briefly at our meetings held in my house and would answer questions from us. All three of our kids have read portions of this manuscript and have given us permission to use their stories. We have disguised the names of some of their friends and identified others who have also given us permission to use their real first names.

Catherine's goddaughter, Alex, who is nineteen, and her niece, Maeve, twenty, were a unique source of perspective. They were enormously helpful in providing us with stories about their own friendships growing up. Beyond that, they had the psychological maturity to share observations about their history with their parents and how that played out in their social development. Catherine also had a rich source of anecdotes from the students at Chapel Hill–Chauncy Hall and from her essay-writing class at the Middlesex School. We have used these students' stories and writings. I was privileged to read the essays on friendship written for Mr. Zamore's senior writing class at Belmont Hill School, where I am the consulting psychologist.

Without the first-person testimony of many children, *Best Friends, Worst Enemies* would be as dry as the proverbial dust. If we have done our job, it will be the stories of children that make this book a memorable journey for the reader. We hope you will see children discovering their capacity for love, suffering from arbitrary and painful rejection by their peers, and developing their social creativity. The richness of children's friendship is the source of inspiration for this book. The pain of rejected children gives *Best Friends, Worst Enemies* its sense of mission. We hope the reader will leave us with new insights about the misery and the magic of childhood social relationships.

Acknowledgments

We would like to thank the many children and adults who shared their stories of friendship and social cruelty with us. There would be no book without their generosity. We talked with children from all over the country, but we are particularly grateful to the students from the Lincoln School, the Wayland Middle School, Chapel Hill-Chauncy Hall, Middlesex School, Belmont Hill School, Polytechnic School, Campbell Hall School, the Hill School, and Capitol Hill Day School.

Gail Ross, the coolest agent in the business, brought *Best Friends, Worst Enemies* to Ballantine, where we had the good fortune to have three gifted editors. Ginny Faber believed in the book when it was just an idea, Joanne Wyckoff edited thoughtfully and with a deft hand, and Nancy Miller coached it to the finish line. We want to thank Gina Centrello, publisher, as well as Kim Hovey, Gilly Hailparn, and the entire Ballantine team. Their enthusiasm for *Best Friends, Worst Enemies* has energized us.

Only the "in-crowd" got to read early drafts of the book. We appreciate the time and thoughtfulness of Christopher Leach, Sue Khodarahmi, Ann Northrup, Michelle Anthony, and Gillian McNamee. Writers need friends who support their work. We are grateful to Michael Brosnan, Wendy Fox, Josh Horowitz, Ned Hallowell, and Bonnie Bryant Hiller.

Elizabeth Diggins kept us organized and provided indispensable help with the manuscript. Our families were our readers, consultants, cheerleaders and best friends.

Best Friends, Worst Enemies

Chapter One

An Invitation to a Birthday Party

My daughter's twelfth-birthday party was a nightmare, a social train wreck. It was, of course, a sleepover. I still have the photos of the group at breakfast, seated around the dining room table: sluggish, cranky, ready to go home. And I was ready for them to go. There had been moments during the party the night before when I wanted to send them all packing instantly. "Get out," I wanted to shout. "You're all mean! You're all horrible."

My daughter, Joanna, now sixteen, has long since forgotten that party. It's ancient history to her; she has moved on with her life. When I reminded her recently of the events of that night, she gave a shrug of acknowledgment and went back to what she was doing. I can't forget it that easily.

Let me set the scene—time, place, and characters—for the drama. Joanna's birthday is in late June. That's a good month for birthdays, close enough to the end of the school year so that most of the kids you might want to invite are still around town. At the same time, late-June birthdays don't conflict with the inevitable round of end-of-school events. Best of all, the weather is usually good, which means we can hold a swimming party in our backyard, which borders a lake. When Joanna was nine or ten years old all we needed to throw a successful birthday party were some water balloons, a dock for kids to jump off, and of course cake and ice cream. But parties for twelve-year-olds are a lot more complicated than swimming and cake.

My wife, Theresa, and I had a sense of foreboding about the party when we saw Joanna's guest list. That year our daughter was leaving her public school to go to a private school that offered extensive support for her reading difficulties. Her departure made it inevitable that she was going to lose some friends. Her final social gesture as she left her public school was to invite the entire cool group from her class to her birthday party.

One girl who came to the party was Maria. Maria, like Joanna, was a little different from the mainstream of the class. Her mother was Irish Catholic, her father Korean. They represented an unusual diversity in the town. Maria wasn't absolutely at the center of the cool group either, but she was eager to be, and we had sensed in the past that Maria felt competitive with Joanna. Therein lies the tale of the birthday party.

Twelve girls arrived over about a forty-minute span: Maria and ten other schoolmates, joined by Joanna's lifelong friend, Erin-Claire. Erin-Claire is the daughter of dear friends. She has never gone to school with Joanna, but they have known each other since infancy and share a great loyalty. It would be unthinkable for Joanna to have a birthday party without Erin-Claire, and vice versa. E.C., as she is known, occupies a special category in Joanna's life, that of absolutely trustworthy friend.

Almost as soon as the girls arrived, the political machinations started. There was the usual discomfort and stiffness that afflicts most parties—child and adult—at the start. But there was more than just ice-breaking discomfort here. An invisible divider was up.

The wall crystallized when the girls were shown two adjoining rooms, Joanna's bedroom and the guest room. Maria immediately began to designate which girls should sleep in which room. Naturally, she picked the four coolest girls and said that they would be with her in the guest room. The girls obediently dropped their sleeping bags and backpacks where Maria told them to.

While Maria was upstairs orchestrating the sleeping arrangements, Joanna was downstairs trying to organize some games. The party was slowly beginning to warm up. Girls were swimming, jumping off the dock, and talking. The water balloons were clearly not going to fly. Twelve-year-olds considered themselves too old for those, it seemed, even though Joanna had wanted them. To her it was a tradition. I worried that my daughter's tastes weren't sufficiently sophisticated for this twelve-year-old crowd.

Then word filtered downstairs about Maria's management of the sleeping arrangements. Joanna immediately felt hurt. She began to feel attacked and aggrieved. She physically moved away from the rest of the group. E.C. sat with her. The rest of the girls were uncomfortable. Clearly no one knew how to take the lead in either stopping Maria or reaching out to Joanna. The in-group, including Maria, who had come outside, gathered together more tightly. Joanna and E.C. became a separate group of two. Joanna cried a bit, displayed some anger, and talked with E.C. She was clearly very sad, and E.C. was being a steadfast friend to her.

This went on for about half an hour or more, but it seemed much longer. I watched the scene with intense dismay and a sense of helplessness. I had heard what Maria was doing, but I hadn't known how to intervene when I was upstairs. I saw that Maria, for some unhappy reason, felt compelled to take over the sleeping arrangements.

What happened next was quite wonderful. Joanna had insisted that we buy cans of shaving cream when we shopped for the water balloons. She had seen some boys squirting shaving cream all over one another during a celebration in our town and she had been entranced with their freedom—as well as a bit disappointed that girls apparently weren't allowed to do that sort of thing in public. For her birthday she had wanted the possibility of shaving cream attacks.

Joanna and E.C. began to squirt shaving cream at one another. They started small, working their way up until they were covered from head to toe, hair included. All the other girls, who were hanging out by the edge of the lake, turned to watch and soon signaled that they too wanted to join the action. Joanna and E.C. each picked up a can of shaving cream and began squirting the other girls. I grabbed the camera and snapped pictures. It turned into a free-for-all—and the party was suddenly working. The best thing about it was that all the girls started to seem like girls again, carefree and innocent. Gone, for the moment, was the poisonous political atmosphere. There were only laughing girls covered with shaving cream, creating wild masks and hairdos with the foam all over their heads.

The party proceeded cheerfully for three more hours. The meat-eaters ate hot dogs and hamburgers; the vegetarians ate salad and chips. Things seemed so peaceful that I was unprepared when I heard shouting and weeping coming from the front stairwell. I ran in, and there stood Maria, angry, defiant, and shrieking denials at Joanna: "I didn't do anything. It's your problem!" And then Maria burst into a fury of tears.

Apparently, because of her social success with the shaving cream as well as the steadfast support of her friend E.C., Joanna had recovered enough confidence to confront Maria and accuse her of trying to wreck her birthday party.

Theresa took Maria aside to talk with her, and out poured a story of social misery. Maria felt genuinely overwhelmed by Joanna's accusation and proclaimed herself innocent of any malicious intent. She hadn't done anything, she sobbed; she had just wanted to be sure that she had friends to sleep next to at the sleepover. Maybe nobody liked her, maybe she ought to go home right then.

In my mind Maria had been a power-hungry villain who tried to take over the party from a less socially powerful and more vulnerable Joanna. But it turned out that the "villain" was just another insecure middle schooler. Her "victim," meanwhile, had made a powerful stand of open confrontation.

As Theresa talked to Maria I talked with Joanna, who was accompanied by E.C. (They were inseparable at this point.) Joanna was totally charged up with anger at Maria and even more furious because Maria's outburst had seemed so manipulative. Joanna wanted a full confession and retraction from Maria.

There was no resolution. Despite our intervention—and we went as far as having them face one another and say they were sorry—Maria and Joanna sulked and avoided each other the rest of the night. The party ground on unhappily with videos, many more chips, and finally the mandatory very late bedtime. The next morning everyone was exhausted and very relieved to be going home. I don't think that we were the first parents on earth to watch the departing backs of children leaving a birthday party and think, "Thank God we don't have to do this again until next year."

Was it so uniquely horrible? Was my daughter damaged? The answer to these questions is no. I took you home with me to this terrible birthday party because this one event allows us to see all of the strands in a child's social world, the subject of this book. It's all there: devoted friendships, battles over popularity, parental anguish over social cruelty. These are the themes that we will be returning to again and again in this book. The social lives of children are a complex interplay of the group and the individual, of cliques and status hierarchies, of the sustaining loyalty of a friend to a friend. And the birthday party offers a particularly vivid lesson in the difference between social popularity and true friendship.

All parents experience pain about their children's social lives. There is no escaping it. A mother agonizes over her child's social dilemmas. A father immediately assesses whether his son or daughter is well received by a group of children. (And he's likely to register where his son ranks athletically compared to other boys.) We are social animals, and all of us are able to read the social reactions and strengths of others. Parents beam with pleasure at their child's successes and writhe with anguish over their failures.

Being a parent means feeling helpless a lot of the time: helpless to give your child the reading skills he wasn't born to have, helpless to make him the soccer player he would like to be but never will be, helpless to give him a wonderful classroom teacher every year. The list of things that parents cannot do is almost infinite. As a parent, I am intimately acquainted with the knowledge that I cannot bend the universe on behalf of my children, much as I might want to.

As both a parent and a psychologist, I believe that there is no area in which a parent feels more powerless to make a significant difference than in relation to a child's social life. It's as if our children are stuck in an endless awful birthday party and we're watching helplessly from behind a one-way mirror. That "birthday party" might be the toddlers at play in the day care center, Little League, or a random group of children in the neighborhood. Wherever children gather, a complex group dynamic begins to pick up strength. It may turn into a storm or not, but it has power in a child's life. When a child gets home and says, "He hit me" or "She was mean to me" or "She started a club and didn't include me," our most ferocious parental instincts are aroused (I call them "mother grizzly bear feelings"). And yet there is no one to attack.

If another child unexpectedly hits and hurts your child, you want to hit that child back, but you must not. If other children ignore your child, you want to scream, but you probably will not. If your child lacks the ability to negotiate the complex social currents of the group of which she is a part, you want to hand her the skills to do it, but you cannot. We cannot step in and fix it because children have to learn to do that for themselves.

Children fear adult attempts to fix their social lives. When I asked a seventh grade class in New York, "What role should your parents have in your social lives?" one boy said succinctly, "Your parents should have *no* role in your social life." Kids fear that our interventions will make things worse; they don't trust us to catch the subtleties of their interactions. They have a point. The things we try to do often backfire, making things worse for our child. The things we *can* do—listen sympathetically, stay confident, provide opportunities for our children to connect with others, and remember the power of our own early attachment to and love for our child—feel inadequate. But they are not.

Even remembering this, watching our children suffer socially is very hard to bear. And it does make sense to be concerned or even worried. Research on friendship has found over and over how important peers are to children. Of course, as parents, we already knew this intuitively. And as grown-up children ourselves, we know it from experience. Children need friendship. They need a minimum level of acceptance by the group. They don't need a dozen close friends or one incredibly close friend, and they don't need to be the most popular kid in the class. But they need good-enough peer relationships. Without some friendships, children are psychologically at risk.

You have to live with your helplessness as you watch your child negotiate social terrain, knowing the stakes are high. Sometimes that sense of helplessness arises from misunderstanding the nature of child development, of not knowing what is supposed to happen or not trusting in a child's ability to grow. A physician from Nashville called me four times in one week. He had heard me give a lecture on the social world of children and wanted to talk to me and get a referral for a psychologist in his area "who thought like me." When I finally made contact with him I asked what he was so worried about. He said his daughter had no friends at school. I said I was sorry to hear that. Did she have any friends at all? He told me she had a wonderful friend in the neighborhood and they hung out together all the time. I said I was relieved to hear that. Then I asked, "How old is your daughter?"

"Six," he answered.

I hope you will agree that this father's anxiety was excessive. I reassured him that his daughter didn't need to have mastered all her social skills and have all her friendships locked into place by kindergarten. Development, I told him, would bring greater social ability and more friends in school.

By contrast, a mother from New York posed a painful question following a speech I delivered on the subject of friendship and social cruelty. "How," she asked, "do you help a seriously learning disabled child make friends? My son has severe attention deficit hyperactivity disorder, he gets angry very suddenly, and it is hard for him to keep friends." She looked at me with eyes that were both pained and hopeful. The people in the audience held their collective breath, aware that it might be some of their children who were turning away from this mother's child. I hesitated to answer the question because I thought my answer would be inadequate. I could not offer her the consolation that I wished I could. I did not want to add to her pain. But I took a deep breath and told her the truth. It is tough, I told her, because children react to any difference with avoidance. That is natural and inevitable. Her son may be able to make a friend who is not learning disabled, but first he will have to master his impulsiveness and develop a greater tolerance for frustration. It is likely that she will have to manage her son's social life to a significant degree for years to come, setting him up with groups and opportunities that are supervised so that an adult can get him out of social trouble.

In my experience, parents either overreact to a child's social difficulties or don't react strongly enough and don't do all they need to for their child. For example, the anxious father from Nashville needs to back off and relax. But a bully's parents who ignore all complaints from school need to wake up and get involved. It's not easy—and research confirms that parents have some difficulty responding appropriately to their child's social dilemmas.

Let's return to Joanna's twelfth-birthday party one more time. You'll recall that my daughter had taken a risk and invited the cool group without fully realizing that she wasn't as in as she had hoped. Because they all said yes to the invitation, she imagined herself the social center of the party, in a way that younger children automatically are at their birthday celebrations. The most popular girls had arrived in a bloc and were prepared to enjoy themselves, but Joanna wasn't really the focus of the action. As it turned out, neither was her guest Maria. By playing out her own social insecurities in a move to take over the sleeping arrangements, Maria unwittingly revealed the shakiness of Joanna's strategy.

Throughout the entire party, there we were, the parents. We worried about the guest list, we watched as things developed, we analyzed, we tried to think on our feet, we tried to help. Yet we were helpless to change the nature of our child's social life on this occasion.

The social problems of children present parents with a paradox. Most of the time we may be helpless to change a child's social destiny, particularly when a group's perception of him or her is set. Yet at the same time there is a lot that parents can do to teach their children social skills and support their friendships. And just as Erin-Claire's steadfast friendship was Joanna's lifesaver at her twelfth-birthday party, any child who has a friend is protected from many traumatic childhood social situations.

So how can a book make a difference to parents and children? A book cannot tell you which child would make a good friend for your son or daughter. That choice is your child's to make. A book cannot prevent a group from ganging up on your child, in school or out of school, if that is what the group is driven to do. However, as a psychologist, I believe in the power of insight to heal hurt and to clarify behavior. Understanding what is happening to your child—and what happened to you in your own childhood—can help you help your children.

Understanding brings perspective. Parenting, as everyone quickly discovers, is a lonely, exhausting job for which none of us is fully prepared. We lose perspective several times a day, sometimes repeatedly in the same hour. This may be especially true when you're dealing with a group of boys using swear words or when you find out that your daughter has given in to peer pressure and has begun to smoke. The power of the group to influence your child, to hurt his feelings, or to undermine your values is formidable.

I believe that when you can acknowledge the social power and pain in your child's life, bear the weight of it without overreacting, and ultimately share your sense of perspective with your child through your own steadiness, he or she will benefit enormously. It helps to have insight into what groups of children are actually doing so that you can react to them in a balanced and adult way. Understanding the social lives of children can guide adults to positive action. It can relieve your bewilderment and your fury, even if it cannot always produce an effective strategy for intervening.

In my experience, what interferes most strongly with a parent's wisdom in this area are the painful memories from his or her own childhood. We all wish we could save our children from the pain we experienced, and at the same time we do not always remember exactly what happened to us. Indeed, some awful incident might be totally forgotten yet still be stored in the unconscious, as Freud believed, or in the muscles, as trauma and body-mind therapists believe. In either case, when your own child is attacked or excluded, you suddenly experience a powerful distress. In that moment you face the task of continuing to offer your child support while simultaneously remembering and working through some incident that affected you long ago. Whenever I have very upset parents in my office talking about their child's social ostracism, I always ask, "Did something like this happen to either of you?" It is like opening the proverbial floodgates, as the memories of social cruelty pour out. After thinking through those memories, parents often say, "Oh, no wonder I was so upset about my daughter."

Groups are the highways of childhood. Our kids are swept along, going at the same speed as the majority of the traffic. If the other children in your child's school are going fifty-five miles per hour, then your child can move among them at a safe speed. If the other students are traveling at seventy-five miles an hour, it will be difficult—and socially dangerous—for your child to go fifty-five. So he or she will speed up to stay alongside his peers and may not dare to pull over to the side of the road for a break, as it feels too dangerous when the traffic is moving that fast. (Some do stay at fifty-five, or slower, from temperament or from parental pressure. But they pay a price for it—being left in the dust!) That is why in one school almost all of the eleven-year-old girls are slathering on makeup, while in another school not even the thirteen-year-olds are trying it yet. That's why there is dating in some schools two years before it starts in others. If everyone goes to the prom, your child feels a need to go to the prom, no matter how miserable it may be not to have anyone to ask.

Friendship, by contrast, resembles the side streets and back roads of childhood. Friends can go at their own pace; they can stop when they want to; they can get away from the speeding traffic. A girl who likes makeup and boys when she's at school can stop and play with dolls with an old friend who reminds her of that recently abandoned pleasure. In the shelter of friendship, children can move at their own developmental pace. Furthermore, they can have contact with different individuals, of different ages, with different agendas, from different places and different families. This nourishing multiplicity stands in stark contrast to the enforced uniformity of groups.

It is foolish and nostalgic to imagine that children can just live on the secondary roads of friendship and not have to deal with the highways of group life. We all have to merge onto the throughways when we want to get somewhere. Children want to get somewhere socially as well. There are many times when they yearn to be moving with another group of children. This may happen when a new school, a larger class, and more people to choose from are exactly what they're looking for. They want to get out there and zoom!

Elementary schools are state roads; big high schools are interstate highways. As our children grow, we need to equip them to negotiate the demands of both environments. At the same time, we need to see that our children are not just speeding along and eating at fast-food joints. They need to learn to negotiate the red and green lights, the frequent turns, the interesting sights, the unique and hidden byways of friendship.

At the end of the day, it is friendship that will nourish the soul of a child. If parents can learn to recognize, support, and celebrate children's friends, they will give their sons and daughters a great social foundation.

Chapter Two

Family Matters:
Secure Attachment in the
First Friendship

How do children learn to connect with other human beings? How do they learn to welcome, and to trust, social contact? How do they learn to enjoy other people—indeed, to love them? Let me present three scenarios to show a remarkably powerful force, the force of parent-child attachment, at work.

Anxiety runs high on a transatlantic flight. The 767 is crowded and uncomfortable. It's noisy, bumpy, and the air conditioning's too cold.

Everybody on board has been thrown out of their comfortable routines—except the baby in row 47, seat H. That baby isn't crying. He's not fussing at all. As the plane races toward London in the darkness, the baby's mother smiles at him, coos to him, rocks him on her knees, pats him, smoothes his hair, and praises him unceasingly. She plays with his fingers and allows him to play with her necklace, all the while keeping up a running conversation of nonsense syllables and endearments. The baby remains calm and, smiling, drops off to sleep. When he sleeps, she reads her book, but if he wakes—as he does once or twice—she sets the book down and resumes their "conversation." Soon he falls back to sleep. As the infant slumbers, the mother continues to stroke and cuddle him. The mother, too, is calm and happy. Her obvious attachment to the infant on her lap calls forth a smile from everyone who passes by in the plane's narrow aisle. In fact, the soothing influence seems to ripple out to the people in neighboring aisles, who seem less anxious and uncomfortable than the rest of the people on the plane.

At a West African restaurant in New York City, a young couple is attempting to have an adult dinner with friends. There's one problem—they have brought their young toddler along. The toddler is cheerful, excited to be out in the grown-up, brightly lit world of a restaurant. She's interested in everything, reaches out for everything, chatters and crows and laughs. Her parents and their friends can't get an adult word in until the waitress scoops their daughter from her booster seat and walks away, settling the child comfortably on her hip. The toddler is delighted. She rides the waitress's hip from table to table, watching as orders are taken and food delivered. She disappears into the kitchen, wide-eyed, and reappears laughing. The adults eat their dinner and catch up with each other as their toddler and the waitress circle the room. Occasionally their daughter looks over at them with a slightly quizzical smile, as if to say, "This *is* okay, isn't it?" She's happy as a clam; the adults are delighted and grateful, happy as clams themselves.

On another plane, this one bound for Washington, D.C., from Boston, a young, harried mom is sitting with her toddler, who has just learned to walk. "Down, down!" the toddler calls as soon as the plane takes off.

"Down!" he shouts as the pilot comes on and says that the passengers will need to keep their seatbelts fastened through the slight choppiness ahead. The little boy's words turn to piercing, angry sobs. He wants to get down! His cries are earsplitting—and his mom is at the end of her rope. It has already been a long day, and they have quite a way still to go before they get home. For the moment, comforting her son with their usual ritual of songs and peekaboo games is simply beyond her. She needs someone to comfort *her* before she has the resources to comfort her child.

Then the pilot clicks off the fasten-seatbelt light. From a few rows forward, an older woman walks back and looks down at the screaming baby. "Let me take that boy for a while," she says with a smile. Without a second thought, the mother relinquishes her son. The stranger looks down at the toddler, who looks up at her, then back at his mom. His mom smiles, as if to say, "It's okay, you can take a little walk. I'll be right here." The kind stranger takes the little boy's hand, and the pair begin to walk up and down the aisle. It's clear that this lady is willing to walk the child all the way to Washington.

The mom can close her eyes and rest. She hasn't been the most responsive parent this morning—but she didn't need to be. Parents don't have to be perfect. She has received compassionate help, and she let her toddler connect for a time with another adult. She's usually a warm and responsive mom, so the groundwork had been laid for her son to be happy and confident connecting with someone else for a while. The bond of the mother and child stretches the length of the plane.

What do these scenes have to do with friendship? An enormous amount, say psychologists. When the umbilical cord is cut after birth, an infant's literal, physical link to the mother ends—and emotional and psychological attachment begins. That attachment provides the psychological underpinning an individual needs to make his or her way through childhood and into adulthood. Since babies show a strong preference for one caretaker at the start, and that person is usually the mother, it is the mother who becomes the child's first friend. Research suggests that the quality of that first attachment has a profound impact on how children later get along with friends, perform in school, and react to unfamiliar situations. The first friendship becomes a template for future human connections.

A securely attached baby feels that his mother is a safe harbor from

which to cast off and explore the world. When Mom is near, the baby feels secure. Even the inevitable upsets and frustrations are manageable if she is available for comfort. If that comfort is reliable and consistent, the baby can manage longer and longer periods away from Mom, storing up confidence and security for explorations out into the world. An insecurely attached baby also needs comfort. But since he feels less secure about receiving it, he may cling tightly or withdraw from contact. Either way, the fears and hurts of childhood are harder to recover from without that solid attachment.

Attachment theory teaches that through the interactive experience of being cared for, an infant forms a representation of the self and the other. It is that internal image of "me" and "you" that allows a reciprocal relationship to exist. If all goes well, the child has an image of herself or himself as safe, lovable, competent, able to get basic needs met without too much delay. Other people are seen as benign or benevolent—like the waitress at the restaurant, who was assumed by the toddler and the parents to be safe and friendly. On the other hand, if the early attachment is rocky, a child might see himself as unsafe, insecure, even unlovable. Other people are seen as potential dangers or as unreliable. In other words, those internal images of one's self and of others, which are the products of thousands of tiny interactions between a baby and its caregivers, make up the basis for how children will approach all of their relationships. Attachment isn't about being "one"; it is about being a pair. It involves interaction. But attachment is not just about relating. It's also about what psychiatrist Stanley Greenspan calls "taking pleasure in relating"—something most parents and infants do naturally.

There are times later in a child's life when a parent may feel that she is not helpful or effective in helping children over the hurdles of their social lives. It is the purpose of this chapter to remind parents of how much they did at the start of their children's lives to help them develop into competent social beings. In the relationship between mother and infant, there is much that foreshadows the intensity of friendship. Simply put, mothers and children are incredibly social.

A large body of research undertaken over the past thirty years backs up the critical importance of secure attachment. The quality of the relationships children form with primary caregiving adults not only provides them with the internal working model of relationship; it also allows for

the construction of relationships with peers later on. Through secure attachment, children learn the language of intimacy with and pleasure in another human being. Attachment equals a sense of security and safety.

A controversial critique of attachment, Judith Rich Harris's book *The Nurture Assumption: Why Children Turn Out the Way They Do: Parents Matter Less than You Think and Peers Matter More*, suggested that parents have little power to determine the sort of person their children become. Rather, Harris argues, it is what children experience outside the home, in the company of their peers, that matters most. She believes that parents don't socialize children; children socialize children. Yes, peers influence each other tremendously, but children don't hit the playground or the day care center or the classroom as empty slates. They approach other children complete with their attachment history. What Harris misses is that parents have had a huge role in shaping the social abilities of the child who goes out to meet those other children.

Unlike Harris, I believe parents *do* matter. They matter profoundly. Being securely attached matters. The closeness between parent and child matters. Experiencing the delicate interplay of a relationship with a parent matters. Parents make a huge difference in their children's connections with others, for good or ill. Parents influence what children's peer relationships will be like, and those peer relationships in turn influence the kind of people—and friends—children will become.

Initial attachment between infant and caregiver—traditionally with the mother, but more and more often with the father as well—has a particular intensity. It is, after all, about biological survival. (Later on, in middle school, children's attachments—this time to friends—will once again feel like they're about survival.)

What does good attachment look like? As you can imagine, the parents of securely attached children have been studied extensively. They tend to be responsive to their child's needs. This can be as simple as feeding a baby when he's hungry or as complex as recognizing that she likes quiet time after lunch. The responsive parent does not anxiously hover, satisfying the child's every whim and impulse. Rather, she calmly meets most needs as quickly and fully as possible, acknowledging that there will always be frustrations and tears. Responsiveness involves give-and-take, as in the "conversation" of the mother and child on the transatlantic flight. It involves empathy, such as matching a child's facial expression with an appropriate action. And it involves careful observation, such as knowing when the toddler in the arms of the waitress needs a smile of reassurance that this stranger is okay.

A secure child sees him- or herself as lovable and experiences others as loving. Also critical to children is the knowledge that their parents are thinking about them when they're not around—that they hold them in mind. Good parents are able to convey the sense that families—indeed, all human beings—are connected even when apart. Just think how quickly you can summon the face or the voice of your dearest friends to mind. And think of how annoying it is when someone close to you forgets your birthday. There you have the essence of holding someone in mind, and how important it is.

Just as sensitivity and responsiveness are the parental behaviors that promote good attachment, they are the qualities that promote good friendships. A securely attached child believes that his or her attachment figure is open to communication and will be responsive if help is needed—not a bad definition of a good friend. Good and loving social experiences with a parent, repeated hundreds and thousands of times, form the child's expectations of what social life will bring.

Secure attachment gives a child an internal model of the other as available and trustworthy. This creates a sense of the self as deserving of care. On the other hand, insensitive treatment means insecure attachment, which creates internal models of others as unavailable and untrustworthy and a model of self as unworthy. This is a recipe for trouble in the social world of children.

If secure attachment can prepare a child for good peer relationships, insecure attachment can make these relationships difficult. A child will approach a potential friend, for example, and be clingy, demanding, or bossy. Another child might withdraw, avoiding the kinds of interactions that lead to good friendships. Or a child who expects to be rejected, punished, or hurt might lash out first, making friendship all but impossible. Peers can be seen as frightening or unreliable, as punching bags or obstacles to happiness, instead of as potential friends and acquaintances.

When psychologists talk about attachment, we often talk about *unmet attachment needs*. Children need to be given a sense that their caregivers are reliable, consistent, affectionate, loving, and responsive. Children need to be cuddled and also encouraged to explore the world. When children meet each other in day care, on the playground, or in the classroom, their interactions will depend to a large extent on how well each child's attachment needs have been met. As I said above, they are not blank slates when they head out of the home and start to influence each other as peers. A group of children with well-met attachment needs will be able to play happily and creatively. Children whose attachment needs were not fully met might be inhibited, aggressive, or unable to share or take turns. Of course, even the most securely attached children experience the ordinary ups and downs of peer interactions, as we shall see.

Sometimes, however, unmet attachment needs have a positive impact on future relationships if those later friendships are experienced as second chances. Eager to love and be loved, eager to meet those basic needs for caring and affiliation, children can make up for their unmet needs by being outgoing, having strong leadership qualities, and becoming devoted friends. So insecurely attached children are not doomed to a life of desperation, withdrawal, clinging, aggression, or insecurity, but they may need some additional help negotiating the complex terrain of the social world.

The deeper a child's unmet need, the harder it may be to ever have it filled later on. Expecting rejection, neglect, or smothering, the child may respond to peers with passivity, withdrawal, or aggression. Children who are afraid to assert their own needs may follow along with whatever the friend or the group says. I see such children in schools regularly. But it is not just children who reveal, through their behavior, that their working models of friendship are inadequate or even destructive. Over the years I have had a number of patients in therapy who have great difficulty developing and maintaining satisfactory friendships. Listening to their life stories, I realized that they had anxious attachments to their mothers—and the long-term result has been social anxiety and instability. One patient, Rebecca, never knew what to expect from her mother when she came home. Her mom could be funny, interested, and at times extravagantly loving. She would take Rebecca to F.A.O. Schwarz and buy her spectacular toys. The next day she would scream at her daughter because of some "bad" thing the girl had done, and Rebecca would not be allowed to play with the toys they had purchased. That very same night the mother might wake up her daughter to lie on her bed while she battled insomnia. They would sit together, watching late-night TV, the mother talking and smoking, while the four-year-old daughter was expected to be a calming influence. Rebecca's mother's attachment to her was built on shifting sands. It left the little girl feeling profoundly anxious about what was going to happen next.

Little wonder, then, that Rebecca found it hard to trust friends or lovers and often either avoided them or attacked them. Because of her own wariness, the friend or lover would in time be driven away. Rebecca's troubled friendship style left her terribly lonely, but it was difficult for her to change her working model of relationships. One of the things therapy did for her was provide a reliable and responsive person in her life, one who wouldn't suddenly pull the rug out from under her.

It doesn't always have to be that way, however. Later friendships can offer a second chance to finally get those old needs met. I often ask adults in therapy how they managed to cope with some of the terrible traumas they endured. The ones who coped best, even with horrendous histories of abuse and neglect, were those who found a friend or supporter. Somehow, even through the betrayals and abandonments, these individuals managed to connect with someone, usually a very special person who saw through the child's surface layer of aggressiveness, withdrawal, or fear, and persisted in offering a helping hand. For some survivors of abuse this connection came from a peer, perhaps someone whose own suffering made them especially empathic. Others were supported by an adult, someone who didn't abuse or neglect them but treated them with respect and dignity. Still others were shut out of human connection but managed to find a friend by connecting with a pet, a doll, a character in a favorite book, or an imaginary friend.

There are many reasons, other than neglectful or overly anxious parents, that a child can have an insecure attachment. There may be a poor temperamental fit between mother and baby. That is, the child may be outgoing and loud, the parents shy and quiet, or vice versa. A child may have trouble on a neurological level that makes it difficult to maintain and sustain contact. A parent who is depressed or stressed may not be able to provide the responsiveness necessary for secure attachment. A grieving mother who recently miscarried a baby or lost her own parent may find it hard to be responsive to a child's needs. In fact, one study found that *even before a child is born* it is possible to predict how secure the child's attachment will be by interviewing the mother about her own history of loss and grief. If she has unresolved losses, her child will have a hard time being securely attached. Similarly, when a child loses a caregiver, no matter how wonderful the new caregiver may be, he or she may have a hard time attaching securely.

Children's original love relationships with their parents teach them vital lessons about how to be friends. But many parents are confused about their role. Mothers especially often feel pressured to let go of their children too soon. They are pressured by "experts," by the youth culture that sucks their children away from them, by the demands of work, and by their children themselves ("Butt out, Mom!"). Fathers, on the other hand, have traditionally been cast as bit players in the drama of attachment: playmates and buddies rather than primary caregivers. Mothers and fathers are eager to get it right, with moms figuring out how to stay engaged and connected and fathers trying to be more involved in the daily nurturing interactions that build secure attachment.

Larry Cohen has spent most of his daughter's life as a stay-at-home dad, scheduling his practice and his writing around her needs. When Emma was a toddler Larry organized a fathers' group so they could learn together how to take on a more active, nurturing role with their small children. The fathers in Larry's group had not had fathers who were involved in their babyhoods and toddlerhoods. As boys, they had been discouraged from playing with dolls or caring for younger siblings. They expressed a profound desire for closeness—for attachment—with their children. Yet they felt anxious, almost panicky, about not having the physical or emotional equipment to handle a crying baby.

"I had a problem with my son crying," said a dad in the group. "The sound of a one-year-old crying will drive you up the wall very quickly, and I guess it's calculated to do that. It's very much an attention-getter! My initial impulse was to quell the crying, just get it to stop, and now I realize that sometimes the child simply needs to cry. Sometimes I just hold my son and he cries. And at the end of a good cry, he feels better."

Connection with their small children enriched these dads' lives as it made their kids feel more securely attached. "I think being a dad has really helped me in my work," said one father. "One of the things I've gotten to do as a father is be silly, roll around on the floor, and lose my dignity. That attitude of being a little more lighthearted and taking everything less seriously has filtered through to the rest of my life."

Another father said, "One of the most surprising things for me about being a parent has been the level of unconditional love that one grants to one's children. You literally can't do enough for them. And it brings tears to my eyes sometimes just to go to the door of the room where Ethan is sleeping and look at him sleep, or now to hold Connor, who is seven months old."

That's attachment.

The parent-child interactions described by these men build a foundation for a child's future competence and confidence with other people. The responsive mother on the plane to London embodies a role as her child's number one friend. She gives her son a sense that the world is safe—even when you're thirty-five thousand feet up in the air. Her behavior lets him know that he is entirely lovable. She conveys to him that he is somebody, as later on his friends will reassure him that he is somebody.

Not only that, the mom's attachment behavior makes everyone else near her on that plane feel safer. Her responsiveness to her baby is socially expansive. It radiates into the space around her. Her attachment shows, and everyone wants to be part of it. How calmed we all feel! How evocative her behavior is of our days with our own babies—and our days with our own mothers. No matter what our own infancy was like, most of us have a corner somewhere inside of us that responds at a very deep level to being soothed and comforted.

That tiny baby sleeping at thirty-five thousand feet is learning a security that will eventually allow him to move out of his mom's arms. For a central paradox of parenting is that we securely attach with our children so that we can someday let them go. It's tempting to hold on to your children for dear life when they want to try their wings. But expressing confidence and optimism about how the world will treat your child helps ease the transition. Humor can help also. If your five-year-old hangs back at the thought of attending a birthday party, for instance, you can reassure her of your love and your abiding presence by saying, "Hurry up and leave so I can miss you and count the minutes until you get home!"

It seems contradictory, but if you want your child to be adventurous, you need to cuddle her more. If you want your child to always be close, you need to applaud her explorations. Some children need a little push out of the nest—but never give this shove without an unlimited free pass for coming back home. Children of all ages need to be able to regress sometimes, pretending to be younger than they really are. They need to know they can cuddle with you or check back in with you anytime they want. Other children will race away recklessly and need to be held in check a little. Don't hold them back, however, without a clear message that you are eager for them to try their wings once they can do it a bit more safely. Otherwise the clingy children will just cling tighter or stumble out into the world unprepared. Conversely, the reckless child will just rush out even more impulsively or catch the parent's anxiety and become fearful.

I recently observed a little boy and his mother at a neighborhood restaurant. No one was next to them, so the little boy could race to the very edge of the booth they were sitting in and stop with a squeal of delight. He thought this game was great fun. His mother kept an eye on him as she ate her hamburger but she didn't stop him or anxiously call him back from the edge. Then the boy got a little too rambunctious. Throwing himself into his mom's lap on his return from the edge of the seat, he bopped his head against hers with a loud crack. Her head flew back and struck the wall behind her.

Tears erupted from the boy, although I imagine the mom wanted to bawl too. She had cracked her head hard. But she turned first to comfort her son. She smoothed his damp hair off his forehead and kissed the place where they had bumped heads. He calmed down—and started right back into his routine of racing to the end of the banquette. Then he remembered something. He turned and walked back to his mom. He leaned over to her and kissed her bump.

Now everyone really was all better—and the little boy had learned a vital lesson in reciprocity and empathy. He's on his way to a future playing field where he will be the kid who runs over to a soccer player on the other team who has taken a kick in the shin and asks, "Are you okay?"

Besides responsiveness to the child's needs, parents teach children about social life by being sociable. A mother who hands her baby confidently to visitors to hold teaches the child that other adults can be a source of comfort. The parents of a five-year-old, both teachers at a boarding school, encourage him to wander from table to table in a noisy, crowded dining hall looking for his favorite tenth grader to sit with. They've taught him that older kids can be a source of learning, laughter, and friendship. He also knows that he is worthy of their welcome. Children who feel confident in the bedrock foundation of parental attachment are able to believe that they will be similarly supported in the wider world.

Teachers, too, can be parental stand-ins, offering children a foundation of care and responsiveness that paves the way for future social success. In his book *Connect*, Edward M. Hallowell, M.D., recalls teachers whose attention, he says, "saved a child from despair." With these teachers, Hallowell writes, "the topic was always life itself."

On your own child's journey through school, he will meet many such dedicated and sensitive teachers. My coauthor Catherine O'Neill Grace knows a fourth grade teacher from a Montessori school in Virginia who had matter-of-factly arrived in his classroom one day with his head shaved. It turned out that one of his students was returning to school bald from chemotherapy for leukemia. His gesture of solidarity with his student not only showed friendship but also gave the rest of the class a way to talk about a strange and frightening aspect of a classmate's struggle.

Day care providers and baby-sitters are also important parental stand-ins for children. Carollee Howes, Ph.D., of the University of California, Los Angeles, has conducted a series of studies about how the attachments children form with their paid caregivers resemble the attachments they form with their mothers. Howes and her colleagues also found that in a group of forty-eight four-year-olds, children with secure attachment to day care teachers were more gregarious and more likely to engage in pretend play with peers. Children with insecure teacher attachment were more hostile, aggressive, antisocial, and withdrawn from their peers.

A child with secure attachment at home is likely to have secure attachment to his or her day care teachers too. But teacher attachment doesn't undermine attachment to parents. The most consistent finding is that for disadvantaged children, good day care is a tremendous boost to development and later achievement, both social and academic. And for middle-class children good day care can enhance peer social skills. This will come as a relief to mothers who want to or have to work—and it emphasizes the pressing need for high-quality child care.

Social learning continues as your children grow. When they are adolescents, your chances to connect with them will happen less around the dinner table or at bedtime than during late-night pizza snacks in a darkened kitchen, on long car journeys, or on single-file hikes on a woodland trail.

Good attachment stretches to allow children to move away from parents and find their own places in the world as they progress through the predictable developmental stages of growing up. It is also the foundation for a range of skills that children will need to be competent, caring friends and successful members of their communities.

Like many researchers, Alan Sroufe, Ph.D., a psychologist at the Institute of Child Development at the University of Minnesota, has found that infants who securely attach to their mothers become more self-reliant toddlers and have higher self-esteem. Sroufe's findings go a step further, however, to the school years and into adolescence. He has been following a group of 180 disadvantaged children for nearly twenty years, beginning with interviews with their mothers before the children were born. He's interested in mother-infant attachment and a variety of other measures, including the children's expectations from relationships with their parents and friends. He has also observed the children's life stresses, their school success, and their peer relationships.

Sroufe's research shows that even though these children lead unstable lives, with more life stress and less social support than most middle-class kids, those with a secure mother-infant attachment were likely to be self-reliant into adolescence. A measure taken in infancy remains an excellent predictor of adjustment eighteen years later. The securely attached children showed lower rates of mental illness, enjoyed successful peer relationships, and did well in school. (His research also offers hope for children whose attachment in infancy was less than ideal, as it shows that anxious, poorly attached infants can become more secure if their mothers enter stable love relationships or alleviate their symptoms of depression.)

Of course all kids, including those with the most secure attachment, will face hard and painful social situations. Their playmates will grab away their toys or shove them. Their best friend will betray a secret, their peer group will reject them or scorn them, and so on. So why bother to build secure attachment? Secure attachment helps children cope with these universal awful scenarios and helps them maintain a sense that the world is basically a safe and nurturing place, even though they may be going through a bad patch. This paradox puzzles parents, who wish desperately that their deep love for their children could somehow protect them from all social harm. It doesn't, and it can't. But it is still remarkably valuable.

The interaction of a securely attached child with his or her primary caregiver builds the solid hull of the little boat the child will eventually pilot away into adulthood. The child may encounter storm-tossed seas and rocky shorelines along the way, but you can help make sure his boat is seaworthy. You can outfit him with the qualities and skills he will need to make friends. The securely attached child:

- Can enjoy the company of others
- Can learn to take turns and share
- Can empathize
- Can regulate aggressive impulses
- Can cooperate
- Can "read" emotions
- Can trust or believe that we hold him or her in mind

Children hold parents in mind as well. I'm thinking of Hannah, now seventeen, who was the longed-for baby of older parents. She attended the same school for years and was the center of a group of student actors there. During a college tour of the Twin Cities her godmother asked Hannah what she thought it would be like to start school in a place where she didn't know anyone.

"I want to be the way my mom is with other people," Hannah said. "She makes people feel so welcome. They feel like they're the only people in the room when she talks to them. She asks them questions and always seems to know something special about them. She's a really good friend."

A few hours after that conversation, Hannah walked into a painting studio at Macalaster College. Approaching a student who was painting there, she said, "This is such a great painting! It doesn't look like student work at all. I'm so impressed. Are you a painting major?" The student put down her brush and began an animated conversation about her artwork and about Macalaster. When Hannah left the room, she had the girl's name on a scrap of paper from a sketch pad. If she decided she wanted to go to college there, she had already made her first friend. The internal model of her mother that she carries with her had served her well.

Hannah's confidence and competence began early, says her mother. Her mother tells this story about her:

"We live in California, and kids begin swimming very early in our neighborhood. Hannah was a fish from the time she was three! She started competing in races and other contests at the pool before she was in first grade. I remember the summer she turned six. I was sitting at the side of the pool watching Hannah jump off the low board over and over again.

"Our pool was a big one, with three levels of diving platforms. Hannah glanced over at me after one of her jumps. I remember she was wearing a little red one-piece suit. Then, without another look, she marched over to the second board—the high board, though thankfully not the highest one! She marched to the end of the board and plopped right in. I remember thinking, 'She's moving away from me.' It was a bittersweet moment."

The idea that early attachment is crucial to a child's future success is one that parents will recognize intuitively. But as you struggle through the day-to-day drama of your child's social life it can be easy to forget that you ever had an influence on her connection with her peers. Those early days of repeated, responsive action—all that peekaboo—fortified your child for the inevitable give-and-take of social relationships.

I don't want to give you the idea that attachment determines everything about a child's future social history. Other factors are important too, especially a child's basic temperament. Some children are more outgoing, almost from birth, while others are shy or slow to warm up. Parents often worry or get confused when their child's temperament does not match their own. A child of outgoing parents may happen to be slow to warm up and may be mistakenly seen as lonely because she isn't constantly surrounded by a stream of friends.

A shy parent can also be pulled along by a more gregarious child. My friend Esther, for example, was constantly embarrassed because her daughter Clara would make instant friends and not understand that Esther couldn't make friends with the other mothers that quickly. One time her daughter made an enemy instead of a friend. They were visiting my house, and Clara was playing at the nearby park. She was very proud, at age seven, to walk to the park alone. She came running home, though, and insisted that her mother come with her to go yell at a boy who had teased her and to talk to the boy's mother. "I know where they live," she insisted. "I saw them go home." Esther was mortified at the idea of going to a stranger's door and demanding an accounting of the playground fracas, but Clara thought this was the most natural thing in the world.

My experience with even the most competent parents is that at stressful moments with their children they may suffer a collapse of confidence. When that happens, it helps to remember everything you did at the start. Count on it: Back when your preschooler or middle schooler or teenager was a baby, your parenting installed a lot of useful equipment such as sociability, confidence, and resiliency. Your child won't lose those qualities, even if he's having difficulties—and taking you with him. You may feel helpless, and your child has certainly felt helpless, in his social world. But you need to have faith that what you did in the early going continues to make a difference.

There are so many moments when parents cannot have any direct impact on their child's social life. In a social crisis, even a small one, parents often momentarily lose faith in their child's social ability. If you sense that your child is being given the brush-off in a phone call with a friend and you are not sure she knows what's happening, your internal experience is one of helplessness ("Oh, God, she's being given the brush-off and she doesn't see it"). And in that moment of feeling helpless, parents can suddenly lose the knowledge that their child is socially capable. They forget their son or daughter has been able to make friends since infancy, ever since he or she could smile at a stranger on a bus and get a smile back. Indeed, parents forget that their child developed that social ability in their full view, in the relationship with them.

Memories of your daughter's early social competence are not likely to be in your mind as you drop her off at college and leave her in a dorm full of strangers. At that moment you can only hope that things go well. You can only hope that your daughter's roommate is a kind person ready to reach out in friendship. You have to have faith in your child and in the situation, just as you once hoped that the kindergarten class would be welcoming and the teacher alert and protective when you dropped this same child off at school thirteen years before.

Remember, things worked out in kindergarten. But your confidence rarely stays solid, because what you are feeling and what your child is feeling are not the same. Yet you consult your own feelings first, and those feelings may spring from painful memories. "Is she feeling as bad as I think I did when I was young? Does she want to be reassured as I wished I had been by my mother?" you ask yourself. For these reasons, parents often misread the social ability of their own children.

A parent's experience of a child's social competence and the child's experience of his or her own ability can be very different. Steven, now eighteen, recalls how his mother used to push him forward at Christmas gatherings. "She'd insist, 'Say thank you, Steven,' before I ever got a chance to open my mouth and say it myself! It used to make me so mad because it looked like I didn't know enough to say thanks on my own. I couldn't get credit for saying it on my own, even though I was just about to."

As children move away from parents into their own social orbits, it can be tempting for a parent to hold on for dear life. When I feel this way, I try to remember the wisdom of a Buddhist teacher, George Bowman, who says, "Don't deny your children the pleasure of reunion." And I think of a boy I know who, struggling with homesickness during his first experience of sleepaway camp, pictured his mom's face in the darkness of his bunk. The next day he made a friend.

Sometimes parents have to look for the small signs that show how attached their older kids are to them. A friend of mine was divorced when his son was in middle school. Maintaining contact with the boy, who lives with his mom in another town, was more and more difficult—especially when his son reached high school age. But at a family gathering my friend noticed that his son was wearing a bow tie. My friend touched his own bow tie—his signature neckwear since college—and smiled.

Other times parents have to accept that their kids try on different styles of attachment. Last summer I picked up my daughter after three weeks at camp. I watched as some girls barreled into their parents, bowling them over with their hugs, while other girls pretended to ignore their parents completely. Miranda, who was Joanna's best friend at camp, approached her mom slowly but steadily. She worked her way over to her mom silently, subtly, playing it cool, but ultimately leaning against her and nuzzling her in greeting and reunion.

As kids venture away from home, their attachments can sometimes seem angry. On the night before leaving for a semester in China, a college student insists on going out with her friends instead of spending time with her parents. When she finally gets home, she throws a tantrum worthy of a toddler after she discovers that her mother has not spent the time folding and packing her shirts. The message here is "I am scared to leave so I'll pretend I don't care about you, but I can't quite pull off pretending that, so I'll have a temper tantrum to show how much I need you." Not surprisingly, parents tend to see this kind of behavior as selfish or obnoxious instead of as an expression of attachment.

The fact is that you never really send your children off for good. They never really leave you. They act grown-up (more or less), but they take you with them, and knowing that you are there refreshes them. In fact, they might not let on, but they need you to be there, available for their call, even if it never comes. I have always offered the same advice—only partly tongue in cheek—to parents of college-bound kids: "Stay in the same house, the same marriage, and the same career, and stay sitting by the phone—but never be reproachful when they don't call."

There is no guarantee for your child's social future, but attachment is the best insurance policy you can provide. Of course, good attachment doesn't equal smooth sailing. As parents, we must prepare our children for what might be a rough voyage with an uncertain destination. Rather than trying to beat back the waves, we need to concentrate on building sturdy boats with stout sails for our children, and providing them with the skills to choose a crew of congenial fellow sailors. Those friendships will serve them well as they weather the storms of growing up.

Chapter Three

Children and Friendship: A Developmental Tour

Anyone who wants to understand childhood friendships needs to know that children of different ages possess different capacities for friendship as they grow. So you can see this in action, let me take you on a tour of my town and my neighborhood, looking in on children of different ages as we go. It's a beautiful October day, two days before Halloween. The leaves may be yellow and red and ready to fall, but friendships are blooming and visible everywhere in my town.

We are in a midsized suburb of Boston, only ten miles from Boston Common. In 1776 the British returned here from their battles in Concord and Lexington, and there is a statue of the Civil War's Uncle Sam at the corner of Massachusetts Avenue and Pleasant Street. Pleasant Street is a broad avenue of houses, many more than a hundred years old, some of which have been put to new uses, one as a funeral home, another the headquarters for the visiting nurses. Among them is a handsome brick home with a hand-painted sign out front announcing the day care center the Apple Tree.

As at many such day care centers, the front entryway is a mixture of warm welcome and sensible security precautions. Inside the front door is a second door with a combination lock on it and a sign saying, "For your children's safety, keep this door closed at all times." It is tightly locked, and one must wait to be let in. We are greeted by the center's director, Rosemary Higgins, and taken to the infant room, situated in what was once the dining room of the old home. Now the floor is covered with a brightly colored and very waterproof rug. You have to step over a white baby gate to get in, and you are greeted with the cautious stares of six infants, four sitting up, one lying down, and one in the arms of Betsy, the infant room teacher.

In some academic circles there is controversy over when true friendship begins. Among day care providers there is no such controversy. Most of the children in this youngest group don't have clearly identifiable friends yet. But some do—and the friendship is unmistakable.

We have come here to look for the first signs of friendship among children, because the research tells us that the most important preconditions for infant friendship are geography—that is, proximity—and familiarity. Before very young children can begin to make friendship choices, they have to get together regularly with a group of children from whom they can make a choice, and they have to see each other often enough to be able to develop a relationship. This can happen at home, too, when a baby is exposed on a regular basis to another baby its own age through regular visits.

There is one more skill a baby must have in order to demonstrate friendship. At a minimum, a baby has to be able to crawl, so that she can move toward another baby whom she likes. A child might have strong feelings about another enchanting baby across a crowded room, but until he can crawl—or unless an adult spots his preference and plunks him down next to his buddy—he's stuck in one spot, waiting for mobility.

In this small group, there are four crawlers, but only one close relationship has developed so far. Jonathan and Eleanor like each other. They are just eight and ten months old, respectively, which places them at about the youngest ages at which children can display friendship that psychologists can observe and measure.

On Monday, Wednesday, and Friday mornings, Jonathan is often already there when Eleanor arrives with her mother. When she is put down next to him he smiles and wiggles his toes. He is clearly pleased. The babies look at one another and Eleanor picks up the cap of a baby food jar. She waves the cap around and puts it in her mouth. Then she looks at Jonathan again, makes eye contact with him, and holds out the slobbery cap. He takes it and waves it up and down, hitting the floor with it. Then Eleanor leans over and drops onto her hands, assuming a crawling position. She heads off toward a small loft structure. Jonathan seems puzzled by her sudden departure but soon follows suit. She disappears behind a toy box, and by the time he gets there she has turned herself around and greets him, eye to eye, wet nose to wet nose. They both smile and laugh with pleasure.

Is this friendship? Other babies in the infant room are often set down beside one another. They will look at each other and from time to time will make socially inviting gestures to one another. What makes Jonathan and Eleanor's connection different? How does offering a toy begin to metamorphose into a meaningful relationship? The problem, from a research point of view, is that infants are not able to speak and therefore cannot tell us, "I really like her. She's my friend." We have to judge from their behavior.

Researchers videotape infants and record how many times they seek each other out and how much they look at one another, gauging the warmth of the interaction. But these day care teachers do not need research. Betsy, the classroom teacher, knows Jonathan. He's been here most school days since he was six weeks old. She understands what his friend means to him. She describes Jonathan as being at loose ends on the days when Eleanor isn't there. When she is present, his mood is brighter and he is more active. All of the adults at the center are happy for Jonathan and Eleanor and take pleasure in their friendship.

We can't really know if Jonathan and Eleanor just happened to both be developmentally ready for friendship or if they found in each other some mysterious chemistry, the infant version of soul mates. Are the other children missing something because they do not yet have a friend in the classroom? No, no more than a toddler is missing out by not being on a soccer team. Some of them just aren't developmentally there yet. You only have to look at these children to see that they're not interested. In between their rare invitations to make contact with each other, their eyes track the adults. They are monitoring who is getting fed, who is getting played with, who is getting diapered. They cry if the attention another child is getting reminds them that they are hungry or wet or just want to be held. Or they play contentedly on their own, moving brightly colored balls up and over looping roller-coaster rails mounted on wooden blocks. They are mastering their world and maintaining their attachments to adults. All is well for them. Friendship isn't missing; it just isn't on the radar screen. Yet.

Some of these infants won't be significantly more interested in friendship even a year from now, though they will be socially much more capable. For infants, there is always so much to be mastered on one's own or with an adult, emotionally and cognitively. Children get to friendship at very different rates. The friendship between Jonathan and Eleanor is lovely to watch, but it is not a standard to which other children should be held.

When I was in graduate school in the seventies I was taught that there is no real friendship before the age of three because children are not able to coordinate their play. But videotape and longitudinal research conducted in the eighties and nineties established that friendship emerges during the first year of life and that such friendship choices are very stable. Mothers of two-year-olds in one study reported that 75 percent of their children's relationships had lasted thirteen months—more than half of their children's lives. Another longitudinal study of four-year-olds found that friendship preferences had lasted an average of two years. It's easy to imagine Jonathan and Eleanor staying friends that long, or even longer.

The classroom across the hall from the infant room is filled with nine children, age twelve months to eighteen months, looked after by two teachers, Alison and Pam. The teachers tell us that there are no close friendships among the children here, and indeed we don't see any pairs of children playing together for any sustained period of time. Yet there is a lot of social interaction going on.

Penny and Andy sit near one another on the carpeted step. Penny, who is looking at the pictures in a book, sees that Andy is not busy with his toy, and so she holds the book out to him. He grabs the edge and looks at the pictures for several seconds, checking Penny's face momentarily to see if he has met the requirements of the social moment—but neither of them knows how to sustain the interaction. Perplexed, Andy drops the book and wanders away. Penny's gestures and facial expressions suggest that what she wants to do is say, "Andy, take a look. Isn't this a fascinating book?" and have him reply, "Yes indeed. Thank you for showing it to me. Why don't you read it to me?" But of course neither can read, nor can they carry on such a conversation, and so the social attempt falters. Nor can they find at this moment a type of play that they can keep going.

There may not be any friendship pairs, but there is plenty of friendliness. Of the thousands of interactions every day among the children, only a few end in shoves or tears or angry words. Unlike the younger infants, who mostly keep their eyes on the adults, every child in this room is aware of what the other children are doing. They are all looking to see if someone finds something particularly interesting to play with. Nathaniel waves a clear plastic tube with red plastic ends. He then stops to pick up a ball and pops it into the tube. It drops to the bottom with a satisfying noise. He follows it with two others—*plop, plop.* Kayla has watched this with interest and goes to find another tube, which she bangs on the edge of a table so that it makes a satisfying *whomp.* Meanwhile, Nathaniel has turned his tube upside down and dumped out three balls on the floor. They roll in several directions. Kayla picks one up and pops it into her tube. They both reach for another loose ball, and Nathaniel beats Kayla to it. She looks disappointed and stares at him angrily for a moment, as if to say, "Not fair! You got me interested in this game, and then you snatch it away from me!" Nathaniel is oblivious to Kayla's distress; his focus is back to the ball and the tube. Kayla turns her attention back to her own tube, apparently deciding not to press the point.

There is conflict elsewhere. Pam, one of the teachers, is sitting down cross-legged to read to two girls, Molly and Sue, each of whom is perched on a leg. Justin wants to join. He approaches, turns slowly, and, like a cautious driver backing into a parking space, backs into a sitting position on Pam's calf, just in front of Molly. Unfortunately, he sits on Molly's feet and crowds into her space. Her protest whine is immediate, and she shoves him away with both hands. He bumps onto the floor, stands up, and looks to Pam to settle the conflict, which is exactly what she does. She manages to find space for three on her lap, reseating Justin, Molly, and Sue. This is, of course, the negative side of toddler social interaction: fights over interpersonal space, competition for the teacher's love, the assertion of "I got here first." It is hard to share a teacher's lap— or anything at all—when you are just fifteen months old, because most toddlers are so full of neediness from moment to moment. However, being able to share is a basic precondition for friendship. That is one reason why it is difficult for toddlers to maintain these relationships. And this tension remains throughout our lives. Think about older children or adults trying to balance the desire to do something they really want to do with the desire to be with a friend who wants to do something different.

In this toddler room, the friends start with the same foundation we saw in infants. They are familiar with each other, have the ability to engage with each other, and have preferences. But in toddlerhood a new layer is added as the children begin to move toward each other to coordinate their play and then sustain it. They just don't all get there at the same time.

The teachers point out Ian, a thin boy with blond curly hair. He is the most socially capable boy in the class, ready for a more mature kind of interaction than are the other children in the room. We watch Ian cruise the room, approaching other children with offers of play. His eyes are more socially alert than those of the others; he stares into their eyes for a longer period of time than they can look back. He initiates block play with Sue, and she watches with interest, adding blocks to the structure he has begun. Ian sets a block on top of her block and checks her face for approval. For a moment, Ian and Sue are playing together. Soon, however, her focus switches to the water table, which a teacher is setting up for play. Sue gets up and toddles over to where the action is. Ian watches her go with a mild sense of bewilderment. His face says, "How could you leave? We were just getting something going here." For Ian, initiating and maintaining play is the challenge that commands his fullest attention. Unfortunately, at the moment no one in the class is developmentally ready to match his interest in mutual play. Ian's classmates are busy discovering the world of things, and it's too much for everyone but Ian to discover how blocks stack and do it in harmony with a peer. He'll have to wait for the others to grow up a bit. In fact, he may need to wait until several of his peers catch up in this area, so he will have a choice. Just because a classmate has the social skills to be a friend doesn't mean he and Ian will click.

Ian has the skills and is just waiting for someone to catch up. Eliza, on the other hand, has not yet developed the confidence she'll need to establish peer interactions. During our time in the classroom we notice how anxious this little girl seems. Her face tells the story: she is constantly vigilant, scanning the face of every adult who comes into the classroom. Not surprisingly, this inhibits her play. Not only is she uninterested in her classmates, but she cannot sustain interest in play itself the way other children her age are able to do. Pam tells us that Eliza has trouble separating from her mother first thing in the morning. She screams and grabs on when she senses her mother is about to leave. A teacher stands by every morning to pick her up and comfort her during the departure. For the first hour after her mother leaves, Eliza is fragile, crying easily and recovering slowly. A teacher often keeps the little girl next to her, offering herself as a substitute attachment figure. Sadly, however, Eliza often remains on edge for a good part of the morning she spends at the center. It is rare when she can "settle in" fully. Eliza is a child with mild separation anxiety, and it affects both her capacity to play with other children and her ability to take comfort from play itself.

In fact, Eliza's parents have recently been in for a conference to see if they should keep her in school or look for home care for her. At the conference, Alison tells me, she and Pam explained to Eliza's anxious parents the research on day care and home care. Most children get over separation anxiety fairly quickly. Those who don't may need some extra help with separation or, if it's possible, they may need to stay home with a single, consistent caregiver. Another possibility is that the social situation, rather than the separation, is the source of Eliza's anxiety. The teachers suggested to the parents that they have several children over to their house, with Mom sticking around to supervise the play, to see if social interactions are easier when Mom is nearby. Maybe they should try having a play group meet at Eliza's house a few times to see whether separation is the problem or if she has trouble dealing with the social situation.

Eliza's parents were confused because their older child, a boy, loved every single second of this same preschool from the moment he stepped through the front door. The teachers told them that sounds like normal variation within the same family. Both their kids will learn to play and to connect with other children, the teachers reassured Eliza's parents. Eliza may need just a little more time at home or more time to adjust to the rhythms of the day care center to take advantage of its opportunities for play.

Learning to play is essential for children. In fact, play is the essence of childhood. It is a child's mental health. It is work. It is recreation. I know from my work as a child psychologist—trained to conduct play therapy—that the mental disorders of childhood often interfere with a child's capacity to play, and that the job of therapy is to restore that ability. Once a child is playing again, you know that his or her mental health has returned. Child psychiatrist Edward Hallowell says that you know when child therapy has done its work because the child's play becomes "boring" again. By "boring" he means developmentally normal. The play is no longer as vivid, angry, or as full of messages as it was during the time of distress.

Although separating from her mother is painful for Eliza, she does not need therapy per se. However, she is getting therapeutic treatment from her teachers, because her anxiety requires it. Her mother is also aware of the situation and is trying to arrange for baby-sitting coverage at home so that Eliza can at least remain in her familiar surroundings when her mother goes to work.

If you are a parent with a child like Ian, you do not have much to worry about in the area of social relations (I am aware that all parents worry anyway). He is developmentally advanced, able to relate both to adults and to children. His only problem is that not enough children have reached his level yet, though they will get there soon. Perhaps Ian is showing us that he will always be a social leader. Eliza is at the other end of the spectrum. Without the sense of a "secure base" that she can carry with her, she is not yet able to enter the world of preschool with any confidence. Our hope is that she will grow in confidence and master the separation anxiety that afflicts her. The rest of the children in this class of twelve-to-eighteen-month-olds are somewhere in between Ian and Eliza on the developmental scale. As they play they are gradually becoming more aware of the social possibilities that other children offer.

Keeping It Going: Learning to Sustain Play Between the Ages of Three and Seven

Where do we go next in our developmental tour? We need to see a group of three-year-olds in action, in a larger setting than the intimate and protected quarters of the Apple Tree. That requires just a short journey on our part. Eight blocks away, on the other side of Massachusetts Avenue, is an old brick building that is instantly recognizable as a public school, but it is no longer used by the town. One half is now the town's Arts Center, the other half is the Park Street School, which encompasses children age two through nine, toddlers through third grade.

The wide hallways, the high ceilings, and especially the oversized wood-frame windows that leak cold air in the winter give Park Street a much different feel from the Apple Tree. Even if you never went to a school like this yourself, you have the feeling that this is *elementary school*, not home. The classrooms dwarf the smaller children. To them the spaces must look huge, like indoor playgrounds, with two-story lofts and separate play areas for dress-up, blocks, water table activity, and painting. There are about twenty-one children in a class, with three teachers. Michelle, the lead teacher of the three-year-old class, tells us that out of her twenty-one students she has two pairs of friends who come immediately to mind. One is a girl-boy pair, Amy and Joseph, and the other a friendship of two boys, Andrew and Curt. In her five years of experience as a teacher of three-year-olds, Michelle relates, "You usually only see two pairs of friends in a class. The other kids mostly switch off play with the other regulars in a group of four or five. It's unusual to have two children always seek each other out, but that is the way it is with Amy and Joseph and Andrew and Curt."

Let's observe them. Amy and Joseph, both three years old, have made the transition to the classic pastime of childhood, collaborative play, and in their case they also engage in shared fantasy play. Their friendship is absolutely unmistakable: they fall immediately into their accustomed roles. Amy is the scriptwriter. She fills Joseph in on the drama of the day. "I'm the mommy, you're the daddy. We're going to have a baby." This is a script he understands. It is close to his experience at home, where there is a little brother four months old. He is willing to go shopping and do the cooking. "We need to go to the grocery store," she says. "We have to buy milk," he adds helpfully. And so they go to a steering wheel conveniently mounted on the outside of the loft structure and drive to the store. Happily, the school has provided a well-equipped kitchen and a well-stocked grocery store, complete with a small plastic shopping cart. There are plastic oranges and bananas and baby bottles to be purchased. Nothing that Amy thinks up makes Joseph self-conscious or offends his sense of being a boy, nor is there any source of conflict between them. Though they sometimes differ on what they should do next, they take turns reading the intensity of purpose in the other, and each adapts easily to it. They don't exactly take turns deciding who will get his or her way, the way a teacher or parent might tell them to do. Instead, they do something much more sophisticated. They read each other, the way all friends do. "How much does this mean to you, and how much does it mean to me? It looks like you are really set on buying eggs, so I'll drop my preference for bread. But you don't really care who diapers the baby and I really, really want to, so I'll insist on doing that." They are wonderfully compatible.

Amy and Joseph's play is so well formed and trusting that it is almost startling. They have mastered complex play at the symbolic level, which is a psychologist's way of saying that they can play pretend together. Their play reveals that they are capable of social imitation, cooperative problem solving, and role reversal. Each recognizes the other as a partner who can complement the first child's actions. All of these skills are developmental achievements.

Amy and Joseph are not the only children in the classroom with these abilities. There are many others who have discovered similar social skills but who are not friends to the same degree that Amy and Joseph are. This poses a conceptual dilemma. We must recognize that social skills and friendship are not the same thing. Having social skills makes establishing friendship easier. Poor social skills can make it impossible for children to develop friendships. This suggests that social skills are an important but not sufficient condition for friendship. Ultimately, friendship has to be defined by children choosing each other, trusting each other, loving each other.

The bond between Andrew and Curt is as magnetic as that between Amy and Joseph, but their play is not as complex or as interactive. Andrew is a quiet boy age three years, seven months. The phrase "mature for his age" springs immediately to mind when you observe him. He is the only African-American boy in the class, and for reasons of temperament or perhaps from some sense of being in the minority, he radiates a sense of self-consciousness and dignity. He is big for his age, and when he is indoors, he moves deliberately. Curt could not be more different. He is skinny, wiggly, white, younger—three years and two months—and relatively immature for his age. He cannot stay out of trouble and doesn't seem to hear much of what the teachers say. He constantly has to be reminded of things and receives time-outs and other consequences that Andrew never gets. Andrew appears to understand that Curt cannot stop himself, and it makes him sad, but he doesn't know what to do to help. The self-control gap between them seems so large that one wonders why they are friends. Yet they choose to be at each other's side from the opening moments of the school day until one of them goes home. They play shoulder to shoulder, though often in parallel. They are together at the water table, their arms touching, calling attention to their individual play and eliciting appreciative comments from the other, but their boats are not involved in the same drama. An undersea monster (a brontosaurus doing double-duty as the Loch Ness monster) threatens Curt's boat. Andrew sees what is happening and watches Curt's play with interest but does not come to the rescue. His boat is involved in a drama as well but doesn't cross the line into his friend's emergency.

Clearly these two boys don't enjoy the level of sharing and complex symbolic play that Amy and Joseph do. Does that mean that they are not as close as Amy and Joseph? Does that mean that their friendship is not as strong? The answer to both questions is no. Their play may not be as developed as that of Amy and Joseph, but the feelings of intimacy and affection are real, as is the sense of hurt if there is conflict between them. If Curt is angry with Andrew, he cannot articulate it, so he acts as if Andrew doesn't exist. He turns his back on him, refuses to acknowledge him, and plays at the side of the room. The effect on Andrew is very powerful. He is bewildered and lost until their bond is restored.

Whatever mystery exists about the basis of the boys' friendship in the classroom is explained when they leave the building and go out to the playground. Andrew is cautious and hangs back. Curt is a little tornado. "Come on and catch me," he shouts at Andrew. The energy of his running is irresistible. It pulls Andrew right in, and he is immediately more uninhibited than he has been all day. Soon they are both running and laughing, taking turns chasing and being chased. Their pleasure in their play and in each other is unmistakable. It makes you smile to watch it. And you wish for every child to have it.

Sadly, as Michelle tells us, not every child in her three-year-old class is part of the social scene. This is how she describes her students. "There are the good friends, like Curt and Andrew and Amy and Joseph. There are the kids in groups who regularly play together, and then there are a few children who are socially clueless. When they try to join in the play with other children, they are so awkward it just grinds to a stop. You see them try—it is painful to watch. And it happens over and over. All you can hope for is that they find one other child who is as awkward as they are and that they stay together, so they're not lonely." For the first time in our tour, we see that children with less social competence are not only socially behind but lonely. Unlike the children at the Apple Tree, where only a rare infant or toddler pair has a close friendship bond, three-year-olds are expected to play together, and unless they truly enjoy playing alone, they can have a painful time of it if they don't have the ability to make friendly connections. Again, a best friend isn't necessary for happiness, but positive interaction with peers is necessary.

The painful reality that Michelle points to is that by age three, some combination of attachment style, temperament, developmental skills, and life experience has produced children with a wide range of friendship possibilities. Some children may not have the same innate ability to read the social cues that others have, which limits their ability to coordinate their mood or interests with another child. Other children may be thin-skinned or have a low frustration tolerance that results in blow-ups that frighten potential friends. Temperamental and activity differences between children are not necessarily a barrier, as we saw with Andrew and Curt. Indeed, opposites can sometimes attract and complement one another. Though Andrew is developmentally ahead in terms of maturity and focus, Curt is ahead in terms of physical confidence and ability, so overall they are developmentally well matched.

Finally, as I discussed in Chapter 2, a child has to bring a sense of confidence and trust to a relationship in order for it to become a friendship. Carollee Howes writes that "friendships among very young children are social contexts that resemble harmonious mother-child dyads." What characterizes the two friendships we have observed in this classroom full of three-year-olds is a sense of goodwill and trust that re-creates the attachment that these four children have almost certainly enjoyed with their mothers. When that sense of harmony is missing, friendship founders.

Now let's travel down Massachusetts Avenue to another part of town, to a house this time, to observe the sometimes edgy relationship of two five-year-old girls, Gina and Karen. In this older, more urban end of town, you would expect people to know one another. Wooden three-decker houses with narrow driveways between them create a sense of closeness and potential neighborliness missing in the widely spaced houses at the suburban end of town. Here the children can move easily and quickly from one house to another on their own, secure in the knowledge that the street is safe and that there are many trusted adults close at hand. The yards are small and there is little play space, so children tend to congregate in those yards where there is grass to play on and no tomato plants to knock over.

Gina and Karen were born three weeks apart and have known each other all five years of their lives. They live next door to one another. Their fathers are first cousins—which makes the girls second cousins—and the girls' great-grandparents live four doors down the street. Both girls made appearances at family summer barbecues in carryall baskets when they were infants, and crawled around under their great-grandparents' Christmas tree when they were ten months old. Their extended family thinks of itself as warm and close, and the adults are thrilled to have Gina and Karen so close in age. "How lucky they are," says their great-grandmother, who grew up close to her own cousins. There is the easy expectation that they will be friends, and to all appearances they are.

For the first five years of their lives they have been one another's most consistent playmate. When Karen gets lonely she usually goes next door and finds Gina, as she has just done. In the first moments of their meeting they are somewhat cautious. Karen stands silent and shy at first. Her unexpected arrival has forced Gina to give up her individual fantasy play with her Barbie dolls, and Gina hesitates momentarily as she emerges from her bedroom. Gina wasn't feeling lonely—unlike Karen, she tends to enjoy long stretches playing on her own—and it takes her a few minutes to shift gears and become the hostess. Karen has arrived without her Barbies, so they are going to have to play with Gina's Barbies. Gina's mother greets Karen and supplies some of the warm-up conversation while her daughter makes the mental transition. It isn't always easy to switch from being an only child, or even happily alone, to including a friend in one's play.

Gina and Karen bring a broad range of skills to their interaction. They have all the basics in the friendship toolbox: proximity, familiarity, the ability to coordinate play, and the ability to sustain it. In addition, they have another skill, one that becomes more and more crucial as children develop. That skill—and it is one they will use throughout their lives—is the ability to resolve conflict. The issue of sharing is paramount in play at this age. In order to coordinate their play, two children have to be willing to give up their individual greediness, neediness, and need to control in order to collaborate in a fantasy game. Gina has to be willing to let Karen undress her Barbie dolls and dress them up in a different way than she might choose to do.

It is a developmental achievement to be able to share. Most children younger than three are not able to share consistently enough to make regular reciprocal play possible. By five, most children have taken that developmental step. What lures them out of their early self-absorption and into mutual play? The answer is that playing with someone else is more creative, and ultimately more fun, than playing by oneself. There is someone there to admire what you built; there is another person who can add her excitement to something you love: "Oh, that looks good. Why don't you put the purple hat on her?"

It is difficult for young children to climb onto what psychologists call a "play plateau" with one another. They have to clamber up there together. What's a play plateau? It's a mutually created space that doesn't completely belong to either child. You have to give up private play space that is completely under your artistic control without losing yourself too much to the other person's vision of the play. And that is the case with Gina and Karen. Once Gina's mother has excused herself, giving the girls some space, they seem to circle one another, almost sniffing the other out, before they can play. And the first thing that needs to be settled is the Halloween costume. "What are you going to be for Halloween?" asks Gina, in a tone that implies, "I have to know the answer before I let you play with my stuff; we have to get the competitive and envious stuff out of the way."

"A princess," says Karen. "My mother made the costume." Gina has three instantaneous feelings. First of all, she is glad that they don't have the same costume, but then she is sad that she isn't going to be a princess like Karen. She is also confused to hear that Karen's mother has made the costume. She had looked at the princess costume in the store and had really liked it, but had settled on being a genie with a veil. She doesn't know if having your mother make the costume is a better thing than buying one in a store. Maybe it is and maybe it isn't.

Similar dramas are being played out all over town at this time of year. Halloween is a very important holiday in the minds of children. It is adventuresome: They go out into the world at night, and they get to be "bad" by becoming witches and devils. They also know that they are making a public statement and are being viewed by strangers. It gives most children a sense of self-consciousness and competitiveness that they do not generally experience. Kids want to succeed at Halloween.

What Gina and Karen could not possibly know on a conscious level is that they are playing out a competitive drama that also belongs to their mothers. There are long-held feelings of competition and envy between the cousins-in-law. Karen's mother is a fastidious housekeeper; Gina's mother is not so tidy, but her husband has a better job. Karen's mother is very close to her husband's grandparents and is tremendously solicitous of them; Gina's mother maintains a certain reserve with the larger family that hasn't escaped notice. These two girls have the advantage of proximity and family support for their friendship. They have the disadvantages of mixed parental vibrations surrounding their play.

Nevertheless, after Karen sees Gina's costume and says, "That's nice," in a genuinely appreciative way, the two settle down to play. They start with the Barbies but soon set them aside and begin to play pretend. All of a sudden they are on the same wavelength and absorbed in the flow of their play. Both girls are totally devoted to developing their fantasy. And so it goes for an hour or an hour and a half. A couple of rooms away, Gina's mother is intuitively aware that things are going extremely well between the two girls. She is glad that they are such good friends, even though things are not always so comfortable with Karen's mother.

Then, suddenly, both girls are in the kitchen looking unhappy. "Karen says I always have to be the groom and she gets to be the bride," complains Gina. Karen freezes. It is hard to be criticized and not have your own mother there when you are five (or forty-five)! "That's not true," Karen says slowly, with anger in her voice. "You chose the game." Gina's mother feels instantly helpless. She dislikes it when there is conflict between the girls, and she doesn't want Karen's mother to hear of it or to comment on her handling of it. More than that, she has no idea how to settle their dispute. She cannot possibly know who has been the groom and who has been the bride and for how long. Indeed, Gina's mother did not even know that there was a wedding going on in the house!

Her first impulse, which is to say, "Now, girls, take turns. How about if you each get to be the bride for a few minutes?" feels pretty lame, even to her. So she decides to buy time. She says, "Would you like some juice?" Yes, they would, and soon both are draining their plastic dinosaur cups and asking for more. Karen asks if there is anything to eat, and Gina's mom finds some peanut butter crackers. Karen says, "I'm going to be a princess for Halloween." "Oh, that's wonderful," says Gina's mom, with a glance at her daughter. She is reassured to see that Gina does not seem to regret her choice of the genie costume. They begin to talk together about picking costumes, about the selection that they all had seen at Toys R Us and Walgreens. When Karen says that her mother has made her costume, Gina's mom feels a pang of guilt, but only for a second. She knows she is not the kind of mom who is ever going to sew Halloween costumes. As long as Gina is satisfied with her store-bought costume, she feels okay about both girls.

Suddenly the two girls get up and return to their play. Their brief conflict seems to have evaporated, catching Gina's mother off guard. While they drank their juice and talked about Halloween, she was still racking her brain for a way to help them be friends again. Gina's mother thought she was just stalling and distracting the girls by offering them juice, but in fact the break has provided them with something very important. The juice and the snack and the conversation have restored them (and their little-girl egos) so they can resume the sharing and creativity that characterizes play between children from age three all the way up to age seven. This is their greatest happiness. As much as they love their parents, they don't count on their parents for play like this, even when it gets stuck. It is very difficult for most adults to get on the same play wavelength as young children. We adults tend to be too controlling, too self-conscious, or too time-bound to become involved in the flow of childhood play. If affection and a sense of specialness are the first gifts that children give one another in friendship, the give-and-take of reciprocal play is the second great developmental achievement of childhood friendship.

Measuring Up:
Finding a Place in the
Eight-to-Twelve-Year-Old Crowd

What are the eight-year-old boys in town up to? Do they compare costumes? Are they engaged in fantasy play? Are they competitive about Halloween? On a dead-end street up in the Heights, the highest point in the town, five boys are playing out in the street. They range in age from seven to eleven, and three of them are brothers. The brothers are extremely athletic; all have skateboards and are attempting to do tricks on a ramp, the seven-year-old practically killing himself to impress his older brothers. Two neighborhood boys, Mark and Fernando, both eight years old, are watching and talking, their skateboards resting on the ground; they have brought them out to show that they have them, and have made a couple of lackluster runs. However, it is clear that this is not their thing. They are discussing Halloween. "I'm going to be Darth Vader," says Mark. "The mask is really cool. And I can do the breathing. Ahh-hhaaaa. Ahh-hhuuuu. It sounds even better with the mask on. Do you want to hear?" "Sure," replies Fernando, and then, without being asked, he volunteers, "I'm going to be a Ninja. I've got a sword. It's plastic, but it's really strong. I'll get it and meet you at your house. Do you want me to bring my Gameboy?"

"Yeah, and bring the Yellow version and your cable. I want to trade!" shouts Mark over his shoulder as he heads for his house.

Fernando is also running for his home, where he collects his Ninja mask, his sword, and his Gameboy with the Pokémon Yellow version game in it. The skateboard is dropped by the door and forgotten; after all, it was never really a toy for Fernando, but a prop. It made a statement to the neighborhood that said, "Hey, I may not be as athletic as the Olson brothers, but I am a boy—look at my skateboard." The Gameboy and the Star Wars fantasy play with Mark are where Fernando's real interests lie. He heads out the door to meet Mark at his house. When he gets to the door it opens slowly before him and he hears Darth Vader's ominous breathing; "Ahh-hhaaaaa, ahh-hhuuuu." Suddenly Mark jumps out from behind the door, armed with a lightsaber. Fernando is momentarily startled; however, with his Ninja sword in his right hand he is prepared to defend himself. They battle briefly and without any intention of hurting each other. They are giving action demonstrations of their costumes—and their friendship.

They tire of this sword fight quickly. These two boys are not as committed to physical play as are the three brothers in the street. They set down their costumes and their weapons and pick up their Gameboys. "How many have you got in Yellow?" asks Mark.

"A hundred and fourteen," replies Fernando.

"I have ninety-seven in Blue," says Mark.

"That's cool. Here's my cable. We could trade some." Fernando picks up the black cable, plugs it into the side of his Gameboy, and offers the other end to Mark. Mark plugs it in and they both sit down, intently staring into the little screens, diving into the mysterious world of Poké-mon that is so compelling to boys of this age. While these two friends sit together they trade information, swap pocket monsters that the other boy hasn't yet captured, and talk about the progress that other boys in their third grade class are making with their Gameboys. "Charlie is a Master now, you know," observes Mark. "Yeah," says Fernando, "but he got his Yellow right after Christmas." Competition and cooperation alternate easily in this friendship. They show off to each other and they coach each other. Success gives you bragging rights, and lagging behind allows you to ask for help without being teased for it. They commiserate about being left in the dust by Charlie, who has qualified for the exalted Poké-mon Master status that both Mark and Fernando yearn to achieve.

Later they will snap new games in and share information about them. "Why is the third level so tough?" asks Mark. " 'Cause of the acid raindrops," observes Fernando. "You have to watch out for them." "I get lost," says Mark. "No, you can't," says Fernando. "It's an oval; you just keep going."

An adult listening to this might have a hard time telling whether this exchange was friendly or hostile. There is a lot of bragging and putdowns. The tone of voice sometimes implies, "How can you be such an idiot?" But watching the boys, you can easily see that they are friends.

As we leave the boys playing Pokémon, traffic has picked up, with moms and dads bringing kids home from soccer practice. Let's eavesdrop on two nine-year-old boys talking in the backseat. They are talking—gossiping—about other boys at school. At first it is all about Pokémon and who has what. All of a sudden, however, the conversation turns to rule breakers. "Did you see that Matthew had to sit in for the whole of recess?" one boy asks his friend in a tone of mixed fear and admiration. (Nine-year-old boys have not universally embraced the "risky shift," the change to antisocial behavior as a way to gain status. They are still little boys in their relationships with adults.) "Yeah, but he hit Sarah. She cried and told the teacher." Every boy understands that punishment is inevitable when you hurt a girl and she reports it to the teacher. The boy does not judge Matthew because of his punishment or the girl for her telling.

The subject of crying, however, prompts the first boy to ask his friend, "Did you see Mike cry at lunch? He really cried a lot." Now they are discussing the big issues of boy life. Is crying okay? What are the rules for boys? Should they condemn Mike for crying in public? Was he weak? When would other boys judge you as weak if you cried? "Yeah, but you know, the swinging door really hurt his wrist. He had to go to the nurse. She thought it might be broken. Eddie says that Mike's going to have a cast on his wrist."

Allow me to translate this exchange into its underlying elements of coaching and mutual discussion of the appropriate gender norms of behavior. The first boy is really saying, "Mike cried. We all know that boys aren't supposed to cry. He broke the rule of cool for boys. Should we despise and condemn him as a crybaby?" His friend replies, "Look, ordinarily we would say that Mike was a total loser for crying in the lunchroom, but in this case he was actually physically hurt. He ended up with a cast, a badge of courage." There is also an element of self-protection here from the second boy. "Indeed," thinks the friend, "even I—cool boy that I am—might have cried if my wrist had been broken. We'd better give Mike a waiver on this one."

This is what friends do for one another between the ages of seven and twelve. They review the correct rules of behavior for their gender, they analyze the traits that make boys popular, and they affirm one another. Two girls might say, in effect, "Yes, we have these important traits (hairstyle, clothes, correct attitudes) that make us cool. We lack some things that other girls think are important, but the two of us agree that those things are not all that important."

A lot of the conversations we adults overhear among children age seven to twelve make us despair. The children seem so superficial and so mean to the ears of the eavesdropping driver of the carpool or the parent serving pizza at the party. "Why do kids have to talk about other children in such a cruel way?" parents ask me. Well, some of it *is* cruel. They are trying out their social power, and that includes the power to hurt. Some of it, however, is precisely calibrated self-assessment used to compare themselves with what is considered cool by the group: "Do we have what we're supposed to have? Are we all right?" they're wondering. Groups set the standards for kids this age. In conversations with close friends they figure out the standards and learn to meet them.

I remember hearing a conversation between my daughter, Joanna, and a friend when they were about eight. "You're the better reader and the better student and I'm the better gymnast," said Joanna. "You should be a model," said her friend. "You're blond." Two friends, comparing and contrasting their traits, are holding gender stereotypes up to one another the way they might hold up clothes in front of a mirror: "Is this me? Does this fit?" What they're really saying is, "This gender stereotype looks better on you and that one looks better on me. Wearing this will help me be popular." (The group's requirements for popularity are demanding and the criteria rigid; the pain of not being one of the in-crowd or the cool kids can be severe.)

What is the best defense against the code of cool? Without a doubt, it is having a friend. When I interview school groups, the third, fourth, and fifth graders define a friend as "someone who doesn't tease you when the group does," "someone who really likes you for you," and most explicitly, "someone who does not care if you are popular."

Ironically, even a friend who likes you just for you will still say, "You can't wear that!" or "Don't act like a baby at the baseball game," but the meaning is quite different. The message of the group is "You have to look and act this way or else we'll reject you. And we might reject you even if you do it right." The message of the friend is "Have you noticed what's in and what's out? Let's practice and get it right so we'll be in!" As adults say, a friend is someone who will tell you when you have spinach in your teeth.

Between the ages of seven and twelve, friends continue to be playmates, much as they were in an earlier time. But over time friendship takes on deeper levels of meaning than just having fun together. The important role friends play in providing mutual respect and affirmation about their shared life is the reason children seek each other out with such intense longing. Children can give one another a kind of support that parents cannot give. That is why, no matter how wonderful a family vacation may have been, the kids run for the phone to call their friends as soon as you're back from a long trip away from home. Once they've checked in with their friends, they know who they are and that they are all right. They also want to catch up on the gossip. What happened while they were away? What will they face when they return to the group at school?

Parents must not underestimate the power of such friendships. They can be extraordinarily meaningful. Two thirteen-year-old boys in Wisconsin killed themselves in a suicide pact some years ago because one family had moved away from the town and the boys were separated. Their feeling must have been "We cannot live without one another," because they waited until there was a weekend visit by one of the friends back to the old hometown to complete their tragic act of friendship. Though their suicide was a rare and extreme act, I believe many childhood friends have had milder versions of these same feelings. Certainly most children, at one time or another, will use the dramatic language of life and death—"I'll die if I can't go to that sleep-over"—even if they don't intend to harm themselves. The boys had become so important to one another that each felt he could not face his respective school group and life without the other and had no other way to express it. They did not want to face adolescence alone, without their best friend and coach.

Friendships in Adolescence: "Clothesese," Identity, and Secrets

Most teenagers have intense feelings about their friends, or lack of friends. After all, they trust their friends with their secrets. Let's look at two pairs of adolescent friends: thirteen-year-old girls, Melanie and Claire, and seventeen-year-old boys, Jack and Hal.

Melanie and Claire have to decide whether they're going to celebrate Halloween at all this year. Some of the cool girls in the eighth grade have announced publicly that they aren't going to go out trick-or-treating on Halloween. In early October the most popular girl in the class said, "We're going to a party." Everyone else understood from this declaration that it was to be a sophisticated party, a high-school-type party, not anything with costumes. That left Melanie and Claire undecided about whether they should do Halloween at all. Were they too old now? Would the other eighth graders see them and judge them if they did go out? How much effort should they put into their costumes?

Clothes are extremely important to the two girls. They spend much of their time together trying on each other's tops, bathing suits, and baggy pants. You might say they speak to each other in "clothesese." Sharing clothes is a way of expressing their closeness, a way of announcing the changes in their bodies and a way of affirming each other's attractiveness. Mark McConville, a psychologist who specializes in adolescents, has written that for teenagers, "clothes are the psyche worn on the outside." Certainly that is true for all children at Halloween, but for two adolescents the choice of Halloween costume becomes an advertisement of what age they think they are. The holiday becomes both one last chance to be a kid and a symbolic move toward being more grown-up.

At first they avoid the issue. "Should I come over on Halloween?" asks Claire. "Yeah," says Melanie. "Are we going out?" inquires Claire. "Yeah, maybe . . . yeah, probably, just in this neighborhood," replies Melanie in code, signaling that they will go trick-or-treating, but just in her neighborhood, not where any other eighth graders might see them. That evening Melanie asks her mother to take her uptown, and once there she buys a fluorescent pink wig. Why that choice? "I just like it." She won't announce to her mother that she is going to go trick-or-treating. Meanwhile, Claire is beginning to work on a costume, something inspired by the musical *Grease*, which she and Melanie have seen together on video many times but which was also the fall production at the high school. She asks her mother to help her with a poodle skirt. Her mother is thrilled. She knows that this is probably the last time she will get to help Claire with a costume for Halloween.

Ultimately, Melanie puts together a costume that includes the pink wig, a short black skirt and a pink feather boa. "I'm going as Julia Roberts in *Pretty Woman*," she crows. Claire comes dressed as a fifties girl in a poodle skirt. Melanie's costume, with its not-so-hidden message about sexuality, appalls her parents. It seems to announce a headlong rush into adolescence. But Claire's costume pleases her parents, since it emphasizes her identification with them and with a simpler, more innocent time. Both costumes, however, make identity statements. Together, the disguises add up to a joint announcement: "In combination we are both young and almost grown-up, we are both innocent and sexy. We are friends who express the hidden sides of one another."

The girls go out trick-or-treating between 7:30 and 8:00 P.M., when the little kids have all gone home. They return to Melanie's house with full buckets, since the neighbors know that when the eighth graders come by, the evening is over and it's time to get rid of all the remaining candy. These two girls, tall and beautiful, are the last children who come to the door at Halloween. It is very likely to be the last time they make the rounds at Halloween themselves.

When the girls return they go upstairs immediately and close the door to Melanie's room. Melanie's mom is tempted to stand at the door. Is it better to know or not to know what they are talking about? But she steps past and goes downstairs, leaving them alone—the right choice, in fact the only choice. Adolescent conversations are private, which is perhaps the most important thing about them. There's a simple reason why parents can't tell you what gets said: Adolescents don't want their parents to know.

Indeed, when the girls heard Melanie's mother's footsteps in the hall, they stopped talking so as not to be overheard. Melanie's mother is keenly aware that she has become an intruder in her own home. She wants to tap on the door and call in, "I hope you're not eating all that candy right away." But the mental image of the two girls rolling their eyes at one another in response to this maternal warning—a warning they have heard every Halloween since they were three—stops her. Melanie's mom doesn't want to be an outsider, she doesn't want to be a nag, and she doesn't want to appear totally uncool to these two girls, whom she loves very much. She is aware that in an effort to achieve even greater privacy, on warm nights the girls move out to a flat part of the roof with pillows, blankets, a CD player, and bags of chips. They talk there in whispers, sharing important information about themselves. Being on the roof makes them feel separate and more private.

What is the need for all of this privacy? The essence of adolescent conversation is personal disclosure, opening the heart to a friend in a way that a boy or girl has never done before. The privacy and secrecy is about safety: You share this only with people who will totally understand, which leaves parents out immediately. Parents' adolescence was back in the Dark Ages, after all.

What do these young people tell one another? What are they saying? I cannot give you the dialogue itself, and to be honest, much of it would come across as extraordinarily banal. (Have you ever read the e-mails or instant messages that adolescents send one another?) But I can tell you something about what is in their hearts: thoughts about themselves, fears about their future, disgust with adults, and most especially secrets about their lives with their parents. This is the age when children begin to open up and describe to each other the tough things about their family lives.

Children under the age of ten are extraordinarily loyal to their parents. Even if they come from the most dysfunctional family, children remain loyal and silent. Little boys and girls under the age of five sometimes blurt out embarrassing things in public. However, they soon learn the rules of family loyalty and keep the family's secrets, often at considerable cost to themselves. I know from my work as a therapist that it is often close to impossible to get nine-year-olds to acknowledge their mother's depression or alcoholism, and they will lovingly minimize a father's explosive and violent outbursts. Young children in families are always hoping that their parents will improve. Indeed, kids often struggle as best they can to prop up flawed parents. However, as they begin to separate from their parents and see more of their flaws in comparison to other adults in the world, they may become critical of how their parents handled them. At the very minimum, and even from the most loving and obedient child, there is the complaint to a friend: "My parents still think I'm a baby. They don't trust me."

Teenagers may trade pretty powerful observations about their respective families. Personal disclosure and empathy are the glue and the currency of teenage girl friendships. Girls refer to each other's troubles and are at pains to tend to a friend when some event presses on the sore spot in that friend's life. If a girl's parents are divorced, then her friend is particularly attentive to her during a period when the parents are fighting over money. Boys know a great deal about the secrets in one another's lives too. However, guarding information about a friend's family is often a test of loyalty among boys. Can you know a friend's secret—for example, that his father has rage attacks when he drinks—and still keep it a secret? That is the measure of a true friend. He doesn't refer to your secrets in public; he doesn't even necessarily let you know that he has noticed.

My college friend David remembers bringing a couple of pals home one afternoon when he was in middle school. When they entered the house, it was clear to the visitors that David's mother was drunk and had been for some time. But they didn't say a word, instead proceeding up to David's room as if nothing were amiss. Later, the two visitors talked about it to each other. They decided to protect David from knowing that they were aware his mother had a drinking problem. Only two decades later, as adults, were they able to talk about it with him. And even then David found the shame of the memory, and of his friends' knowledge, scalding.

You can be sure that behind that door on Halloween night Melanie and Claire are talking about their lives, their disappointments, their hopes, and about who each of them is in the world, even if the surface content of their conversation is all about candy and clothes and crushes. Erik Erikson said that all adolescent conversation is about identity. Everything that teenagers say comes back to "Who am I?" "Who are you?" "What does being your friend say about me?"

Does this mean that teenagers are not really deep friends, that they are always looking in a mirror, fundamentally self-absorbed? It does not. Any reader can test that hypothesis against his or her own memory of friendships in adolescence. My guess is that you will remember very intense friendships, as meaningful as any in your adult life and not so very different from these more mature relationships. Adolescent and adult friendships are structurally similar. It is trust and personal disclosure that distinguish a friend from an acquaintance in adulthood; so too in adolescence. For that matter, our middle schoolers in Chapter 1 defined a friend as "someone you can trust," someone who likes you for who you really are. Children recognize the core of friendship relatively early. As they grow, their capacity to like one another, to trust and to support one another, grows apace with their development. Friendships between teenagers—and of course romantic relationships as well—may even survive cultural differences, changes of school, and the powerful group pressures that will be discussed in the middle chapters of this book. They may also hold up through the separations of college or of membership in different crowds.

Of course, these separations and differences do make it hard to maintain friendships. Up in the Heights on the north side of town, there is a small deli and grocery that stays open until 10:00 P.M. In Arlington, as in most towns, the last kids out on Halloween night are older teenage boys. At 9:50 on this Halloween night, an imposing, heavyset football player with a baby face walks into the deli and goes to the counter to buy a pack of cigarettes. Everyone in the store notices him because of his size. Many of the adults know him. He is Jack Carroll, the star tackle on the high school football team. The grown-ups try not to notice that he is buying cigarettes. If they let themselves think about it, they would remember that Mr. Chojnacki, the coach, forbids his teams to drink or smoke.

Jack is struggling with his addiction to cigarettes—and with his conscience. Like all the members of his team, he pledged to his coach not to smoke or drink during the football season. It has been difficult to keep the pledge, and he is using Halloween as an excuse. It's a holiday! All the little kids in town are eating candy. It seems like a night when kids get to be kids. For Jack, that means taking a night off from his varsity team pledge. He had hoped the store would be mostly empty so that no one would see him buying a pack. He doesn't want someone in this medium-sized town to tell on him to his parents. They too went to the high school, and most of the long-term residents in town know his family.

What the adults don't notice, because the two look so different, is that the young man behind the counter is exactly Jack's age. Hal is also a high school senior, though less imposing, thinner, and somewhat more mature in the way he carries himself. Jack is surprised to see him and more than a bit embarrassed. The two of them, Jack and Hal, were best friends all the way through elementary school and middle school. Even after Hal transferred to the Catholic high school at the beginning of ninth grade the two managed to stay close right through the spring of tenth grade. Ultimately, Jack's athletic career, his bond with his teammates, and the acclaim he was getting in high school made them grow apart. They might have survived even that had it not been for the smoking and drinking. Hal didn't like the friends that Jack was making, and he couldn't stand the fact that he wasn't able to stop his friend's self-destructive behavior.

Jack put his three dollars on the counter and said, "Hey, how are things going?"

"Good, real good," replied Hal. "We're closing up soon. Do you still smoke Marlboros?"

"Right, good memory," said Jack quickly, trying to get away from the subject. "Do the little kids trick-or-treat in stores? They were all over town tonight. Remember we always used to do that together?"

"No, no kids in here. I saw them go by," said Hal. "I guess we can't give candy away when we're selling it too. Yeah, I remember. We used to get buckets of the stuff. You always gave me half of yours because you hated chocolate. I gave you the candy corn. I couldn't stand it." He pushed the cigarettes and the change across the counter to his friend "This shit'll kill you. Go back to candy corn."

Hal has said this casually, but both boys feel the weight behind it of a friendship with a long history and a sad trickling-out ending. Jack held up his hand to stop his friend's words. "Hey, we should get together. Football season's over soon." He is making a subtle overture of friendship that both know will go nowhere. Still, the feeling of affection between the two is real. They miss each other, yet neither knows exactly how to say that.

Jack is dying to say to Hal, "You've been in my mind. I just wrote an essay about us in my English class. I wish you could read it." His boy code won't allow him to tell his friend that he expects that they will be friends again. That's what he wrote about in his English class. You might be surprised that Jack, the athlete struggling with cigarettes and alcohol, has the sensitivity to write an essay about his lost friendship with Hal. His English teacher, who has seen the sensitive boy lurking under the tough guy, shares the essay with me, with Jack's permission. Here is an excerpt:

When I was young my best friend was Hal. He lived across the street, I at 60 Green Street and he at 61 Green. He would look out his window and wait for me to return from baseball practice or whatever it was that I had left to do and the moment I entered the door the phone would ring and he would be at my house in a matter of minutes. We had our first sleep-over together and we watched our first R-rated movie together. His mother drove us to the movies every weekend and I was the one who named his dog.

In the last few years we have grown in different directions, however. While Hal does not adapt to misbehavior very well, some of my actions that I do on weekends would make him uncomfortable as well as embarrass me, not because I am ashamed of my weekend activities, but because he knew me when I was just like him. I took him out with me once and he couldn't handle my friends' cigarette smoke. I always thought that there was something different about Hal. He is perhaps thirty years ahead of his time, a fifty-year-old in a teenager's body. I don't know why he is the way he is, but I can only respect him, because when I am past the craziness of my adolescent years, I can join back with him and perhaps we can become friends again.

Jack is right to be hopeful. Friendships do continue to develop and change, even into late adolescence and adulthood. Intimacy, and the bittersweet missed opportunities for intimacy—like Jack and Hal at the cash register—continue to play central roles in children's lives as they build friendships and lose them, create conflicts and resolve them.

Chapter Four

When Kids Have Best Friends

Kate and Ann, a pair of seventh graders, sophisticated and boy-crazy at school, spend their Saturday afternoons pretending to be horses. They canter up and down a wooded hillside in their neighborhood, making convincing whinnying noises as they retreat from the pressures of middle school to the predictable pleasures of a childlike game. They play for hours.

Just three months ago, Kate was a newcomer to her school, her neighborhood, and this relationship. Now the two girls are self-proclaimed best friends. But Kate still has the wrong clothes and listens to the wrong music. She's never been to a make-out party, and she didn't spend the summer at the right camp. She doesn't know the rules of softball, and she doesn't have a bra yet. The ways of boys are still mysterious and threatening. To her, the world feels full of tricks waiting to be played.

Ann, on the other hand, has gone to their school since first grade. She's athletic and popular and gets good grades. She was a leader, the coolest girl of all, at the right camp. Last summer she was a rebel who instigated daring nighttime escapades, yet walked away with a handful of achievement and popularity awards at the end of camp. But this fall, her parents are moving through the first difficult stages of a divorce following an on-again, off-again separation. The sands are shifting beneath her feet.

When they are together, these two girls feel solid and centered. Although they have left childhood behind in many ways, they remain fluent in the fantasy language of play. But as young adolescents, they are also becoming adept at the language of intimate self-disclosure—the exploration of feelings—and each has a host of feelings to talk about.

Their friendship is reciprocal. They give a great deal to each other above and beyond the companionship and affection they share. Away from school, secure in Ann's undivided attention, Kate is buffered from the ravages of group disapproval that she faces in the hallways. Ann, escaping the painful atmosphere of her own house by spending time at Kate's, gains a respite from the increasing tension between her parents. The girls' connection, their closeness, provides them with a degree of stability, predictability, and trust that both need badly at this point in their lives.

Ann loans Kate clothes, confidence, and status in the group. During the school day Kate is able to say things like "Ann and I bought a bunch of magazines this weekend" or "Ann and I went swimming." The other girls in their class remain a bit mystified by the whole thing. But those precious words, "Ann and I," render Kate worthy of their attention. If Kate has the Ann seal of approval, she can't be all that bad, can she? And her clothes *have* been looking better lately.

Why does a social powerhouse like Ann need an outsider like Kate? Because Kate offers Ann an important perspective on life beyond the ingroup. Playing imaginary horse games with Kate gives Ann a break. It's as if she has turned her speeding car off the superhighway of seventh grade for a quiet amble down two-lane roads familiar to her from earlier in her life. Kate's friendship helps Ann step on the brakes and slow down her headlong rush into adolescence.

The girls' retreat into play happens in a wooded ravine that forms part of a park across the street from Kate's house. When they cross the street and move through the trees down toward the creek at the bottom of the ravine, it's almost as if they're entering some kind of enchanted forest. Among the trees, they escape from the pressures of wearing the right clothes and playing up to the right boys. They can be children, not adolescents, for a restorative hour or so. Being there makes Kate feel as if she is back in the predictable world of childhood that was lost when she moved to a new neighborhood and a more sophisticated school. Galloping around in the woods makes Ann feel as if she were back in the apple orchard at her grandparents' house while her parents sat together up on the front porch.

Yes, these best friends may be regressing to a time before adolescent anxiety caught up with them. But the hours they spend in that place are healing and helpful. When they're back in the real world of divorcing parents, confusing sexual feelings, and conflict-ridden seventh grade social rituals, their closeness provides additional reassurance. They are at a major transition in their life, and friendship is a vehicle for it.

The psychiatrist Harry Stack Sullivan, who pioneered the modern study of friendship in the 1950s, noted that friends are as important to young adolescents as parents are to infants. After separating somewhat from their adult caregivers and exploring the world around them, teenagers are driven by a need for intimacy to devote themselves to close friendships. This new level of intimacy does not replace shared interests, reassurance, and a sense of identity—the basics of friendship we saw in Chapter 3. Rather, it enhances them.

Ann and Kate played this out in their own relationship. One rainy afternoon Kate and Ann broke their usual after-school pattern and went over to Ann's house to pick up a book. As they entered the house they saw Ann's mother sitting all alone in the living room. No lights were on, although it was a dark day. Ann's mother didn't speak to them. She didn't even seem to notice them as they clattered into the front hall. She was just sitting, staring down into her lap.

The girls tiptoed by her. Once upstairs, Kate waited for Ann to decide whether they were going to talk about her mother or not. Ann did, hesitatingly telling her friend about what home had been like lately. She unburdened herself to Kate, describing the scenes her mom and dad had made, and admitting how much she feared for her future. Would she have to change schools? Would she move away? What would happen to her? She trusted Kate to listen, to comfort and support her, to care about her. She trusted Kate to hear her fears without ridiculing her. Ann believed that Kate could help her feel better—and she did.

Friendship Quality Versus Quantity

According to the psychological literature, the reciprocity and commitment that characterize Ann and Kate's relationship are essential components of friendship. So is the spontaneity that allows them to partake of some of the qualities of childhood play. So too is the giving and sharing in their more intimate, personal exchanges, which are characteristic of adolescent friendship.

As we saw in our tour of my town in Chapter 3, the nature of friendship evolves over time. At all ages friendships come in many stripes and colors, from casual to close to complicated. For most children—and adults—the term "best friend" captures a specific quality of closeness and endurance. For children, particularly girls, "best friends forever" is part of the rhetoric of friendship. They expect their close friendships to be of long duration, in spite of the reality that the average childhood friendship lasts a year or less. One eight-year-old boy I know expresses the essence of this feeling when he says of his neighbor and best friend, Zachary, "We've known each other our whole lives. We've known each other since we were zero!"

The phrase "best friend" can take on an almost mystical significance for children and adults. Even parents of kindergartners worry when their child has no easily identifiable best friend. Others, of course, worry because a child is so close to one friend that she doesn't have enough other friendships. I think the best antidote to all this worry is to look at what we mean by a good-quality friendship. It really is the quality, not the quantity, that's important.

We adults tend to romanticize friendship—just check the "friendship" section of any Hallmark card store. Ask a group of adolescents what makes a good friend, and you run into some predictable, warm-and-fuzzy clichés. But kids are also able to move beyond platitudes to express the importance of close friendships in their lives. Catherine asked her class of juniors and seniors to write a single sentence about their close friendships. The results were inspiring. "My best friend gives me a vicarious life . . . an open ear . . . ten thousand hours of unjudging therapy . . . a slap in the face when I need it . . . a different perspective on me," one wrote. "My best friend gives me absolutely no slack," wrote another. Another: "My best friend gives me the power to talk about anything in the world." And "My best friend gives me food for thought, and always something to smile at (usually me)." Finally, "My best friend gives me hope."

Strength. Courage. Trust. Self-confidence. Perspective. Hope. A listening ear. These are powerful, life-sustaining gifts. No wonder making and keeping friends is a central task in the lives of children.

Does every child have a single best friend? *Should* every child have such a friend? Those are questions I'm asked often as I travel around the country speaking to parents. As in so many other matters pertaining to children and their relationships, the answer begins with "It depends." It depends on a child's age, on his or her temperament, and on what the rest of his or her social connections are like. Some children are comfortable and satisfied with a single, intimate friend (although you may be concerned that exclusivity can cut children off from other social opportunities). Other children regard a wide circle of companions as their close and intimate connections.

Best friendship is subjective. A teenage boy may report, "I have ten best friends." A student at a boys' school where I have worked as school psychologist for many years even said that the entire senior class was his best friend!

A group of preteen girls may be in constant flux (not to mention constant phone and e-mail contact) over who is best friends or second-best friends with whom this week. When we hear the adjective *best*, we understand that the friendship it describes is close, trusting, intimate, and sustained. But we shouldn't necessarily assume that this best friendship is the *only* one with those qualities that the child enjoys.

Early on, children know that promising "I'll be your best friend" means something special, although they don't yet realize the irony of offering best-friend status and taking it away so casually. Negotiations about best friendship have great political currency in elementary school. Children promise it to others, withhold it, and speculate on it. There's a huge amount of negotiation involved. Being someone's best friend is a product traded as energetically as any commodity on the Chicago Board of Trade!

Best friendships can be remarkably fluid, but they can also endure. At a school where I spoke, two fifth graders came up to me hand in hand and shyly told me that they were best friends. "How long have you been best friends?" I asked them. "Since third grade," one answered. "Except one year someone else was my best friend."

A range of research has shown that the average school-age child has about five close friends. As with all averages, it's important to remember that this means some children have far fewer than five and some more than that. Five is not a magic number. Some children have best friends, some don't. Friendship quality, not exclusivity or raw numbers, is what really matters.

It's troubling for parents to watch their child stand alone when everyone else seems to be declaring best friends on the playground or at the birthday party. On the other hand, it can also be troubling to see a child concentrate his or her social activity on a single best friend, no matter how compatible or how completely that companion meets a child's need for approval, security, and fun. Some children are just temperamentally suited to concentrating their love, trust, and loyalty on one child or even a small circle of friends. When it comes to counting up your children's friends, remember that there's a wide range of normal. Some parents can't resist the tendency to micromanage peer relations or to worry that their child isn't making the right connections. It's more helpful to ask basic questions such as, "Is my child happy?" or "Is he lonely?"

Marjorie, a tenth grader who attends a large public school near Washington, D.C., has run into some conflict with her dad over their differing concepts of friendship quantity versus quality. "My dad thinks that I should do stuff with lots of people and have them over. He'd like me to be more social. He thinks that if I'm not more social, I'll be sad. Whenever he was at home as a kid he always had somebody there—always. So if I'm alone or with just one of my friends, he assumes I'm sad, but I'm *not*! When I have my birthday party there are a lot of people here, and he would like it to be like that all time. There were twelve people at my last party, and I realized that's about how many people my dad had at his house all the time because he comes from this really big family. So a big crowd seems normal to him.

"With my best friend, we talk every day. We talk about what's been going on in school. We talk on the phone a lot and that's fine with me. Having friends is really important. You can call them and talk to them about stuff, you can tell them your problems, you can lay stuff on them. If you don't have friends, you keep stuff locked up inside. But you don't have to have a crowd of them."

In their daily lives, children will encounter a broad array of acquaintances, classmates, teammates, and neighbors. From these they choose and ally with individuals they term "friends." From the very start the nature of these friendships has a huge impact on their lives. That impact can be positive or negative. Remember Jonathan from the Apple Tree preschool? He generally had a great day if his friend Eleanor was there but was somewhat lonely and at loose ends on the other days.

When your children leave your house and disappear into school for the day, they face an array of tasks and an array of opportunities for pleasure, frustration, and pain. In one sense each child faces these challenges alone. But in another sense they do so in pairs or in groups. Even lonely or isolated children are deeply affected by the status of friendships—or the lack of them. Connecting with a close friend or friends provides them with companions on the journey, allies, cheerleaders, someone to offer feedback to help them figure out just how well, or badly, they're doing at this business of growing up.

Friendships help define us. Through the lens of a chosen friend, we see ourselves and become ourselves. For children, having friends matters, and the quality of those friendships matters. Late in her life, the writer Mary McCarthy told her biographer, "In examining my life history you probably don't give enough importance to friends. I would date my own life more by friendships than by love affairs on the whole. Friends and teachers; for me it has often been the same thing."

Think back to an early, close friendship. What role did that friend play in your life then? How does that friendship affect you today? It probably provided a safe bridge between the small world of your family and the huge world of school and society. Harry Stack Sullivan coined a term to describe that kind of connection. He called it "chumship"—a close, intimate, mutual relation with a same-sex peer. Chumship, he wrote, offers the first opportunity "to see oneself through the other's eyes" and to experience true intimacy.

Sullivan sees chumship as having an enormously powerful developmental function. Chumship shapes not only your sense of self-worth but your actual sense of self. It offers a context for overcoming previous bad experiences. These friendships offer validation of your interests, hopes, and fears. They provide affection and opportunities for intimate disclosure. They help you learn to be sensitive to others, and they serve as templates for later romantic, marital, and parental relationships.

Catherine has a friend whom she has known since second grade. Together in their chumship, they felt brave enough to explore beyond the boundaries of their own houses, venturing out on bikes to explore the larger world. For a while they were next-door neighbors, and they rigged up the classic tin-can-and-string telephone across the wall that separated their backyards. Today they are both involved in publishing and have sometimes worked together on projects. But their business telephone conversations still retain the flavor of that old tin-can phone.

The notion of chumship is an appealing one; I often find myself returning to the work of Harry Stack Sullivan for the poetry and drama of his descriptions of childhood friendship. For the specifics, I look to the more recent research of people such as Willard Hartup, a psychologist at the University of Minnesota. Hartup has moved from the "friendships are good for you" stage to trying to define specific qualities of friendship. He differentiates between "companions" and "friends," finding that friends have a greater sense of one another's needs and capacities. For Hartup, "being friends" implies a special sensitivity and responsibility for another.

According to Hartup, the essential qualities that support a friendship are reciprocity and commitment between two people who see each other as equals. When asked to describe their best friends (or ideal friends), both younger children and older adolescents almost always mention loyalty and commitment.

Because children use terms like "best friends" to mean so many different things, Hartup and other researchers tend to refer to these relationships with different terms, such as "close friendship" or "acquaintanceship." To avoid the confusion inherent in the word *best*, let's refer to these intimate, reciprocal, committed relationships as close friendships.

Close friends are emotional resources. Children draw on their friends for the security they need to strike out into new territory. Close friends also act as buffers against negative events. At a boarding school where Catherine taught, her classroom was right down the hall from the mailroom. On the day that college acceptance letters began to arrive, she observed that students—both boys and girls—approached the mailboxes in pairs. That way, if the letters contained bad news, the friend was there as a comforter. If the news was good, there was someone there to share the celebration. No matter what, the friend was a supporter.

Research has shown that adolescents who perceive their friendships as supportive are more likely to be popular and considered socially competent; they are also more strongly motivated to achieve and are more involved in school. Supportive friends, Hartup tells us, contribute to a child's feeling good about himself and make him feel connected. This equates with a positive outlook about the future and success in subsequent relationships, especially romantic ones.

Close friends serve as informal classrooms. Good friends teach each other through example, through collaboration, and through conflict. Research has shown that both cooperation and conflict actually occur more easily in friendships than in other social contexts. This makes friendship central to the development of social skills.

Adults may be surprised or confused by the level of conflict that arises in many close friendships. In fact, one of the best things about a good friendship is the ability it offers to air conflicts and resolve differences, which enables friends to work through problems together. After all, a nonfriend can just walk away from conflict or escalate it out of control. There's nothing to lose.

Friends are better teachers of one another than nonfriends, Hartup believes. They contribute to each other's ability to solve problems—especially difficult problems. Performance on difficult tasks was made easier when friends worked on it together because of a "free airing of the children's differences in a cooperative context." In other words, friends can disagree, take risks, try things out, and support each other as they work together to solve a problem.

Conflicts are inevitable, but friends feel a special obligation to each other in managing them. "A good friend is someone you fight with, but not forever," an adolescent told researchers investigating friendship quality.

Kate and Ann lived through such a fight. At a year-end seventh grade party, Ann found the pressure to affiliate with her cool crowd overwhelming. When Kate arrived, wearing a plain navy blue dress instead of jeans, Ann joined in the teasing. "You look like a nun," Ann said to Kate. The other kids immediately started calling Kate "sister."

In her rage and pain, Kate pulled Ann's hair, and the two of them had to be dragged apart by other party-goers. For the rest of the night they pointedly ignored each other. The next day Kate didn't answer the phone. But by Monday afternoon Ann and Kate were ready to talk it through. It wasn't easy, but they did it. Ann apologized for the teasing. Kate apologized for the hair pulling. They shared blame for the fight. Both realized that their closeness was too important to them to be permanently broken by the incident.

Friends, Hartup writes, are talkative, and all this talk serves a purpose, creating a "we" concerned with a mutual task. The two halves of a "we" may argue, but they tend to be equitable in managing their conflicts. That sense of equality in the relationship is characteristic of close friendships.

Good Friends Are Good for You

Let's look at some of the ways in which close friendships benefit children. The full story of this research is not yet written, but the current understanding of Hartup and others is that specific good friendship qualities lead to specific good outcomes.

Loyalty is one of them. In high school Larry wrote a controversial article for his school newspaper. His good friend Doug was the assistant editor. He called Larry from an editorial meeting, which was in an uproar over the piece. The editor, anticipating pressure from the paper's faculty advisor, wanted to cut it. But Larry's friend, champion of free student expression, wanted it included. Faced with a standoff, Doug made it clear to the editor that he was willing to quit the paper—which he loved—to stand in solidarity with Larry. Larry says that he would have backed down if the editor had told him privately that the article was too controversial. But with Doug behind him, Larry stood his ground too. The editor agreed to publish the story with a few minor changes. Larry ended up getting in trouble with the principal over the article, and Doug once again came to his defense, writing an editorial about free speech in the next issue of the paper. Larry and Doug became closer friends as a result of their struggle. The next year Doug became editor of the paper—and Larry was his assistant editor.

Most children, maybe all of them, fear rejection. That makes it hard to show other people who they really are, what they really think, how they really feel. With a close friend, you can reveal yourself without the same level of risk. Vulnerability can be a sign of trust in the friendship, rather than a dangerous opening to humiliation. The *mutual support* in a close friendship is a buffer against rejection. I am thinking of a pair of football players who came to my office together. I was expecting only one boy, the one who had been referred to me by his teachers. An African-American, he was one of the best wide receivers the school's football team had ever seen. He was struggling academically and his response to the stresses of school life was to become a clown, which further hampered his academic progress. His clowning masked a very real depression and despair that his academic struggles were causing.

Why were *two* boys at my door? The wide receiver's teammate, a white boy, voluntarily accompanied him to the session. He remained in my office, which made it possible for his friend to stay there too. His presence mitigated the shame of being referred to the "shrink" and shored up his teammate enough to allow him to stick around for the help he so badly needed. The wide receiver discovered that a close friend is the opposite of a "fair-weather friend." When he was in difficulty, his friend stuck around. And his friend discovered the profound satisfaction that comes from lending a hand. We usually don't give boys much credit for being emotionally sensitive, but these boys knew that solidarity was more important than confidentiality, that there were limits to the male stoicism of keeping a stiff upper lip.

Friends help children grow wings. They widen perspective and allow children to experiment. Close friends accept you for who you are, and tolerate—or even like—things about you that your parents might not approve of or even understand. A reader from a family of TV viewers finds a home away from home with his bookish friend's family. An athlete from an intellectual family finds a place to be valued for his sports ability when his friends' parents cheer for him at the games his own parents ignore.

In addition, *friendship exposes children to different social norms.* When your child leaves your home and enters the home of a close friend, he will inevitably be exposed to a different culture, with new ways of behaving and new kinds of language. Spending time with trusted friends' families gives your child a chance to try on different ways of being in the world. Do you have a house with a family room crammed with books? Your child's best friend may have a house that spills over with athletic equipment. Do you have a formal living room where people sit down only for special occasions? Your child's best friend may take him into a home where the kids are allowed to jump on the living room sofa, and so is the dog.

Larry remembers that when he was growing up in New Orleans, he learned to call adults "ma'am" and "sir" at the home of a proper southern friend. His own parents were horrified when he came home and tried this out on them. But Larry was learning an important social lesson for the milieu in which he found himself. (Of course these "lessons" in how other people behave can be startling. My own horizons were shockingly broadened when I heard a friend of mine swear at his own mother, something that was unimaginable to me. I don't think I ever went to his house again!)

Friendship can compensate for lacks in a child's life. Catherine, who has one brother six years older than she is, yearned for a larger family. She made huge piles of yarn dolls, named each one, and divided them into families with at least eight children apiece. She also found a way to connect with a real-life large family. Each day when she arrived home from fifth grade, she'd walk in, notify the housekeeper that she was home, and then walk out the back door. Across the alley lived a family with eight children. Catherine slipped easily into this crowd of boisterous siblings, choosing the one closest to her in age as her best friend, and spent the afternoons there until her own mom got home from work and called her home to dinner. Years later, in a conversation with a member of this family, Catherine talked about how much their rowdy, warm house with its triple bunk beds had meant to her. "And we always envied *you* for having your own room," her friend laughed. Close friendships thrive on these kinds of differences.

Close friends hold each other in mind, and trust that their friend holds them in mind. This quality can confer the security and safety that allows young people to try new things and face difficult experiences. Catherine's niece Maeve, a sophomore at a large university, had attended the same public school from sixth grade through high school graduation. While there, her best friend was a Vietnamese girl, Trinh, the daughter of recent immigrants. Maeve herself is multiracial, with a white father and a mom who can claim both African-American and Native American roots. In a school and town environment that was diverse by race, culture, and language, Maeve and Trinh were brought together by their proximity in one neighborhood. They walked to elementary school together, and sometimes it seemed that they never left one another's side.

After high school, Trinh and Maeve headed to the same university—much to their relief. Catherine checks in with Maeve frequently. Recently Maeve was full of excitement about an apartment she had rented with some new friends. "No Trinh?" Catherine asked her.

"No, she's premed and she's working really, really hard," Maeve said. "I hardly ever see her." Then she paused. "But just knowing that she is here on campus gave me the confidence to make new friends." (I suspect that for Trinh, knowing that Maeve is on campus makes it easier for her to put in the long hours of grueling work that her premed program requires.)

This holding-in-mind quality can be enormously helpful for younger children too. A friend tells a story about taking a walk around a pond near Boston with his daughter, Sarah, then age six. "We were chatting away and she was noticing everything as usual," he remembers. "Suddenly a plop of seagull poop landed right over her eye. She said, 'Eew, eew, eew, get it off.' She tried to stay calm, but I could tell she was heading toward hysterics. I wiped the poop off with my handkerchief and we raced toward the water fountain to wash the hankerchief. After it was all washed out I gave her a big hug and said she was very brave. She looked at me and seemed about to burst into tears, remembering it. Then she smiled and said, 'I can't wait to tell Crystal about this.'"

Crystal was Sarah's best friend. My friend isn't sure if Sarah ever actually told Crystal the story, but just being able to think about telling her best friend about her horrible adventure transformed it from a trauma into a tale to share with a friend.

Friendship keeps children connected. In a changing world, close friendships help provide children with a sense of continuity and stability. As any parent knows, some kids make a great effort to stay in close touch. (For Kate and Ann, that means calling each other on the phone as soon as they're in their rooms after school, even though they have just ridden the bus home together.) Today, technology has made keeping in touch easier—including with friends far away. A thirteen-year-old I know moved to the Boston area against her will from a city four hours away. She has, with difficulty, made some friends here but is still very much attached to her old friends. Her stepmother says, "She comes home from school and turns on the computer to chat with her old friends online. And she picks up the phone to call her Boston friends. We have two phone lines and she's on both of them at once!"

Rob and Adam:
A Case Study in Adolescent Friendship

Rob and Adam, seniors this year, have been close since freshman year, when they were both new at their small high school. Rob is from South Boston, a close-knit, predominantly Irish Catholic neighborhood where he attended parochial school. Adam comes from a predominantly Jewish community west of the city, where he attended public school. In an interview, the boys narrated the history of their relationship with a degree of insight and attention that is characteristic of adolescent friendships. (I am always pleasantly surprised when boys, who often have a tough time articulating their inner lives, are suddenly eloquent when describing the emotional qualities of their friendships.)

Becoming close friends is a creative act that requires imagination, reciprocity, and trust. The act of becoming friends brings a new unit into being. Adam and Rob's friendship is more than the simple sum of Adam plus Rob. It is a new entity, a friendship, anchored in the flow of school, home, and (in this case) two very different communities.

"We met on a bus ride," Adam recalls. "We were going up to Mt. Monadnock on the second or third day of school. Rob was sitting at the front of the bus and I was sitting at the front of the bus just because I don't particularly like riding in back."

"It smells in the back of the bus," Rob says.

"Yeah, it does. And so we were just sitting up there and I looked over at him and he was of course all dressed up and looking dapper and whatnot, and I asked him if he was a teacher. He sort of gave me a snide remark back and said no. And I said okay. I think we sort of let it be at that point."

The boys didn't hike together that day, and they didn't connect in class. Even though they didn't connect that first day, the story of how they met is part of the history of their friendship. Listening to the story, one gets the sense that it has been told many times before. A few weeks later, however, they found themselves working the light board in the theater.

"We were both interested in doing a lot in the theater and working for the school, so I think we just sort of clicked at that point," Adam says.

From that point on, the boys worked in the school's theater program together, spent time exploring Boston together, got to know each other's families. (Adam's mother laughs that the Catholic Rob has learned to say "Oy!") The boys have gotten to a point at which they can interpret each other with dead-on accuracy.

"We read each other really, really well," says Adam. "Rob and I sort of have these looks like, what the hell does that mean, or why is this happening? At assemblies we have to sit so we can see each other. If we're not sitting next to each other, we always sit so we can see each other. So if someone gets up and says something that we just think is totally ridiculous, we just give each other a look."

Adam and Rob are very much aware that they come from different worlds and that their friendship has broadened their horizons. It has also, Rob says, helped him learn to face and accommodate change. During their freshman year, the longtime head of the school announced his imminent departure.

"When we had the change of headmasters there was some moderate turmoil that was going on throughout the year," Adam recalls. "I knew there were going to be a lot of changes. I saw a lot of people overreacting around me. I put that aside because I saw a lot of good things happening. And I think Rob got caught up, through no fault of his own, in a lot of that negativity."

"The difference comes back to our backgrounds," says Rob. "The South Boston community does not accept change very well. I came to school here, and I'd never dealt with so much change all in one short period of time. Because from kindergarten to eighth grade I had never dealt with such a change before. Everything had always been the same. I had always had my fork on the left and my knife on the right.

"But Adam always said, 'Oh, don't worry about it. It's going to be fine.' I always said, 'No, it's not. Something's going to happen.' "

"He's the pessimist around here. I'm the optimist," says Adam.

"Sort of like the Odd Couple," Rob adds. "I'm the one who's neat, and he's the one who's the newspaper reporter who's just a slob."

"I'm not a slob, I'm just laid back," Adam protests in what is clearly an ongoing shtick between these boys.

Rob has faced more than administrative shifts during his high school years—and Adam has proved an important support for him.

"Just this past summer my uncle passed away. That made a major impact on me. Adam came up to Boston for the wake. He and his mother came over from Martha's Vineyard, where they were on vacation."

"You want to try and do as much as you possibly can because you feel bad," says Adam of this decision to leave his vacation to support his friend. "I think in many respects, especially during that time, I tried to get Rob out as much as I possibly could—take him to different places, try to get his mind off what was going on, doing what we usually would do. I think he caught on to what I was doing a little bit, but that's okay."

As graduation approached, Adam and Rob were beginning to think about what would happen next year. Would they stay in touch?

"Yes. Oh, yeah," says Adam. "I think that'll be pretty easy to do."

"The friendship definitely will remain," says Rob.

Thinking of the future, and the different roads he and Adam will be going down soon, Rob conjures a comforting image: "We'll all go up a hill and we'll have this one big house where we all meet together. I'm visualizing this. We all get this one big house where all the different roads meet."

Adam and Rob's close friendship shows us how complex, layered, and thoughtful relationships between young people can be. The boys live out those qualities of intimacy, reciprocity, and commitment that Hartup and others deem essential to friendship. Adam and Rob are loyal, accept each other, and even enjoy their big differences and occasional conflicts. They have supported each other in successes, failures, and tragedies. They have helped each other.

But Adam and Rob's friendship is more than an exchange of commodities—you give me confidence and I'll give you reality checks. It starts and ends with liking each other, enjoying each other, with *being friends*. The benefits flow naturally from that.

Inevitable Losses

As seniors in high school, Adam and Rob are particularly aware of a bittersweet aspect of best friendship that can occur at any age. Inherent in any close connection is the loss that life's inevitable separations and changes will bring. These losses are very real, including those for the youngest best friends. The power of this was brought home to me by a scene with my own son, Will.

When Will was two, his favorite friend was Casey, the daughter of my wife's best friend, Jann. Jann and Casey would come over to our house two or three times a week, and when Will was informed of their arrival he would always exult, "Casey's coming, Casey's coming." He would greet her at the door, they might hug, they would look fondly at each other, then they would retreat to separate sides of the room, one to play with her Jasmine doll and the other to play with his Power Rangers figures. They may have been playing in parallel, but their mutual closeness was unmistakable. They sought each other out frequently for contact and they greeted adults as a pair; they presented themselves as friends.

Sadly, Casey and her family moved away when Will was just three years old and he missed her terribly. One day about a month after their departure, my wife stopped at the mailbox on the way to the car with Will and found there a letter dictated by Casey to her mother and intended for Will. My wife put Will in his car seat and began to read him the letter. It was short and simple. "Hello, Will," it began. When my wife glanced in the rearview mirror, she saw that tears were pouring down Will's face.

Sometimes the loss of a friend comes about when that friend makes a social move that excludes previous connections. This terrible blow happened to a boy named Paul when he was entering fifth grade. His best neighborhood friend, Michael, a boy with whom he had spent hours playing Legos and then Pokémon and who had been his tennis partner at camp, suddenly turned on him in the hallway at their public elementary school.

"Stop following me, Paul! Get away from me," Michael yelled.

Paul didn't understand. He didn't know that in middle school, peer influence becomes all-powerful for kids. He hadn't noticed yet that as a group identity began to form in his class, kids were required to look and talk alike. He hadn't caught up. He wasn't cool. Michael had made the move, and he had become extremely judgmental about shades of popularity and coolness.

"Stop following me!" he yelled again. "I don't want the other kids to see me with you!"

Paul's pain at the betrayal of his friendship was real, sharp, and shocking. But he recovered quickly, finding other boys to connect with in his after-school tennis camp. It still hurt to see Michael, but Paul was able to move on. Soon he had three new boys in his life that he thought of as best friends.

Parents should not be concerned when a child does not match some magic number of friendships, unless he or she also seems depressed or is being rejected by peers. (I will go into greater detail about rejected children in Chapter 6.) But there can be a darker side of best friendships. At times, these connections can become suffocatingly close, verging on a *folie à deux* that shuts out the rest of the world. For example, extreme possessiveness in a close friendship can be destructive, isolating children from ordinary social contact. Instead of providing reality checks for each other and coaching each other to make their way in the group, they create their own new reality, quite distinct from the one the rest of us share. When two troubled children form an exclusive bond, it can play itself out in extreme pathologies such as the killings at Columbine High School in 1999. But it's vitally important to remember that this is not the norm.

Troubles with exclusivity can be difficult to handle. A friend's daughter, Lisa, had a college roommate whose possessiveness, which at first seemed flattering, finally grew overwhelming. Eventually the roommate made scenes, crying and throwing things, if anyone else was included in everyday activities such as walking to class or going out for a pizza. When Lisa went to class, she often came back to find her roommate wearing her clothes or trying on her jewelry. Needless to say, this connection had to be broken and Lisa opted for a single the next year.

If friendship is a container, good friendships are roomy enough to accommodate each person as he or she changes and grows. But even the most positive friendships can't be expected to contain everything that happens in two lives—especially lives as full of change as those of children, adolescents, and young adults. On the other hand, good friendships can grow to contain change. Kate and Ann's close friendship endured the shocks of middle school. When Ann's parents divorced, Ann went off to another school in another city. But the connection between the two girls stretched to accommodate the change. Kate grieved at her loss of daily contact with Ann, but she discovered something new. When she and Ann got together one weekend after not seeing each other for many months, it was just like old times. They had put away their childish game of horses for good, but their genuine pleasure in each other's company remained. Kate said to her mom, "It's as if I saw her just yesterday."

Chapter Five

In the Jungle:
The Power of the Group in
Children's Lives

The strength of the Pack is the Wolf,
and the strength of the Wolf is the Pack.

—RUDYARD KIPLING

Once I was speaking to an assembly of sixth, seventh, and eighth grade children at a regional middle school in western Massachusetts. I asked them, "Have your parents ever warned you about peer pressure? If so, please raise your hand." The vast majority of children indicated that they had been so warned—but only after looking around first to see who was raising their hand and who wasn't.

"Why," I continued, "are your parents so worried about peer pressure?"

"They're worried we'll get into trouble," said one boy.

"They think the group will be a bad influence on us," declared a girl.

"They don't think I'll stand up for myself," reported another girl.

"They think I'll do drugs," shouted a boy.

"So," I said, "your parents think that peer pressure is a bad thing, right?" Three hundred heads nodded.

"That's not true," I asserted. "Your parents love peer pressure. They really love it." My audience looked shocked. This was news. Everybody knows that parents disapprove of peer pressure. I continued. "They love for you to be influenced by your friends as long as your friends do their homework, are planning to go to college, and are well behaved. They really hope that all of that peer pressure will have an effect on you. That's why they may have moved to this town, because it has a good school system, which means that kids are doing their work and your parents thought the kids here would have a good influence on you. Parents *love* good peer pressure. They only hate peer pressure when other kids pressure you to try drugs and sex."

Children always like to have the curtain pulled back to reveal inconsistencies in their parents' rules and beliefs, and this time was no exception. My audience saw immediately that what I was saying was absolutely true. Their parents love good kids. Their parents even love suck-ups. Their parents hope they'll hang out with responsible children who do their homework: "Why don't you have Susie over?" a girl's parents ask. "She's so nice." Your parents hope that the nice, good kids will pressure you to be nice. They want you to feel the peer pressure. It's a conspiracy!

"I have another question for you," I said. "Do your parents give in to peer pressure?" The children stared at me. Some shook their heads. This was another thought that they were unaccustomed to having. Peer pressure happens to kids, not to grown-ups, right? Their parents have given them the impression that adults are strong enough to stand up to peer pressure.

I put my hand on my tie and told them, "You know, if I am invited to a party and I don't know how the other people are going to dress, I call ahead to ask whether the men at the party are going to be wearing a tie and jacket or not. I don't want to be the only person at the party wearing a tie if no one else is, and I certainly don't want to be the only person without a jacket if everyone else has one. And if I show up dressed the wrong way, I think about it the whole evening and it spoils the party for me. No one has to have said anything to me about the way I am dressed, but I feel uncomfortable if I am different. That's peer pressure. And adults feel it all the time. Adults feel it just as much as kids. Adults gossip about other grown-ups who do things differently from them, and they try to get them to behave in the same way."

I could see that the children were thinking of examples in their own family life. Yes, parents do act like other parents. Parents sound like each other, they dress like each other. Parents aren't all that different from kids, even though they pretend to be. Grown-ups even run in packs, just like kids!

Adults often ask me why children in groups are so cruel. I am always astonished by the question. What about groups of adults? What about the Holocaust? What about the Serbs and Croats? How could neighbors who had lived together for hundreds of years suddenly turn on one another and begin to see each other as enemies? Why have Protestants and Catholics in Northern Ireland been willing to plant bombs in each other's neighborhoods and kill people only blocks away? What about the Hutus and the Tutsis? During the genocide in Rwanda, a Hutu man beheaded his Tutsi wife and his three sons in front of a crowd when the Hutu chief in his town told him that he had to kill all Tutsis. What force could make a person do something like that? Peer pressure. Peer pressure in a horrible group cause.

The Laws of Group Life

All human beings who live in groups are subjected to invisible, neutral forces: the laws of group life. And if we are going to understand why children do the things that they do to each other—especially the cruel things—we have to know what these laws are. Without knowledge of these social forces we make the mistake of thinking that tragic events are driven solely by "bad kids" or "gangs." We won't understand that "good kids" are often responding to exactly the same set of underlying principles as "bad kids" or that there are gangs of "good kids" in our schools as well as gangs of "bad kids."

Identifying and studying these laws is the province of social psychology. When I talked with the middle school children about peer pressure and told them that their parents feel it too, I was introducing them to a central insight of this branch of psychological research: The invisible norms of group life are everywhere. No matter how grown-up or smart you are, you are subject to them.

Law 1: "Be Like Your Peers"

Many parents mistakenly believe that peer pressure is overt and coercive. They imagine that their child is at a party and other kids surround him, hand him a glass, and say, "Drink. You have been a nondrinker too long. If you want to be one of the group, then drink this. We're all going to stand here and make you do it. And if you don't, we're going to tease, humiliate, and reject you."

Nothing could be further from the truth. It is the magnetism of the group that exerts pressure; it is the desire to belong. The motivation to conform comes from within each child; it doesn't have to be imposed from outside. Very rarely is there any coercion. A teenager who goes to a party very likely knows in advance whether people will be drinking there. She has made the decision to put herself in harm's way because she wants to be a part of that particular group, or she wants to put herself in a risky situation to see how it feels. She feels pressure to drink long before she arrives at the party because she has already imagined herself in the situation of watching others drink. And she tests herself internally: "I don't have to do what those other people are doing. I can be independent." Or perhaps she says: "I'm not so young anymore. Lesley says this is a great group of kids. She drinks, but she gets better grades than I do. It doesn't hurt her." She may be ready to join the group by drinking, or she may want to be part of it without drinking and believes that she will be able to stand up to the invisible, omnipresent peer pressure. And she may well succeed. But the lessons from research on the power of group behavior are humbling.

One famous social-psychology experiment was conducted by Solomon Asch at Swarthmore College back in the 1950s. It captures perfectly the power of peer pressure. I like to describe it to children. Asch recruited a young man from nearby Haverford College and offered to pay him to participate in an experiment in visual perception. The young man was then asked to come to the psychology lab at Swarthmore. When the subject arrived, he was immediately introduced to eight other people his age whom he had never met before, all confederates of the researcher. The young Haverford man was the only true subject of the experiment.

The undergraduates were then shown a card with an eight-inch-long line on it, followed by a card with four lines on it, five, six, eight, and nine inches long. They were asked which of the lines on the card was equal to the line on the other card. (This wasn't a hard task, and it wasn't supposed to be.) After a few trials with everyone giving the right answers, the confederates—as trained—unanimously began to give the same incorrect answer. The group was seated so that most of them spoke before the real subject did. Around the circle went the interviewer, and the confederates all said B was equal to the first line, even though clearly it was A or C that matched the original. The subject was likely to give the wrong answer as well. Indeed, only one in three people tested stuck to their guns and contradicted the group. Two-thirds of the subjects went along with the group, choosing the popular wrong answer over the evidence of their own senses.

I described this experiment to middle school students in Montreal, Canada. Once the children heard the setup of the experiment, they were intensely interested in what the subject was going to do. I repeated the confederates' deceptive assertions of "B ... B ... B ... B," and then I asked the students, "What did the college student say?"

An eighth grade boy was waving his hand excitedly before I had even finished my words. "B," he declared confidently.

"That's right. How did you know that?"

" 'Cause I've done things like that!"

Turning to the girls, I asked, "Why did he say B when it was obvious to him that the lines were of different lengths?"

"He wanted to be a member of the B-Line Club," a girl said.

We've all done things like that because we wanted to feel that we were part of some B-Line Club. Our fear of not being included is so great that even when our eyes are telling us one thing, we are willing to say something different. The subjects of the experiment never changed their perceptions; they knew that what they were saying was wrong. They did it because they didn't want to look "different." They reported later that it made them doubt their vision or their sanity. If they did hold to their perceptions and give the right answer, they felt embarrassed about seeing the right thing, because apparently no one else saw it.

Later studies using the same format reveal that conformity increases if people feel incompetent or insecure or if they admire the group's status or attractiveness. Is it a mystery that so many children in middle school, already insecure for developmental reasons, are destined to be conformist and conventional? Middle schoolers are insecure because of all the changes going on in their bodies and in their lives, and they are totally dedicated to the group. For both reasons they are strongly pulled toward conformity.

Many parents have said to me, "We'd like to raise a child who is so morally secure that he or she can stand up to the group." This expression of hope always makes me wince, because I know from the research that we are all subject to the universal laws of group life, the need to be part of a group, and the need for a group to stay together. I know that the forces of conformity are very powerful. In his study of adolescents and their families, Stuart Hauser found that a small fraction of adolescents—only 4 percent—seem to be able to make moral decisions by looking inward to their own conscience and values, instead of outward to the behavior of the group. They are able to divine their own points of view and understand moral complexities from an early age. That leaves 96 percent of children who are routinely susceptible to group pressure and are likely to say, in a difficult social situation, that the answer is B just because everyone else has said it is.

Law 2: "You Must Belong to a Group"

The second law of group life mandates membership in some kind of affiliated gathering of people—an "us." All of us hunger for group identity and closeness. I travel around the country a lot, and if I go to Texas and have a talk with a native Texan, inevitably he tells me what Texans are like. He describes how all people in Texas supposedly behave. If I tell that person that I'm from Boston, he says to me, "Oh, Boston. That's a nice city, but I hear the people are pretty cold up there. Well, we're real friendly down here."

Texans, and all other human beings, like to feel they're part of a group that has a distinct identity. They like to feel that they are good at something, in this case friendliness, and they like to define themselves as different from other people. So in a few brief sentences a Texan announces what he is good at, namely, being friendly, and by the way, he knows that people from my group, folks from the Northeast, aren't quite as friendly as Texans. Folks from Boston, he regrets to inform me, are colder than Texans, but he's going to rise above that and be friendly to me anyway! He has notified me that there is an "us" and a "them," Texans and Bostonians, an in-group and an out-group. He has revealed his hunger for group cohesion and displayed the universal tendency to define a group by who isn't in it. We all do this. We all want to be in, members of the B-Line Club, as that student in Montreal observed. And once we're in it, we have a mild contempt for those who are not: "Too bad about those Bostonians. They're not friendly like us Texans."

My conversations with Texans are benign and joking. But there is a darker side to group cohesion, which was dramatically demonstrated by a famous piece of experiential learning developed by a teacher, Jane Elliott, in Riceville, Iowa, in the 1960s. Elliott wanted to give her all-white third-grade class, none of whom had any experience with children of other races, a sense of how easy it was to develop prejudice and how destructive the forces of prejudice could be. One day she announced that brown-eyed children were more intelligent, better people than blue-eyed children and should therefore be the "ruling class." She helped the brown-eyed children create rules that would keep the inferior group "in their place" in the new social order. Blue-eyed children were made to sit in the back of the room and stand at the back of the line, and they were told they could not use the drinking fountains but had to drink out of paper cups. Superior children were accorded privileges that inferior children were not, such as extra recess time.

The effects of the experiment were felt immediately. Within minutes the blue-eyed children began to do poorly on their lessons and became depressed, sullen, and angry. They described themselves as "sad," "bad," and "stupid." The superior kids turned, almost instantly, from being cooperative and kind children into "nasty, vicious, discriminating" third-graders. When, on the next day, the teacher announced that she had made a mistake, and it was in fact the blue-eyed children who were superior and the brown-eyed children who were inferior, the behavior of the children flip-flopped. Friendships dissolved and were replaced with hostility.

At the end of the experiment, the children were extremely relieved to find out that none of them were, in fact, inferior to other children. When the teacher stopped the experiment, the children crowded around her in one happy, united band, free to accept others, and feel accepted.

Law 3: "Be In—or Be Out"

The third law of group life governs who's "out" and who's "in"—and this law is so powerful that it demands that "out" people create groups of their own.

Inclusion and exclusion are powerful instruments of group cohesion. A friend of mind once said, after we had had a rather gossipy lunch together, "It isn't important whom we like in common. What's important is that we have the same enemies." What she said was true; we felt closer because we hated the same people. We all feel the longing to be part of something exclusive, something that not everyone can be part of, and we imagine we're part of it and they're not. That is the enduring genius in Groucho Marx's joke about not wanting to join a club that would have him as a member. He expresses the wish to be included in a society so special that it excludes himself.

One of the most famous experiments in social psychology was a 1961 study of twenty-two boys at a Boy Scout camp in Oklahoma. The researchers, Muzafer Sherif and Carolyn W. Sherif, discovered that it was not at all difficult to create intergroup conflict. Simply putting the boys in two different cabins began to stimulate competitive feelings between the groups. Assigning them different names (the Eagles and the Rattlers) accelerated the sense of rivalry. Introducing games such as tug-of-war or a treasure hunt led to name-calling and physical friction. Cabins were raided, banners were stolen and burned, threatening signs were posted, and lunchroom scuffles became commonplace. Within days the Eagles and the Rattlers quickly became more like the Jets and the Sharks, the gangs from the musical *West Side Story*, who sang, "When you're a Jet you're a Jet all the way, from your first cigarette to your last dying day." On a smaller, less dangerous scale, these Boy Scouts were subject to the same psychological forces—inclusion and exclusion—that drove the Crips and the Bloods to fight it out for real in Los Angeles during the 1980s. The experiment in creating intergroup conflict had gone better, or worse, than the researchers expected, because they had tapped into a universal force that makes groups come together and distinguish themselves from other groups.

When a child finds himself on the "out" side of the group equation, it can be powerful enough to change his perception of himself. Ben, a sixth grader, applied to and was accepted for seventh grade at an academically demanding private school. In many ways he was an excellent candidate for the school. He was very bright, his parents were intellectual people—so academically demanding, in fact, that they had become dissatisfied with the local schools. Ben loved science. Unhappily, he was not a very popular boy in sixth grade. He was very adult-focused and talked far too much. He did not judge his peer audience very well and was often seen as boastful or pompous. All the way through elementary school he got straight A's. Even he admitted cheerfully, "I'm not cool." He did, however, expect to be a good student at the new school, and he hoped he might be popular at a school that placed more value on academic performance.

When he arrived at his new school, the demands for written language skills were far greater than anything he had faced before. Ben was devastated when he got a D in English at the end of the first semester. Even when he was socially isolated in his regular school, he had always thought of himself as smart. Now the boys in his English class were calling him "stupid" and "dope" and were teasing him about his previous school. Instead of rallying, he also began to do poorly in math, because his math class had many of the same kids as his English section. He began to isolate himself in class, sitting far away from the other children, and he did not try to make friends with the girls, which had been a successful strategy for him in sixth grade. He told me, "I just try not to draw any attention to myself. I try not to say anything." Soon he was getting a C-minus in math, and the teacher had begun to think that he was not academically equipped to handle the school.

Ironically, it was just at this time—in the late winter of a terrible year—that he took a competitive state math test. Though he was at the bottom of his school class, he scored above everyone on the test. The other students were amazed. They had really believed that he was stupid and were embarrassed to find out that he had performed better on the test than they had. He too was surprised. He said to me proudly, "I had forgotten how much I liked math until I took that test." The test notwithstanding, he struggled painfully through the entire year feeling like a social outcast and yearned to go back to the school where he had been miserable but an excellent student.

Law 4: Find a Place in the Social Hierarchy

The fourth law of group life legislates an individual's placement in the hierarchy. If inclusion and exclusion (the in and out of groups) are an ever-present reality, so too is the up and the down of groups, the social hierarchy. Human beings, as well as other primates, tend to configure themselves into a social ladder, with some children being higher up than other children. Think back to algebra class and imagine the up-and-down dimension as a vertical line, while in and out is a horizontal line that cuts across the vertical line to form four quadrants. An extraordinarily popular boy athlete might be in the up-and-in quadrant, while a newly arrived and socially clumsy child might be stuck in the down-and-out section. A shy, reserved child who has been in the school since kindergarten and is therefore known by everyone may be in and down, while a sexy, slightly "bad" high school girl, such as the character Rizzo from the musical *Grease*, might be up and out. She would be popular but slightly dangerous, outside the social norms of the group.

We know that many animals have a social hierarchy, and their behaviors have provided us with words that we use to describe our own social systems. Wolves have alpha males and alpha females. Low-status wolves don't look into the eyes of alphas, and they expose their necks to the higher-status wolves to indicate that they are not a threat. Dog packs have "top dogs." Even chickens have a status hierarchy. Lower-caste chickens have fewer feathers on their tails because they have been pecked off by more aggressive, higher-status chickens. The term "pecking order" comes from this phenomenon. We know that sheep follow one another on narrow paths, carefully following the footsteps of the animal in front of them so that they can automatically avoid holes and rocks and other obstacles. Put a fence in front of a line of sheep, and they will all jump over it. Move the fence out of the way, and the sheep keep jumping. This isn't stupidity on the sheep's part but a simple assumption that the leader must know what he is doing, because he can see farther. We call children who follow others "sheep," with an implied contempt, ignoring the animal wisdom in such behavior.

Young male chimpanzees challenge and fight one another to establish dominance. After these wrestling matches, the chimps know who is the strongest and the challenge matches stop—at least until someone new comes on the scene or a younger male grows to adulthood and wants to prove himself by taking on a higher-status male. Female chimps also have a status hierarchy, though it is not settled through wrestling matches. Their dominance is established with angry looks, raised eyebrows, avoidance, and refusal to groom another female. Through these methods—somewhat subtler than the males' wrestling matches but no less effective—an alpha female is chosen. She gets first choice of food when it is eating time, just as the alpha male gets first choice of a mating partner. The offspring of alpha females grow to sexual maturity faster than do the young of other females. Thus an alpha female can more effectively pass on her genes, just as the alpha male can by having first choice of a mating partner.

Because chimps are our closest animal relative (we share 98.5 percent of our DNA with chimpanzees) their behavior patterns are inevitably instructive for us. Indeed, we do see human parallels: Boys in groups challenge one another to wrestling matches. Young adolescent boys often posture and attempt to intimidate one another by puffing up their chests or heading for the weight room to build up their muscles. Football players who have just scored touchdowns beat their chests in the end zone to celebrate their achievement. In every classroom in every school there is a status hierarchy among boys and a different status hierarchy among girls. All children fight for position. Girls can be cruel gossips, as teachers often tell me. Girls shun one another, give each other dirty looks, and refuse to "groom" one another when they are not feeling close. Girls who are close touch one another and play with their friends' hair and barrettes.

Social hierarchy issues can sometimes be a daily struggle for children. At a small school that had only eight boys in the third grade, the "top dog" was more gifted athletically, academically, and socially than any other boy. Physically he was also the largest. The second most powerful boy in the group was miserable that he could not overtake his rival in anything. The only job left for the number two boy was to be the right-hand man of this class leader, his friend, and yet he could not tolerate being in that role because of his own feelings of competitiveness. At another school he might have been the alpha male, with a totally different arc to his social career. In a large school he and the alpha male might have been leaders of rival groups. Apparently chimpanzees are more accepting of the social hierarchy once it has been established than human beings are, or perhaps low-status chimps just cannot tell us of their misery.

The idea of a status hierarchy among children, in which some kids dominate others, is deeply offensive to many people. We are human beings, after all, and moral beings, not chimpanzees. As one mother furiously asked me, "Why can't all the children in this school be at the same level?" The answer is that a status hierarchy exists in every classroom in every school in the land. Sometimes it's subtle; other times it's overt and highly problematic for children and adults. Status hierarchy is an inevitable phenomenon of groups. The only way to avoid it is to homeschool your children—and even then it will happen on the playground when all the home-schooled kids get together. Indeed, sometimes when I lecture about social hierarchies, parents who are home-schooling their children come up afterward and tell me, "We don't see these behaviors in our children. Home-schooled children aren't like this." I do not have enough experience with home-schooled children to know whether or not this is so, though I imagine that it is possible to avoid many of the severe problems of bullying and victimization, mob behavior, and social isolation that develop in schools when a child is home-schooled. There can be a status hierarchy among siblings who are home-schooled together but I'm sure that a home-schooling environment is not as intense from a social point of view as a classroom can be.

Several years ago I worked with a midwestern school in which a ninth grade class had developed intense rivalry between cliques. The situation was fueled by a couple of boys in the class who believed that, as a point of pride and masculinity, groups ought to compete with one another and that a running score of successful put-downs and other triumphs should be kept. The impact on the class as a whole was to make the boys defensive and aggressive with each other and with adults. When the administrators began to seriously address the tensions in the class, all the boys loudly denied that competitive groups existed. They portrayed the class as one happy family, where all boys were mutually supportive. That was, of course, hogwash. The students, like all children in any school, did not want any adults nosing around in their business— even though they were all pretty miserable. The dean asked me if I would talk with the class, and I agreed. However, when I pictured trying to have a conversation with eighty boys on this subject I knew very well that they wouldn't talk to me. I looked around for a nonverbal way to address the problem and ended up adapting an exercise from family therapy. With some trepidation, and the approval of the administrators, I used it on the entire class.

The exercise is called "family sculpture." In family therapy it involves having one member of a family "sculpt" the other members into interacting positions that illustrate for the therapists how the sculptor experiences the family. With family sculpture, you then have all the other members of the family make their own sculptures of the family. The exercise leads to some intense, wonderful discussions about family life.

I knew that I would not be able to have more than one student "sculptor" do his work, but I suspected that having the class broken down into its different elements might lead to some fruitful discussions. I found a large room that had a rug and emptied it of all its furniture. When the class came in I asked them to sit on the floor. I explained the exercise and asked for a volunteer to break the class down into its groups. A boy who was planning to leave the school at the end of the year volunteered. He was the only volunteer. He attacked the task fearlessly, moving boys here and there, asking them to join this group or that.

It took him about fifteen minutes, and when he had finished, the "sculptor" had laid bare the underlying social structure of the class. Indeed, he had effectively drawn a map of his city, with its racial and social class differences exposed. The center group, deliberately placed in the middle of the room, was composed of boys from three of the affluent suburbs. These were the wealthiest boys in the class and they tended to play the same sports: soccer, lacrosse, and tennis. The second group was a tight pack of boys who, despite attending a private school, were fundamentally identified with the public school they had all attended together in the elementary grades. They were the "townies"—their self-description— and proud of it. Another group consisted of football players. I was surprised at first to see none of the black football players in that group, but then I saw the sculptor's logic: the African-American and Asian boys were together in one group, no matter what sport they played, where they lived, or where they had gone to grammar school. Ringing all of these cohesive groups were boys alone or in pairs or trios—the outsiders.

It was like seeing a skeleton. It was like watching a videotape of open-heart surgery or the pictures from inside the sunken *Titanic*. There is a dreadful fascination with looking at the inner workings of things. And here was the structure of the class, naked and undeniable. The sculptor had done his work and revealed the divisions. I went around asking boys how it felt to be in the group they were in. Almost all acknowledged that they had been put in the right place. One of the African-American boys was relieved and voluble. "This is the way it is here," he said with emphasis, "every day!" It was painful to speak to some of the boys on the outside of the circle, the boys leaning against the wall. I could tell that having their outsider status revealed so openly was hurtful to some of them, and for that reason I would not necessarily conduct this exercise again. The exercise, however, brought the factional feuding to an abrupt end. It made the boys deal with the fact that blacks and Asians were excluded from the inner circle. It pulled the curtain from the self-deluding fiction that they were a mutually supportive, cohesive unit. The hierarchy was visible and upsetting to boys on a moral basis. The meeting ended with boys vowing to bring the class closer together, and many of them worked effectively toward that goal in the following weeks.

Law 5: You Must Play a Role

Hierarchy is a fact of group life. Within that structure, the fifth law of group life dictates that children play other roles besides the basic categories of in, out, up, and down. Every class has a leader, a clown, a suck-up, a goody-goody, a jock, and a flirt. Surely that can't be a coincidence. The laws of probability suggest that once in a while there will be a class filled entirely with gentle and kind children, or an entire class of clowns, leaders, or goody-goodies. But that never happens. Why not? Doesn't everybody just act out their basic nature, their temperament? Not exactly. A person's nature might help determine what role he or she is selected to play, but the fact of different roles is one of those universal aspects of group life.

Why is it that so many classes have a teacher's pet? The answer is that the hierarchy and the roles are "assigned" by the universal forces at work in the group. Many different roles are needed in group life, and the scripts are given to children based on their temperaments and their willingness to play the roles. Any class is a drama that requires different characters. If a child arrives in a class, no one says, "Gee, we need a suck-up here, someone anxious who curries favor with the teacher. Our last teacher's pet moved to another town. Would you apply for the position?" But if the position of teacher's pet is open, so to speak, some child will be pulled into it, just as another child is pulled into the role of class clown and another into the role of benevolent leader. We behave in accordance with the role that is assigned to us. The assignment is not always random; that is, a certain role might fit our talents very well, but children do not choose their roles freely. Ben was assigned the role of class scapegoat in his new school—certainly not a role he chose or enjoyed. But once in that role, he couldn't just decide one day to be an admired risk-taker or cool trendsetter. Meanwhile, the bullies who were tormenting him were also chosen by the class to be the aggressive ones. Without words, without even any conscious thought or decision, these boys were licensed by their classmates to be openly cruel to Ben and other kids in the "acceptable victim" role. Those other boys—the silent majority who don't do the dirty work themselves but get a vicarious thrill out of watching others do the teasing, and sometimes have a guilty conscience afterwards—don't *pick on* the victim themselves. But they *pick* the victim. They decide who will be rescued if attacked by a bully and who will be allowed to go down.

Another experiment in social psychology shows how people in groups behave when they are assigned certain roles. For his "prison guard experiment" at Stanford University in 1971, Philip Zimbardo picked twenty-two undergraduate male volunteers. He selected young men who were white, middle-class, law-abiding, mature, and stable. Ten of these young men he designated as prisoners, twelve as guards. They were locked together in the cellar of a building, in a set of rooms that re-created a prison. The warden (a psychologist) and the guards made a list of rules the prisoners had to obey. Very soon the guards began to think of the prisoners as inferior and began to treat them very badly. The prisoners quickly began to see the guards as bullies and sadists. One guard reported, "I was surprised at myself. . . . I made them call each other names and clean out the toilets with their bare hands. I practically considered the prisoners cattle." Within a few days the prisoners staged a rebellion, barricading themselves inside their cells by shoving beds against the doors. The guards squashed the rebellion and made the prisoners strip off their clothes. The guards took away their beds and thoroughly intimidated them.

The experiment was supposed to last two weeks. On the sixth day the researchers ended it for the safety of all parties. Remember, these were intelligent, stable undergraduates at a fine university who, because of the roles they were assigned, soon acted in sadistic ways toward other young men who had done nothing wrong. The assigned roles of guard and prisoner had driven thoughtful individuals to act in an extraordinarily cruel fashion.

Whenever subjects are debriefed after such experiments, they always express astonishment at how completely they fell into their roles. They are shocked by how cruelly they were prepared to act toward others when they were in those roles. But you do not have to be conducting social psychology experiments to hear that. Time and time again in schools I hear faculty members say, after hearing of a "good" child's cruelty to a low-status child, "I'm surprised to hear that. She's a very moral kid." I also have many kids say in therapy, "I don't know why I did that. It didn't feel like me. I was uncomfortable." It is difficult for adults to grasp the fact that morality is not just an individual trait. Conscience is part of an individual's makeup, but morality is a phenomenon of the group of which we are a part and the roles we are asked to play. Remember, we all want to be part of the "B-Line Club," even if what the people in the club say or do is flat-out wrong and we know it.

In another classic experiment from 1937, Kurt Lewin and his colleagues studied groups of ten-year-old boys. The groups were led by adults who were trained in three different styles of leadership: autocratic, democratic, or laissez-faire. Each group had each type of leader for six weeks; then they switched. When the boys had an autocratic leader, they were thirty times as hostile and eight times as aggressive as they were under democratic leadership. There was much more scapegoating in the autocratic group, because children were encouraged to think along hierarchical lines and have contempt for anyone of lower status. When the boys moved from an autocratic style to a laissez-faire group their hostility increased briefly and then decreased to a moderate level. Lewin observed that the democratic boys helped each other and made group decisions. Children behave toward one another in accordance with the models they have experienced. This experiment is an everyday variation on the golden rule in action: We do unto others as others have done to us.

Finding a Sense of Mission:
Helping Groups of Kids Cohere

Now that we've examined the five laws of group life, let's take a look at what can be done to defuse—and even transform—a group's negative power. For developmental reasons, eighth grade can be a tough year for many kids, and when a school has a cruel social dynamic at work in a class, it can drive even steady, veteran teachers to drink. One year at Jefferson, a public middle school in a suburban town, the eighth grade was the worst in anyone's memory. None of the teaching team could remember when all four sections of eighth grade, ninety-two kids in all, had been so problematic. The popular cliques that ordinarily seemed to lose power at the end of seventh grade were still alive and conducting a reign of terror over the low-status students.

There were several negative leaders among the boys who were openly contemptuous of the teachers and of the administration but who had been careful enough not to get themselves suspended. Rumor had it that there had been a lot of precocious sexual activity in the class, and the adults imagined that some of the obnoxious behavior came from students being overstimulated. Whatever the explanation, the class was strikingly unattractive in its language and behavior, and as a group they relentlessly scapegoated a couple of low-status students who seemed unable to find safety anywhere. In particular, they tormented Peter, a small, sensitive boy with thick glasses. As the spring approached, the eighth grade teaching team began to consider whether things were so bad that the annual musical should be canceled..

At this point, the new music teacher, Mr. Hughes, stepped in and proposed an alternative. Instead of despairing about the class and canceling the show as a punishment, and instead of doing the eighth grade musical in the usual way, with tryouts, cuts, and only a minority of the class participating, he stunned his colleagues with a daring idea. He proposed that every member of the eighth grade participate in the musical, either as actors or as technical support. He described an ambitious production in which leading parts would be double-cast and some class time given over to rehearsal. Furthermore, he made the radical proposal that the production be staged over two weekends (with different leads on different weekends), and that on the second weekend of the run performances would be given at the high school.

The team's initial reaction was that the new music teacher was extraordinarily ambitious. When questioned, however, Mr. Hughes argued that the entire class needed to work on a project, a highly public project, together. He claimed that it would pull the class together. He asked the teachers to support it by giving up on some class time, and wondered whether some of them would be willing to direct parts of the technical operation. Though skeptical and worried, the teachers were so fed up with the class that they were willing to try nearly anything.

And so a special production of *You're a Good Man, Charlie Brown* was undertaken that spring, with every eighth grader participating. The kids were awed by the size of the production, they were very nervous about doing it at the high school, and they were amazed that the teachers were willing to step outside their usual roles and rules to make it happen. They saw their teachers in a different light. Something developed among the eighth grade students and teachers, something that could be described as "school spirit." The schedule and logistical changes (the kids had to take buses to the high school to build the set there) seemed to bring out the best in them. Most touchingly, the scapegoated boy, Peter, turned out to have tremendous acting and singing talent—something Mr. Hughes had known all along. Peter was cast as Snoopy, and he stole the show. The kids could not stop talking about him: "I had no idea he was so good." "Did you see Peter? He was amazing." "He was totally cool." "He made me cry." For the rest of the spring, after the *Charlie Brown* production in early May, no one could remember why they had thought this eighth grade class had been quite so bad.

The misbehavior of that eighth grade had produced angry, frustrated reactions in the teachers. They had punished the eighth grade and exercised their authority, and it had only produced an us-against-them reaction in the kids. The kids were outlaws, the "bad" class, and they acted as if they were proud of it. They trotted their cruelty out under the noses of the teachers. They scapegoated Peter right in front of adults. It was sickening.

Mr. Hughes cut through all of this cruelty not by attacking the group but by proposing a democratic project, and a highly public one at that. Everyone was going to have a role in the ambitious production, and the show could go on only if everyone fulfilled his or her role. It was also the case that everyone would have been embarrassed if the show had been a public flop in front of the parents and the high school kids. Everyone was a stakeholder in the production and it elicited new behavior from the students. Mr. Hughes had tapped into the power of a common mission (the psychological term is "superordinate goal") to make a group cohere and to help it chart a new course and a new identity. Instead of using a scapegoat and defiance of authority to declare their cohesion as a group, they used the superordinate goals provided by the teachers under the guidance of Mr. Hughes.

The same thing happens in the adult world whenever there is a natural disaster or some other tragedy. Several years ago when the Mississippi River overflowed its banks and flooded parts of North and South Dakota and Iowa, neighbors who had never known or liked one another worked side by side to fill sandbags and build dams to keep the river within its banks. Tornadoes, fires, and earthquakes give people a common mission that brings out a sense of community, overriding the group divisions and the sense of "us" and "them" that normally divides a community. When folks are interviewed on TV they almost always say something like, "There are good people here. Everyone pulled together. We support each other in Iowa." In their minds, however, people are often surprised to realize that they suddenly like neighbors whom they had tended to mistrust or dislike. After a natural disaster people often experience greater empathy and compassion for others and a heightened sense of religious faith.

Social psychology has understood the power of superordinate goals at least since the 1961 experiments at the Boy Scout camp in Oklahoma. Remember how easy it was for the researchers to create intergroup competition between the two cabins of boys by simply giving them different names, Eagles and Rattlers, and by holding a cabin tug-of-war? Having created the friction between the groups, the researchers went about trying to create intergroup cooperation. They created situations where competition between the groups would have harmed everyone, where only cooperation would serve the interests of all boys. So, for example, one day the camp truck was "found" to be stuck. All the boys were assembled and they pulled and pushed together to free the truck. Then the experimenters interrupted the camp's water supply and the boys responded by harmoniously working to fix the problem. Each boy was also given a small amount of spending money, but it was only when the boys decided to pool all the funds that they realized they had enough to rent a movie. The two groups enjoyed a happy evening watching a film together, sitting among each other instead of in separate territories.

It is not enough just to put groups together in one place. Indeed, when two groups are in an us-and-them frame of mind, being close together increases the friction. That is one reason why busing as a method of reducing racism has not worked in a psychological sense. When groups think of themselves as very different, simply bringing them together is not sufficient. They have to have a common goal, a common mission. They have to work side by side on some important project together: pulling out a stuck truck, filling sandbags to create a dam, or putting on a play at the high school.

When I was in college I worked as an instructor at Hurricane Island Outward Bound School. On the first day we would place the students in groups, called "watches." There was always an interesting mixture of inner-city kids, public high school athletes, children sent for disciplinary or therapeutic reasons, and privileged private school kids. On the face of it, it would seem difficult to make such a disparate group cohere into a mutually supportive unit, but by the end of the month the groups were always incredibly close. How was this accomplished? On the first day the boys (Outward Bound now has programs for girls and coed programs) were taken down to the waterfront, loaded into whaling dories, each given an oar, and towed several miles out to sea. At that point, the dories were let loose and the boys were instructed to row back to Hurricane Island by dinner. This was a task that could not be solved by one person. Every member of the group had to master his oar and row in unison with the other boys. Getting back to the island had to be an immediate group effort. By the time they had rowed home, they had blisters, the "watch" had complained together, they were cursing the counselors—and they had started to function as a team. The principle of superordinate goals is at work in many of the exercises that are used in outdoor education programs. That's why so many schools try to help a class cohere or break up a bad class dynamic by putting the kids on a ropes course or taking them mountain climbing.

Groups are so important to children that it is difficult for them to act as freethinking, empathic individuals when they are part of one. But adults have found ways to make groups more comforting, cohesive, structured, and purposeful for kids. All groups, however, have their downside. Yes, Outward Bound students will cooperate in rowing a whaling dory to get home that first day, and children will help each other across a ropes course. If, however, a school principal announces that there is going to be an outdoor camping trip, many of the children immediately begin to scheme about who should sleep in whose tent, who should be included, and who should be excluded. Adults are tempted to exclaim in frustration, "Kids! Why are they like this?" Or, as the memorable actor Paul Lynde sang in the musical *Bye Bye Birdie*, "Kids, what's the matter with kids today?" In truth, the behavior of groups is often not about kids at all. Both the cooperative rowing and the rapid-fire planning about sleeping arrangements are part of group life, the upside and the downside of communal living. They come as a package, and when adults work with children they must understand that.

I once interviewed an eighth grade class at a school in northern Virginia. We talked about several different topics, but eventually we settled on parents. The kids rhapsodized about how annoying their parents were and how they deserved more freedom than their strict, overreactive folks were giving them. After perhaps seven or eight children had described how annoying their parents were and how misunderstood the kids felt themselves to be, one girl raised her hand shyly. "I don't know why I'm so different from other kids," she said tentatively, "but I love my parents." "I want to thank you for your courage in saying so," I said supportively. "Right at this moment, in this class, that wasn't the cool thing to say. Nevertheless, I am willing to bet that every child in here loves his or her parents. It is just that not many people except you felt comfortable saying that today."

The group will require children to deny parts of themselves; the group will require a child to say and do things that make a parent feel as if he or she no longer recognizes his or her child. When my daughter was in eighth grade, we had tickets to see a wonderful, athletic dance troupe on a Friday night. Everything was set. On Thursday, however, one girl at school began to talk about going to the mall on Friday night, and soon *all* the girls were going to the mall and they were discarding whatever previous plans they had made. Our daughter's friend had been planning to attend a cast reunion for a play she had done six months earlier with a group of people she loved. Another girl had carefully made plans with her family. Ultimately my daughter said she hated dance, "didn't you know that by now?" None of the girls wanted to go anywhere but the mall, and they all fought their parents ferociously for the right to go with the group. They had a pretty lousy time at the mall (I am delighted to report). However, if there is a powerful group pull on a child, she goes. She wants to be a member of the Friday-Night Mall Club, no matter how much she might irritate her parents.

If you work with children, you must become accustomed to the "us" and the "them," kids versus adults, and you have to understand that there is a certain minimum of tension between groups of children and adults. Research shows that children in social groups begin to act differently around adults by the age of four, and it only gets worse in adolescence. Teachers know this; they live with it every day. If you work with children, you must be philosophical about the invisible forces in communal life that can make a group of tenth graders act in an annoying fashion. A particular group of children can develop a dynamic that is powerfully antiadult, victimizing, or cruel. We will look at severe and even terrifying examples of these dynamics in Chapter 6, "Worst Enemies."

Groups in school can take on a life of their own, and the children follow along like sheep, doing destructive things. I have seen that particular phenomenon so many times in schools that I always question it when someone tells me that their child is in a "bad" class with "bad" kids. There may be a couple of troubled kids, but what I conclude is that there is a destructive dynamic in the group. Because of the human need for group cohesion, kids are loyal to a destructive way of conducting themselves. The vast majority of public vandalism in the United States is committed by boys age twelve to sixteen acting together in groups. I asked a colleague who studies delinquency what percentage of boys in the United States commit some act of public vandalism during their teenage years. He said that it was impossible to know, but that it was probably quite high, perhaps over 80 or 90 percent if you consider shoplifting, graffiti, and other minor acts. Are all of these boys "bad"? I don't think so. But when they are with their peers they can be swept up into the idea of the moment. To not join in, when everyone else is doing it, doesn't feel like a heroic act of conscience. It feels like giving up your chance to be an accepted member of the group, possibly forever.

What saves us from discouragement and despair when we face these invisible forces in group life that have such an impact on the behavior of children? Perhaps it is helpful to look one more time at primates. In his book *Peacemaking Among Primates*, Frans de Waal says that lots of researchers study aggression in primates, but rarely do they look at reconciliation. He states, "Fires start, but fires go out. . . . We know a great deal about the causes of hostile behavior in both animals and humans. . . . Yet we know little of the way conflicts are avoided—or how, when they do occur, relationships are afterward repaired and normalized." As I move into a discussion of the ways in which some individuals dominate others and the ways in which the status hierarchy can result in the rejection and victimization of certain children, it will be important to remember that human communities have the capacity to reconcile, to heal, and to recognize one another's wonderful qualities.

Chapter Six

Worst Enemies: Social Cruelty in the Lives of Children

I hadn't seen my nephew, Jared, since his high school graduation a year earlier. Now that we were vacationing together, I expected that he would want to bring us up to date about all that had happened to him during his freshman year in college. It turned out that he had something else on his mind. He wanted to tell us about a boy he had known, a high school football player who jumped off a bridge in front of a lot of friends.

Jared was clearly shaken by the incident, which happened during the summer after his senior year in high school. He was still trying to understand it. Although he hadn't been present when it happened, he knew many of the kids who were there. And he knew the boy who died. The scene had been described to him in hushed tones. Nine months later, he was still reliving it in his mind.

A group of around twenty-five students from his high school, most of them boys with whom he had graduated, went out to a remote area by a local river. The spot was a traditional drinking and hanging-out place for kids. They were looking forward to watching a few guys take the exciting and risky leap off the bridge into the river.

One of the boys who had promised to jump from the bridge was a tenth grader. He had made the pledge a few days before that Saturday.

"His name was Patrick. He was an amazing kid," said Jared. "He played hockey for the town team. As a sophomore he played varsity football. He had so much going for him.

"There were seniors, sophmores, and others there. They were all drinking. I think some kids had jumped before, but I don't know," said Jared. "They told Patrick, 'All right, it's your turn to jump.' He went out onto the bridge. Instead of climbing to the spot where everyone else jumped from the bridge, he climbed even higher, to the trestle above. I heard they were egging him to jump. At one point when he was headed up he said it was too high and he started to come back down. They all teased him for backing down. They kept urging him to go higher.

"He jumped from about sixty feet into about eleven and a half feet of water. I'm assuming he died on impact. His body didn't surface. Maybe he just stuck in the mud. I've heard that one kid jumped in after him and came back up and said the current was too swift. No one called the police for forty-five minutes. A lot of kids had cell phones. They didn't call right away. I've heard that all twenty-five kids got into their cars and drove away because they did not want to get a $135 ticket for being minors in possession of alcohol. They just drove away."

My nephew believes everyone left because they did not want to get ticketed. But my guess is they left because they felt frightened and guilty and simply wanted to be away from the scene of the crime.

And what was their crime? Drinking was the least of it. It was passivity, failure to act, and worst of all, showing off for the crowd by urging a boy to jump from the top of the bridge. That was not just a sadistic wish to see someone risk his life for their entertainment. The boys who urged him to jump (and I do assume it was boys) were trying to impress their peers with their ability to influence a younger male, to control his behavior in public. They wanted him to risk his life so that they could look powerful to the crowd. That is what they did not want to be questioned about.

I don't imagine that anyone who has been part of some horrible group behavior ever wants to be asked about it, because the internal feelings of responsibility and guilt that come later can be very acute.

I asked Jared if he thought the people who had been at the bridge that day felt a huge amount of guilt over the incident. His voice became more intense. "They ought to. I know one of the guys. He doesn't want to talk about it. Another kid who was there is a big drunk. A big party guy. I don't know how he got through his first year in college. I don't know how he can live with himself."

Jared showed me clippings of Patrick's obituary and the write-up in the local newspaper. There is no mention made in the paper of the role that other kids might have played in the death of this boy.

But when Jared told the story, the role of the other boys was crucial. "If I got drunk and jumped off, would they go in for me? I would have jumped in after him. Friend or no friend, I would have gone in. It doesn't make any sense that they didn't go in for him. It doesn't make sense that they didn't call 911. I wasn't really good friends with him. I don't see what the difference is. I stood next to him on the football field." Jared paused, and when he spoke again his tone was bitter. "I knew the kids who were there. I used to think of some of them as my friends."

Most stories of social cruelty do not end as tragically as Patrick's jump from the railway bridge. But the actions of groups can scar children for life, as many of us remember from our own childhood. If we weren't scarred ourselves, it's still easy to imagine what the injuries feel like as we think about the kids in our school who were bullied, rejected, or cruelly victimized.

The story of Patrick's death tells us how and why the group can be so destructive. The presence of the group, and kids' need for acceptance at any price, gives individuals "permission" to drink more, act reckless, and show poor judgment. Most importantly, however, the presence of the group seems to diminish the sense of morality and individual responsibility that children possess. Children in general, and adolescents in particular, act differently when they are with their peers. When kids are together, individuals can be much less mature and empathic than they otherwise might be on their own. I think that's why Jared can't imagine not jumping in if he had been there, and can't forgive his classmates for running away.

Imagine for a moment that Patrick had gone to that bridge with only one friend. I don't believe that the friend would have pushed Patrick to climb higher than he was comfortable climbing. The friend would have felt personally responsible for pushing him to a dangerous level. The friend would have been in touch with Patrick's feelings of fear. Even if he was not a deeply intuitive person, he would very likely have empathized with Patrick's position. He might even have offered Patrick a face-saving way to back down. Finally, this hypothetical friend would have been aware that if anything happened to Patrick, it would fall on him alone to attempt a rescue or tell the police and the family what happened. Had Patrick jumped into the river and not come back up, a friend at the scene without a group of other guys would very likely have dived repeatedly and frantically to try to help him.

One friend, in short, would have felt individual responsibility for the other friend—responsibility for encouraging him to be safe, for assisting him, for getting help. A friend would have felt empathy—empathy for Patrick's fear of jumping, for the humiliation of backing down, for the moments of terror. Where was that empathy, that sense of responsibility, in the group?

The laws of group behavior created a situation in which the teenagers at the foot of the bridge did not feel their own sense of individual responsibility. Absorbed in the power of the group, they egged Patrick on, taunted him, and then abandoned him. Friendship and just plain human feeling were overwhelmed by the forces of group life. This is not to absolve the kids who were present of their moral failure; it is simply to recognize that the presence of a group can create a situation in which individual moral responsibility and empathy are much reduced.

The forces of group life that I discussed in Chapter 5 often play themselves out in horribly destructive ways. The same force that can make a group cheer on an athletic team can provoke them to egg on someone who is pushing the limits of safety. The dark side of the force that allows a star player to give all the credit to his supportive teammates can diffuse the responsibility in a group so much that no one calls for help. The same force that leads a group to rise as one in a standing ovation can make them act as a mob.

I don't mean to trivialize the tragic outcome of a mob mentality by comparing it to a sports event. Of course, at one level we can never really understand a tragedy such as this one, or deaths from hazing rituals, or the suicides of children who have been bullied and rejected. But to understand these worst excesses of group life, we have to understand the dynamics of groups in general that can lead to such outcomes.

Let's start with the *diffusion of responsibility*. I am certain that when Patrick wanted to come back down from his high perch on the bridge, there were many in the crowd who thought, "Let him come down. Can't you see he's scared?" I am sure that when Patrick jumped into the river and did not resurface, many of the kids sitting on the banks felt the impulse to go in for him. But they were immobilized by their fear of the current or of finding an injured boy and not being able to help him. Some were immobilized by alcohol. But what really immobilized them was the fact of being in a group. No one felt personally responsible for Patrick, and the group was acting out its fear and confusion by standing around stunned into inaction. Everyone was watching to see what the other kids did, and as long as no one did anything, there was no clear group direction. Had someone with natural authority jumped up and yelled, "Some people go downstream and look for him. You, call 911. Someone go out on the bridge and try to spot him, I'm diving in," the group would have been activated.

In this case, tragically, that did not happen. Ultimately the only group impulse was to flee the scene. And once a couple of people got into their cars and drove away, it was okay for everyone to run.

As we have seen, a cohesive group tends to have a strongly defined sense of "us" versus "them," or in versus out. Think about school rivalries, team rivalries, political party rivalries, country club rivalries, national rivalries, and so on. Almost anyone can be recruited to participate in a group persecution of a marginal or excluded person, someone whom the group regards as inferior or different. Even an insider, like Patrick, can suddenly become an outsider—in this case just by hesitating on the bridge. That's how powerful the need for group cohesion is. Cheers for one of our own can quickly become jeers at someone who is outside our circle. The social forces that we have seen at work in group life— cohesion, group identity, exclusion and inclusion—can operate in the service of positive goals or of destructive goals. The cohesive boys' ice hockey team that plays hard together and celebrates a win with hugs and congratulations can also gang up to torment a boy in the locker room, someone whom the group has decided is different, a "geek." The sixth grade girls who gather to comfort a sobbing classmate can suddenly turn on a girl and gossip viciously about her, calling her a "slut."

Another group factor that can lead a group to act negatively is sometimes called the *risky shift*. Groups tend to make riskier decisions than any of the individuals in them would have made if acting alone. That's why some states have laws that newly licensed young drivers must have an adult with them, not a car full of other teenagers. A related phenomenon is called *groupthink*, in which people suspend their better judgment and go along with the group's ideas, values, and ethics. Sometimes all it takes is one strong personality with poor judgment to influence a group to be riskier or more hurtful. On the other hand, a powerful personality with good judgment can influence a group to act with better judgment and more compassion.

Another potentially destructive aspect of groups is that *they all have rules*. When the rule is "Be nice and don't get in trouble," parents are happy. But not all rules are so adult-oriented. In addition, all groups mete out punishment for breaking those rules—and the punishments can be extreme. If you break the rule of cool, you are teased. If you rat or narc on a peer, you are ostracized. If you don't follow the queen bee, you are out of the clique. Why did my nephew's friends tell him the story reluctantly, in hushed tones? Perhaps because they were breaking an unspoken rule not to talk about the group's failure and betrayal of trust. Why did the group turn against Patrick? Possibly because he broke a rule by daring to go higher than other, older kids, or because he considered backing down. There was no rule that said everybody there had to jump off the bridge. But if you did climb up, the rule was clear: You had to jump.

Children suffer at the hands of groups from four painful practices: (1) teasing and name-calling; (2) exclusion, rejection, and scapegoating; (3) bullying; and (4) hazing. These pain-inflicting practices often overlap. Cliques always involve some teasing and exclusion. Rejected children are likely to be bullied as well as excluded. But I have decided to divide them into four categories because I will move from the universal experience of name-calling and teasing to the more extreme damage caused by bullying and rejection and then to the organized and sometimes lethal phenomenon of ritualized hazing.

Looking at each of these types of cruelty, we can see elements of the group dynamics that exist whenever people join together in a social unit.

Teasing is largely about who is up and who is down, which can change from moment to moment. Rejection by the group is an example of in versus out, exacerbated by the diffusion of moral responsibility that happens when a group has agreed to single someone out as a scapegoat. Children who bully feel little or no moral responsibility or empathy. Meanwhile, innocent bystanders suffer from a lack of clear moral direction and are afraid of the bully or the group turning against them. Groups who haze new members, or upperclassmen who haze underclassmen, play out a complex dance of in-out and up-down dynamics. As a group, they come up with riskier and more humiliating demands than any one child would dream up alone. Whistle-blowers, who try to report brutal hazing practices or other rule violations to adults, can be punished severely for breaking ranks with the group. Look at the death threats received by the young man who turned in Bobby Knight, the powerful basketball coach, for physically attacking him.

Teasing and Name-Calling

Teasing and name-calling are universal. There is no reader of this book who was not called a name at some point in her or his school career, or who has not called someone else a name. If you had younger brothers or sisters, you called them names. If you had an older sibling, you attacked him or her verbally. There is no parent whose child has not come home crying, "Mom, Dad, they're being mean to me!" A study conducted by psychologists at Hofstra University found that 100 percent of children had had the experience of being called hurtful names by other children.

In fact, being able to insult someone else is a developmental achievement. Children like to lift heavy things and show other people: "See what I can lift?" Name-calling, an experiment in social power, is a way of testing one's verbal muscles. When a child calls another child a name, it is a demonstration of strength. All human beings have aggressive impulses, and children manifest that universal human tendency. They want to know that they can hurt another child with words, even if they don't actually want to fight. Name-calling is the verbal equivalent of fighting. And it makes the name-caller feel stronger in the moment of aggression. Of course, the price is paid by the person being teased or put down, who feels humiliated, worthless, fearful, vengeful, or all of the above.

Verbal teasing can also be a way to find one's level in the group. A child may cultivate a sharp, hurtful tongue as a way to stay "up" in the social hierarchy if looks or physical strength aren't doing the job, for example. Verbal teasing can even be a way of expressing affection or of basic communication, usually between boys. The Australian novelist Phillip Gwynne captures this communtication between boys exactly in one of his novels: "I never knew what to say to girls. With boys it was easy, if you ran out of things to say you just insulted them. Like 'Geez, Pickles, you've got a head like a robber's dog.' You couldn't do that with a girl, though. Not if you wanted to impress her."

In the early grades children call each other names during conflicts. For young children the motivation for insults is self-protection. They are defending their bodies, their toys, their turf. Over time the angry shout "Go away . . . leave me alone . . . I hate you" turns into the personal insult "You're stupid" because it hurts the recipient more. It "works." Having stung someone else with name-calling, a child may then be tempted to try it again with an audience watching. And when he does he may be doubly gratified, both by the hurt reaction of his target and by the admiring approval of the group. What started as a method of conflict management becomes a tactic in the wars over who is in and out, up and down in the group. At first adult disapproval may be stronger than peer approval or a peer victory. But over time that adult reaction becomes less and less relevant.

Why does name-calling in school seem to get worse as the years go by? The answer is that teasing becomes part of the dominance struggle in the group. Teasing becomes a weapon in the struggle to be cool. It also goes public. Teasing is done by kids in packs, who take turns insulting the victim. Or it may be an individual effort by a child who wishes to impress the group. Children often tell me that the cool kids are the ones who are able to creatively and effectively put down other kids.

I visited a school many years ago where life in the fifth grade was completely dominated by the culture of the put-down. The daily game, at which some children excelled and others did not, involved surprise verbal attacks on a classmate. The recipient of the attack had to return with some quick repartee that showed that he was not hurt by the initial assault and was able to retaliate with something wittier. Then the onus was on the initiator to show that he had not been rocked back on his heels by the comeback; he had to trump the rejoinder. Originality counted. Two books of put-downs had been circulating in the class. If a child came up with an insult that he had learned from the books and the source was recognized, his efforts were loudly devalued: "That's from the book! That's stupid."

The teachers were tearing their hair out in the class, wondering where the kids had gotten the idea of put-downs as an organized blood sport. Any urban sociologist could have told them that these white, middle-class fifth graders were just playing a street game that has been known in the inner city for decades. The original game was played by African-American boys. The insults were called "toasts" and involved attacks on another child's mother in rhyming verse. The game is an early forerunner of rap. "Your mother wears combat boots," is perhaps the oldest such insult. "Your mother has a mustache" is another. The attack on a boy's mother is secondary; the point is to dazzle the crowd with one's wit and power of invention. These inner-city insults, now imitated in suburbia, are a recent manifestation of a much older tradition.

A general change in the level of civility in our society, along with rock and rap music, has made the *f*-word available to any child, along with abundant media models of adults and teenagers insulting one another. If you do not regularly watch television, I suggest that you watch four or five sitcoms in the space of a week and listen to the level of put-downs among adults, among family members, and especially among adolescent children. Our children learn that the way to be funny is to be insulting; they learn that the way to dominate others is by verbal attack. Most importantly, verbal attack is most powerful in front of an audience (on TV, the insults are always accompanied by a laugh track rewarding the name-calling).

No wonder children insult one another. "You're weird," a child might say, which could be translated as "I've never met someone like you before," or "You're not part of my group." They say sarcastically, "Nice shoes," which means "You will never be cool."

Since every child has been stung in this way, why doesn't empathy come into play? If everyone knows it hurts to be teased, why don't they realize that teasing is wrong? They do. If you ask them, they will admit that it is wrong. They know it is not moral. They also know that it hurts. So children defend their actions with a defensive statement, "He asked for it," or "He called me a retard. He started it." What they mean is that it was the only weapon at hand in a situation that seemed threatening, or that they were irresistibly drawn to the temptation to tease.

When parents and teachers look at teasing, some see good clean fun, while others see kids being mean and cruel. No matter what they see, they are missing an important element of the scene. Most teasing happens to enforce the rules of the group. A group of boys, for example, may tease each other viciously and constantly, to enforce the rule of being tough enough to "take it." Children who are different from the group in any way are routinely the victims of more teasing. They have unwittingly broken the number one commandment of almost every group: "Be like us." If you are overweight, wear glasses, study too much, talk with an accent, have a different color skin, eat a different kind of food, or worship a different god, you are going to be teased for it. And if you break the most important rules of all—the gender rules—then you really get it. If you are a boy who is effeminate by the strict standards of masculinity, even in the slightest degree, other boys can and will make your life hell.

This issue of breaking the rules of the group explains why it is so hard for adults to know whether teasing is hurtful or just a sort of verbal rough-and-tumble play. One of the rules is not to show that teasing hurts, and above all, not to be a crybaby or a tattletale. If you have already been targeted for being a geek or a sissy or a bitch, you aren't going to want to compound it by being called a rat or a snitch or a baby. This catches parents in a terrible bind. They hear the sad sobs caused by the pain of the teasing, but they are told firmly—and fearfully—by their child not to intervene. "You'll just make things worse," the child sobs. Unfortunately, they are often right.

All children are teased and called names. That's the bad news. The good news is that most children are resilient and find a way to deal with the insults that rain down in school. They enjoy enough social acceptance so that the insults do not really hurt. They are protected. The great majority of children, even if they are not popular, are accepted in a group. Though their highest social ambitions may not be realized, and despite the occasional pain they experience at the hands of other kids who tease them, they find acceptance. They get hurt, but they bounce back. They have the cognitive ability and sociability to stay afloat, even when the social seas are stormy.

Rejection and Exclusion

A small minority of children are not okay in the social seas. The storm may swamp their boat and send them under. Every once in a while I see a class that has turned one child into a scapegoat, the recipient of all the others' worst fears and impulses. The children project their social anxieties onto that scapegoated child and feel much better about themselves. Saying "He's a crybaby" or "She smells" to justify the cruel rejection, they drive one poor child to the margins, where he may stay for years. We know that such rejected children are at higher risk for depression, for mental illness of all kinds, for leaving school, and most especially for loneliness. What makes this rejection different from teasing is that it involves the whole group—or a sizable subset of the group—against one person. Being teased by a single, stronger child can be painful, but being ostracized by the group is much worse. We all want to be liked and respected, but we need to be accepted.

Before I examine rejection and exclusion in more depth, I want to introduce you to the five basic types of kids: popular children, accepted children, rejected children, neglected children, and controversial children. Children have different experiences socially, depending on their type. John Coie, who recently retired from the Psychology Department at Duke University, and his many students, including Ken Dodge, now at Vanderbilt University, have led the way in the study of the types of children who inhabit the social worlds of school. Popular kids are on almost everyone's like list. Everyone wants to be their friend. Accepted children appear on a significant number of like lists and few, if any, dislike lists. Rejected children are the opposite, appearing frequently—sometimes universally—on dislike lists. Neglected children are not on anyone's list, positive or negative; they are unknown and unacknowledged by the group. Controversial children split the affections of the group. They are very well liked by some and strongly disliked by others. (A small number of children can't be classified by this method; their status is ambiguous.) Once you read the descriptions of these different categories of children in the work of Coie and Dodge, the social dynamics of the classroom or the birthday party are never quite as mysterious as they might once have been. Let's look more closely at each of these types.

Popular children. Children are consistent when they are asked what makes a child popular. "He's cool," they'll say. "He's real good at stuff." "She wears the right clothes." Boys tend to get popularity points for athleticism and being quick verbally; girls get points for attractiveness and sociability. Both genders achieve popularity through wealth and other markers of class status. Fifteen percent of children fall into this category. When psychologists look below the surface, they see some other factors among those who are most liked by their peers. Popular children show higher levels of sociability and cognitive ability and lower levels of aggression and withdrawal. Their social skills draw other children to them and other people have more fun with them.

Accepted children. Happily, the majority of children are liked and accepted by their peers. Forty-five percent of children fall into the "accepted" or "average" category. Added to the popular group, that makes 60 percent who share a variety of attributes that make them attractive to other children. In a positive feedback loop, their acceptance by their classmates reinforces those positive attributes. Like popular kids, accepted children score well on measures of cognitive ability (they're smart) and high on measures of sociability (they're outgoing). Such children also score low on measures of aggression, disruptive behavior, and withdrawal. In short, they are normal, healthy children.

Rejected children. Rejected children subdivide into two groups, which researchers call "rejected-submissive" and "rejected-aggressive." About 10 to 12 percent of children in any school setting are likely to be rejected children, either rejected-submissive or rejected-aggressive. These are the children at highest risk socially. They have a poor prognosis in life, particularly if they have been rejected for more than two years in a row.

Neglected children. Approximately 4 percent of children have very little social impact in the classroom and are neglected by their classmates. Neglected children are neither liked nor disliked by their peers. Generally, adults cannot distinguish between them and their classmates who are in the accepted category, because they seem like "good kids." But in the children's social groups they are off the radar. These children fall through the cracks of classroom life because they are neither disruptive nor overtly distressed. There is some debate about whether they are an at-risk group. Though their social suffering is real, their pain just may not come to anyone's notice. Such children are never the squeaky wheels asking for attention. Neglected children tend to be compliant, adult-oriented, and academically high-achieving, which is another reason that teachers may not worry about them. With so many disruptive children to attend to, it is understandable that a quiet, studious child would escape notice.

Most neglected children would be liked if they were known, but they may lack the sociability to make themselves known. Neglected children may come from families where they have been taught a social style in which withdrawal and isolation predominate, or they may come from families that are simply private. I have known children from both types of families. Some benefit from being drawn out. Others can be helped if the family is coached to support a son's or daughter's sociability in a family therapy setting. It may take a neglected child some years to make contact. Happily, research suggests that by late elementary school, socially neglected children usually have a reciprocal friend.

Controversial children. Neglected children are neither liked nor disliked, while controversial children are both liked and disliked. Some 4 percent of children fall into this category. They are the class clowns, whom some children find entertaining and others find obnoxious, or the queens of the cliques, whom some idolize and others disdain for being stuck-up and mean. They are the bullies, who have loyal henchmen and intimidated victims. They are the rebels, especially the children who defy authority, instilling admiration and envy in some hearts and condemnation in others.

Ambiguous children. If you have been adding up the percentages of the popular, accepted, rejected, neglected, and controversial children, you will find that they do not add up to 100 percent. Truth compels me to state the obvious: Social science research is not perfect, and psychological categories are not conclusive. The reader needs to know that when sociometric research is conducted in classrooms, a large group of children are not classifiable in any category. Thus some 20 percent of children do not make the cutoff point for popular or accepted, yet they are not rejected, controversial, or neglected. They have many of the characteristics of all of the categories but are ultimately labeled ambiguous.

Let's look at some of these types in action. I once sat with a group of eleventh and twelfth graders at a school in North Carolina. The group had been chosen by the dean of students to talk with me about the social climate that they all experienced. The dean had deliberately chosen a group made up of class leaders as well as some outsiders. Whenever anyone said something positive about the school or about the social scene in their grade, one girl would contradict it. "Not everyone is comfortable here," she would say. "This place is a country club." She was dressed differently than the other students, in a style that suggested Greenwich Village more than Raleigh, and she emphasized that she came from a different part of town than the rest of the group. She was blunt and direct, hardly a soft-spoken southern woman. The mainstream girls winced when she spoke, especially when she attacked the notion of the school as friendly and genteel. But almost no one argued with her. After one of her remarks one of the class leaders might say, "Well, that's a little harsh, but . . . " And then she would soften the criticism that the girl had just voiced, acknowledging the truth of it and searching for some middle ground between the socially popular kids and this radical voice. Clearly there was a split opinion about this girl. She had made herself the gadfly of her class. As a result, she was honored by some kids and disliked by others.

Though it isn't easy and is often lonely, it is possible to make a career as a controversial figure when you are in high school. It is much harder to carve out and maintain such an identity in elementary school, because children that age don't have the self-control or discipline to carry it off. Nor do they have a strong enough sense of personal identity to bear a lot of disapproval. For a fifth grader, the approval of the whole class means more than it does to a high school girl, whose support comes from a small clique or a countercultural club. In fifth grade controversial children often don't know why they are controversial. An impulsive class clown may not be able to discern why he is considered amusing one day and a pariah the next. Imagine that a teacher accidentally hands out to her class the same assignment that she had given out the previous Thursday. Every child is holding his or her breath, thinking, "Yes! She's making a mistake and we're not going to have to do homework tonight." The impulsive boy yells out, "But Mrs. Jones, you gave us this homework last week!" Everyone in the class wants to wring his neck. He just can't keep his mouth shut . . . again!

Controversial children can be coached so that they better understand their impact on others. They need maturity and perspective so that they are not condemned to stir up controversy forever. However, with maturity they can still choose to be gadflies if it suits them as an identity, like the radical eleventh grade girl in North Carolina.

Teachers who have to watch the isolation of a rejected child every day often experience acute helplessness. At a workshop I conducted in Maryland, teachers told me that rejected-submissive children and rejected-aggressive children are the most difficult to deal with in the classroom.

The difference between rejected-submissive and rejected-aggressive children lies in how the children respond to their exclusion by the group. A rejected-submissive child knows he's out, and accepts it—with great pain. "My son's class went on a field trip to Plimoth Plantation and I went with them," one mother of a third grader told me. "For the whole day, it seemed, there were twenty-five children standing together, and he was over on the side, standing alone. He hardly talked to anyone all day. It totally broke my heart. I didn't know what to do for him. He is such a sensitive kid. I think that the moment he feels any rejection at all, he withdraws from it. Now I'm worried that he is permanently withdrawn."

Hearing such a story from a mother makes me cringe. For her that day was excruciatingly painful. I could see that the memory of it had haunted her for months. I am sure that she remembered it almost every day as she sent him off to school. But imagine it for the child. He has to live each day. He isn't just alone on field trip day; he is alone all the time in the classroom—even when there are children all around. Children avoid sitting next to him. They draw back their chairs slightly. When he is assigned to their reading group their shoulders slump and they say, "Aww," in a dejected, do-we-have-to-sit-with-him sort of way. The rejected-submissive child, like this boy, sadly accepts this rejection as his fate.

Rejected-submissive children often respond well to a combination of therapy and classroom interventions (see Chapter 11). The angry and disruptive children who scare others and who may have a long history of aggressive behavior are often more difficult to handle. The group punishes such children for being scary or socially disruptive or, worst of all, both. And the punishment can last for years. Researchers have found that aggression and disruptive behavior are major causes of peer rejection throughout childhood and elementary school. Children who cannot control their level of anger, or who regularly interrupt the flow of the class, become candidates for rejection. Once rejected, they are the children about whom teachers despair. Once rejected, they are the children, Coie and his colleagues tell us, who are least responsive to interventions by educators.

No one individual decides to reject a particular child. And it isn't decided by a vote in which the class, or the most popular clique, chooses which child they should reject. It is done through thousands of little incidents, each followed by a gossipy discussion: "Did you see him do that?" "Did you hear what she said?" "I can't believe she did that!" "What a jerk." With younger children it is done without much conversation. Classmates read the fearful reaction in their friends' eyes and they all know the source of it: one particular scary child. Whether verbally or silently, a group consensus is reached that the child is dangerous or excessively weird.

In some cases, rejection comes because the rejected child looks different or comes from a foreign culture. I once asked a group of eighth grade girls whether they teased any particular kids. "Oh, yes," announced one girl. "We tease one boy because he had a funny-looking face. In fact, we teased him so much his parents got him plastic surgery."

"What happened after that?" I inquired

"Well," she continued without apology, "now we tease him about his parents getting him plastic surgery."

Whatever the group decides about a particular child will have profound implications for that child. If the group decides to excommunicate a child, it does. No child has the power to rescind the decision easily.

"Let me tell you about Andy," the principal of an elementary school in northern California said to me. He was talking about a rejected-aggressive boy, the most difficult child they had ever had in kindergarten. "If there were something going on he didn't like, he would start to screech. And he would twirl around and around. We heard about him in the front office right away. It was quite bizarre and other children were very frightened. At first I thought he must be autistic or suffer from pervasive developmental disorder, but that wasn't the case. He made interpersonal contact with teachers and with a few other children when he wasn't upset. He could read other people's faces most of the time; he made eye contact. He was also brilliant. But after the kids had seen him do his screeching thing a couple of times, they gave him a wide berth.

"We called the parents in and they were unusual, to say the least. The father was an extremely spacey musician who didn't have a lot of work;

he didn't seem to be very connected to his son. His mother said she was a Wiccan. I had to check with someone on the faculty to make sure that I knew what a Wiccan was. It's another name for a witch or pagan. Supposedly she was a good witch.

"Later we learned that the parents had serious fights at home. The parents blamed us for Andy's social problems. They called me frequently to accuse the school of favoring some kids or to complain about other children. We couldn't get them to cooperate with our efforts to get help for him. They didn't want him to see the school's guidance counselor."

Luckily Andy had several wonderful teachers who appreciated his great intelligence and helped him manage socially in the classroom. Though it was a lot of work, they kept him from getting labeled as emotionally disturbed. Still, they couldn't make friends for him. He remained isolated and angry. He provoked other children and they provoked him back, needling him subtly until he blew up and threw a tantrum. As he got older he didn't screech the way he had in kindergarten, but it was the same display of temper. The other children got good at provoking it. Where once they would walk on eggshells around him and scatter when he got mad, now they needled him mercilessly. Then when he blew up they would tell him that he was crazy and "belonged in a mental hospital." He was increasingly thin-skinned and required a lot of supervision. "We kept recommending therapy for him but got no response from his parents.

"Finally, in fourth grade some other boys and he really got into it. Some boy teased Andy, who a little while later retaliated by tripping the boy who teased him. After the tripping, three boys chased him until they cornered him by a fence. At that point Andy went wild, really crazy, and scratched a boy across the chest. He ripped open the kid's shirt and left four deep scratch marks. The boy had to be taken to the hospital. I took a photo of it because I knew it was likely to end up as a legal matter. I called Andy's parents and when they came in they started accusing the other child. That's when I showed them a picture of the boy's chest. They were shaken. All they could say was, 'Oh.' He was suspended and reassigned to a class for emotionally troubled youngsters. No teacher felt safe with him in her class after that." (I include a story like this not to scare parents, but to make as strong a case as possible for early intervention.)

I have many times gone into the early grades—pre-K, kindergarten, and first grade— and observed children whom other children are already avoiding. The child may not know why, and when he tries to inject himself into the group, it just makes things worse. The classmates of an aggressive child have no way to express their fear of a child other than through distance. And that fear and distance easily turn to dislike.

Girls as well as boys can fall into the rejected-aggressive category. Two attorney parents in New York complained to the administrators of their daughter's school that their daughter, Helen, was without a friend in kindergarten. They claimed that other kids were "being mean" to her. I was asked to observe Helen in her classroom. Now, observing in classrooms when you are a visiting consultant can be a difficult task. As likely as not, the child does not show you the behavior that everyone is worried about and you are left with no data while still trying to be useful. It can be awkward. I remember Helen because she absolutely relieved me of that problem. Helen was a large girl and verbally skilled. I saw her walk over to another girl who was sitting down and loom over her, interrogating her: "Are you my friend? Why not? You don't pay attention to me! You're not my friend, are you?" The other girl just shrank away from this verbal barrage. No doubt Helen wanted to have a friend, and her parents wanted her to have one as well. At the age of six, however, she had no perspective on her aggressiveness and its impact on other children.

Unless someone coaches Helen and helps her to understand her impact on others, she is likely to be labeled and isolated. Once that has happened to a child, it is very difficult for him or her to escape the "mean" or "scary" designation. Once children are labeled and assigned to their roles and their place in the group, they are treated differently, even when they engage in the same behaviors. Studies have shown that classmates are five times more likely to attribute negative motivations to the actions of an unpopular child in comparison to exactly the same behavior by a popular child. For example, if a popular child pushes someone in the lunch line, classmates will say things like, "He didn't mean it. That's his friend. He didn't push that hard." They will rationalize it. But when a rejected child pushes someone in the lunch line, his classmates will say, "He's mean. He tried to hurt him. He's always doing stuff like that. He's always trying to start trouble." Because of the fixed social perceptions of rejected children, it is an uphill climb for them to get out of their rejected status.

Teachers can find it extremely difficult to feel sympathetic for an overly aggressive or disruptive child in a classroom. These children are hard to be around. Moreover, the other kids in the class—and their parents—struggle with the rejected-aggressive child. Many times I have heard parents say, "It's true, my Johnny isn't very nice to [the rejected child]. But after all, he is so provocative," or "He asks for it." Rejected-aggressive children are often assumed to be the class bullies, and parents feel justified in encouraging their children to defend themselves. The parents jump to conclusions and very often make a situation worse because they cannot imagine the verbal abuse that the group is heaping on a rejected child. They don't want to think about their own child participating in group cruelty.

Without intimate knowledge of a classroom, it is difficult to know exactly which child in a class is the bully. Sometimes the group itself— all those popular and accepted children—is the bully. However, everyone has a caricatured idea of the bully as a purposeful, sophisticated tormentor of other children, particularly one victim. That image doesn't fit the rejected-aggressive child. (We will discuss the classic bully-victim dyad later in this chapter.)

Remember, the research reveals that approximately 10 to 12 percent of children fall into the rejected category. Researchers also report that up to 15 percent of children encounter real social difficulties in school. The problem of the rejected child is not a rare phenomenon. It is a daily sight in schools. When it is portrayed in literature or in the movies it can be painful. I find it difficult to watch the film *Welcome to the Doll House*, which concerns a rejected-submissive middle school girl. Her classmates call her "wiener dog"; her locker is defaced; she is openly mocked in the lunchroom. When I watch this film it makes me so uncomfortable that I want to turn it off.

I think the same thing happens in school. Watching a child be rejected by his or her peers makes us want to turn away, both because it is inherently uncomfortable and because we may feel that there is nothing we can do. That is certainly what children tell me. "You can't do anything about it," they say. "Kids are just like that." The cost to society of losing 10 to 15 percent of children to loneliness, bitterness, and depression is very high. And the highest price of all is paid by the rejected individuals themselves, in the form of adult depression and dysfunction.

On rare occasions, the retaliation of rejected children against the ones who rejected them can reach tragic proportions. Dylan Klebold and Eric Harris, the boys at Colorado's Columbine High School who killed thirteen students before taking their own lives, were by all reports rejected-aggressive kids. News analysis stories suggested that they were teased daily by the higher-status students, particularly the varsity athletes. They were supposedly part of the "Trench Coat Mafia," students who took their outcast status and wore it like a badge of honor. Yet they were apparently not fully part of this controversial countergroup either. Eric and Dylan were extremely disconnected from classmates and adults and utterly reliant on each other's psychological perspective, which was characterized by depression and anger.

I am not trying to absolve those two boys of their horrible crime. There are many children in school who bear the shame and stigma of being socially rejected without becoming violent. Not all of them will become depressed as adults; not all of them will become aggressive in later life. However, all rejected children are at risk. Their isolation starts in elementary school and continues through middle school and into high school. Rejected-submissive and rejected-aggressive children don't just "grow out of it." It takes intelligent, purposeful intervention on the part of educators and parents to reroute these children's lives.

On the social highways of our schools, rejected children drive the battered-up old cars. These are the kids about whom you want to say, "They shouldn't be on the highway." They may drive too slowly, provoking other drivers to blare their horns and force them off the road. Or they drive recklessly, weaving in and out of traffic and having near collisions. They may lack the resources or knowledge to get licenses or inspection stickers. They cause accidents that hurt others, to be sure, but many of them are the ones who—socially speaking—end up dead by the side of the road. We can blame them for not being able to keep up with the traffic, or we can do more to help them.

The issue of group responsibility is crucial in understanding why a child can be brutally rejected year after year. The group, all rejecting together, diffuses the responsibility so much that no one feels the moral pangs that would lead him or her to stand up to the group and stop the scapegoating. That's why many of the most successful school-wide bully-prevention programs focus on the bystanders, helping them take moral responsibility for intervening in attacks and exclusion, and helping them make a special effort to include everyone.

Bullying

Everybody has a mental image of a bully. Most of us actually have the same picture, because the idea of a bully is archetypal: the big, swaggering, loudmouth boy with a gang of followers. He doesn't give a damn about what adults think; he doesn't do well in school; he gets his kicks from tormenting one or several victims. In the movie *My Bodyguard*, Matt Dillon plays the perfect bully. He walks into tenth grade on the first day, walks up to the teacher and—with a mixture of seduction and contempt—hands her an apple. He is ignorant, conceited, and constantly on the lookout for any slight, always guarding his flanks lest anyone undercut his power. He has no real friends, only followers, whom he physically intimidates so they will do his bidding. To use the language of the modern business world—another place where bullies often flourish—he outsources some of his sadism, licensing his followers to do some of the dirty work of picking on victims.

Given how common the stereotype is in popular culture, one might imagine that the classic bully is to be found in every classroom. Research confirms that bullies of this type do exist. But they are actually not very common. Think back to your middle school or high school experience. Can you remember having an archetypal bully in your class? Was there a bully-victim pair, a big boy who hunted and tortured a smaller one? My guess is that most of you answer no. Indeed, our mental picture of bullies is an oversimplification. There is a lot of bullying in schools, but it is rarely the result of one habitual bully. Reality is more fluid.

I have been the psychologist at a four-hundred-student boys' school for the last six years, and I was the psychologist to four coeducational schools prior to this one. I cannot remember encountering any such Matt Dillon–type bully in any of those schools. Yet I have witnessed many serious incidents of bullying by a group, led by a boy or two whom the teachers refer to as "negative leaders." Most bullies are temporary bullies. And they don't operate without the unspoken, and often unconscious, support of the nonaggressive majority.

The metaphor of James Bond is useful here. The double 0 in his code number, 007, means that he has a license to kill. His "civilized" world has assigned the dirty work to him. Sometimes that works fine (it certainly does for Bond), but sometimes we give power to people who are eager to abuse it. We don't have to look much past the nightly news or the daily newspaper to see examples of abuses of power among police officers, prison guards, and soldiers in combat.

I think the group is responsible for creating a climate in which bullying takes place. It is the group that licenses the bully to act the way he does. Sometimes the group finds a child with antisocial tendencies and provokes that child into acting like a bully. The appointed bully isn't always the same child. In fact, it is difficult to identify which children are the bullies because social situations are much more fluid than the static names "bully" and "victim" imply. Even the categories of children that we discussed earlier—popular, accepted, rejected, and neglected—don't always predict who is going to bully whom. When it comes to aggression, the social dynamic in the classroom is constantly in flux. Acts of aggression bubble up to the surface from time to time, as do acts of kindness.

Let me give you an example. I was asked to help sort out an incident of bullying at an elementary school. A fifth grade boy, Trevor, had severely injured another boy, breaking a bone in his face near the eye socket. The injured boy, Alex, was taken to the hospital and Trevor was immediately suspended from school pending an investigation. Many of the parents in the carpool line believed that this was an open-and-shut case of bullying and were talking among themselves about the appropriate sanctions for such a serious injury. "The school needs to take a strong stand" was the general view.

However, things turned out to be a bit more complicated than that. When Alex left the hospital and was interviewed a few days later, along with his friends, they described a scene in which the three friends, all cool kids, had begun to tease Trevor. Why were they teasing him? "Because," said Alex's friend, Jeff, "he's weird and he goes nuts."

Did they tease Trevor a lot?

"Well, not every day," announced Jeff, "but he gets teased a lot."

For how long?

"Since kindergarten," admitted Alex.

Did he always get really angry like that?

"Yeah, a lot of times," acknowledged Alex.

Did the boys know that he was going to go for Alex? Wasn't Alex afraid of Trevor's outburst?

"No, usually he doesn't hurt anybody. He tries, but we get out of his way. Alex wasn't quick enough this time" was Jeff's summary. Alex agreed with this portrayal of the incident and its history, seemingly oblivious to the glaring contradiction between this view and his parents' call for criminal charges to be brought against Trevor for being a dangerous kid.

With a bit of probing, the picture of bully and victim was reversed. It turned out that a group of boys had, over many years, engaged in a form of bear baiting with Trevor. He had become a rejected-aggressive boy and they could count on getting an exciting reaction from him. They knew that Trevor would "go nuts" and attack them. From time to time, if they were not quick enough on their feet, they might get scratched by the bear, but hey, isn't that a known risk of bear baiting?

The fact is, a lot of aggression goes on among children. Smaller children are intimidated by bigger ones, and tougher kids will press their advantage when they see that they have power in a social situation. Educational psychologist Anthony Pellegrini has studied rough-and-tumble play among elementary schoolchildren. In rough-and-tumble play, or play fighting, children wrestle and fight, and yet a level of "pretend" is maintained. It isn't real fighting, and Pellegrini believes that it serves the important social purpose of providing contact and social practice. (Among chimpanzees, wrestling is an important part of development. Male chimps who don't wrestle with peers have trouble later finding a mate.) A few kids, however, use the opportunity of play fighting to inflict some pain on others. They push the envelope, creating tension in the children around them. They have power. They are strong. They stand out from the group.

Dan Olweus, a Norwegian researcher who has studied bullying for many years, describes a common scene among middle school boys. They will jostle each other in the lunch line, while lining up to go into assembly, while waiting for a physical education activity to begin. During the jostling, one boy—usually one who is larger and more aggressive—may happen to push or hit a smaller boy and frighten him in the process. The bigger boy senses the fear in the smaller boy and is gratified by it. Beyond that, other children sense his power as well, and they are momentarily excited to see the fearful child suffer. At the same time, they are relieved that they are not the targets. They are in awe of the big boy and they implicitly give him their respect.

It is out of just such an accidental moment that a big boy may discover a smaller boy whom he might bully when the occasion demands. There may be some readers who wish to part company with me at this point, offended by the idea that children are sadistic enough to enjoy watching other children be hurt. I am not saying that it is true for all children, but it is certainly the case for a large majority. I suggest that you watch one of the following forms of entertainment: professional wrestling, demolition derbies, professional hockey, action or martial arts movies, James Bond films, the Three Stooges, or NASCAR racing. The recent movie *Gladiator* might be a good place to start putting that human need to observe violence into historical perspective.

Even though most children don't bully habitually, almost any child is attracted to the idea of exercising a bully's kind of power if he or she could. Most kids would not consider themselves bullies and would morally condemn the acts, but they reserve the right to intimidate weaker kids on occasion—or at least they reserve the right to urge the bully on. When a rejected child is bullied, most children don't even think of it as bullying. It's just picking on someone because, well, he or she deserves it—"He's a dweeb," "He picks his nose," "She's a bitch," "She was mean to my friend," "Nobody likes her," and so on. Most children regard this as natural and inevitable and they actively resist when adults exhort them to change their ways. Parents may have a hard time seeing their "nice" kids often covertly encourage bullying behavior and even engage in it themselves against certain "acceptable" targets.

We tend to think of this type of behavior as something kids do to other kids, but that is not entirely true. Look at any sitcom or late-night talk show. Look at the jokes adults tell each other. Some groups are acceptable targets for the most vicious "jokes" ("verbal attacks" is the more accurate term): lawyers, blondes, women, men, Jehovah's Witnesses, Bill Clinton. The list of people it is "okay" to tease or humiliate, depending on the context, is practically endless.

Just as the James Bond 007 idea suggests that we give certain members of the group special license to be aggressive on our behalf, we also define acceptable targets. Most bullies learn quickly that it is okay to pick on the lowest-status kid in the class but not the high-status kids. A boy who beats up kids from the rival school after a big game might be seen as a hero—albeit a scary hero. But he's no hero if he beats up kids from his own school.

The research on bullying is not particularly helpful because there is a problem with the definition of the term. Many different kinds of behaviors, from teasing to physical injury, are termed "bullying" and attributed to "bullies." Left unresolved are the questions of whether bullies are socially skilled or unskilled, insecure or grandiose, habitual or occasional, popular or unpopular. As described in the research, kids who bully others tend to be physically larger than average (no surprise), more verbally facile, and, most importantly, at ease with a high level of aggression. They do not seem to experience the level of guilt that other children do when they hurt someone. They do not share the educational aspirations of many adults or the values of teachers. Victims are the mirror image of bullies. They tend to be physically smaller than average, they share adult values, they are often quite close to their parents and to teachers. Most importantly for their status as victims, children who are bullied manifest anxiety in an obvious way.

These are commonsense superficial descriptions, but they go only so far. All bullying situations have to be analyzed closely until the layers of the child's life—bully or victim—are understood and the dynamics of the group have been taken into account.

One bully I remember was a girl. Margie dominated the life of her seventh-grade class. She was the thinnest, best-dressed girl in the grade. More than that, Margie didn't seem to have the same level of concern for other children that most of the girls in the class did. She was detached in a disturbing way. As the leader of the popular clique, she ruled with an iron hand. Other girls had to call Margie the night before to check on the colors that they were intending to wear the next day. If she was planning to wear that color or—on a whim—didn't like the color they mentioned, she vetoed their clothing choice. All of the girls in the class feared Margie's power. Teachers disliked her because they sensed her seductiveness. Male teachers, in particular, felt unnerved by her sexy clothing and her precocious adult manner.

I learned later that Margie came from an extremely troubled family. Her parents were divorced and engaged in endless battles. Her father had a history of serious mental instability. I suspected that he sexualized his relationship with his daughter. He moved out of state, taking his daughter with him, before I could gather more evidence and perhaps file a report on him. Without any hard data, though, my gut told me that she had been sexually abused. What was undeniable is that some family pathology was being played out in the cruelty with which this girl dominated the class.

If Margie was troubled, then why did the other girls respect her, and why did they allow her to run the class? Because she was thin and rich and articulate and the other girls were awed by her capacity to be mean. Seventh grade girls will sometimes band together to depose a cruel tyrant, but it often takes a long time, and sometimes the negative leader successfully prevents a dethroning through a combination of favors and intimidation. Margie had another advantage: She was cool. What I, as a psychologist, saw as pathological detachment caused by a defective bond with her parents, the students saw as cool behavior. The other kids thought Margie was more grown-up than they were. In fact, she was just more troubled and needy, but in a form they could not recognize.

Bullying behavior in general becomes more intense starting in sixth grade and continues to be so up through around tenth grade. Negative leaders often emerge among eighth, ninth, and tenth grade boys who have gotten their growth early or who have decided to take an antisocial attitude toward the high school experience. Eighth grade boys who have gotten their growth and musculature earlier than their classmates may physically intimidate and put down smaller boys, attacking them for their small size, lack of pubertal development, and lack of interest in girls. They attack any sign of empathy or compassion in a classmate as "gay."

Dan Kindlon and I in our book *Raising Cain* called this universal phenomenon among boys the "culture of cruelty." It involves a great deal of daily boy-on-boy bullying. Let me give you an example. I once interviewed a small, musically gifted boy named Brad in the spring of his ninth grade year. He reported that for his entire eighth grade year, whenever he came into close physical contact with a particular group of boys, they would all whisper, "Faggot, faggot, faggot." For an entire year he was subjected to a daily diet of humiliation from the popular, though antisocial, boys in the eighth grade. None of these tormentors fit the stereotype of a bully, but the cumulative effect on Brad was devastating. He literally trembled when he talked to me about it almost a year later.

During the incidents, he withdrew and tried to ignore the taunts. Nevertheless, they got under his skin. He was so humiliated by the repeated attacks that, despite his own misgivings, the following summer he pushed a dear friend, a girl and fellow camper at his music camp, into some precocious sexual activity. As a result, he lost his friendship with her. When I suggested to him that he had pushed her sexually to prove to himself that he wasn't gay, he nodded quietly in agreement. Brad had begun to absorb the bullies' judgment of him and needed to counter it with a heterosexual experience. The negative leaders in his eighth grade gave him a terrible year, and in an effort to recover his self-esteem he bullied a girl and went on to have a sad summer as a result. Brad could not be seen as a conventional bully, even though he bullied his friend into a sexual experience neither of them was ready for.

Sometimes a rejected-aggressive child may act like a bully but not really be one in the conventional sense. If a child is constantly beaten up by others, he will pick on someone smaller than himself when he is given the opportunity. A child may be rejected at school and then come home to the neighborhood and bully smaller children. I have often seen three or four kids in a class who are far down the social ladder take turns bullying the child on the absolute lowest rung. Their motivation, whether conscious or unconscious, is to prove to themselves that they are not at the bottom.

On the school bus one morning one such boy, a rejected seventh grader named Tony, pulled a screwdriver out of his knapsack and threatened another boy. It turned out that Tony had finally snapped after being tormented all year. The ironic thing in this case was that the boy he threatened to stab, Justin, was considered to be very low-status himself. Nevertheless, he had sure tormented Tony. "They went through my bag every day," Tony told me. "They'd take my stuff and make fun of me."

For the higher-status boys, watching two low-status boys fight was gladiator-style entertainment. They watched as the socially unskilled and aggressive Justin taunted Tony, an outsider no one liked. They were thrilled when Tony fought back. Then they stepped back and watched Tony take the punishment.

There is a debate among psychologists, and among educators and parents as well, about whether bullies are insecure and socially unskilled or whether they are in fact quite skilled. Both types exist. The so-called insecure bully is a child who lacks social skills and makes a clumsy bid for popularity by picking on others. Such bullies are trying to compensate for their fundamental lack of social ability by acting the part of the leader, stepping into shoes that they cannot really fill. (Remember that popular leaders use win-win strategies. Bullies use win-lose strategies.)

In my experience, children see through these bullies and mock their efforts. An unskilled bully is likely to lose popularity as a result of clumsy attempts at domination. Or the group may decide to totally reject a boy like Tony, thus empowering Justin to bully him. (One of Tony's classmates told me, "Tony is practically the name for 'stupid' in our grade. You just say someone's like Tony and everyone knows what you mean.")

Another line of research suggests that bullies are quite skilled and have a unique social gift. They possess a capacity that is first cousin to empathy. But the bully puts this skill to destructive rather than compassionate uses. Bullies of this kind are able to intuit how other people feel and then exploit their insights. They know when people are going to be ashamed, guilty, or malleable. They sense when peers are eager to please. They know what buttons to push in order to dominate others. Indeed, a bully of this type needs to have political savvy. If he doesn't, he can misread a situation and get himself in trouble.

One bully who misread a situation was Franco. Franco was new to seventh grade and was anxious to score some social points. He was walking down the school hall one day and saw Thomas, a small seventh grader whose mother had died the previous year. Thomas was standing with three other, considerably bigger boys. Franco had just learned about the death of Thomas's mother. He came up to Thomas and singled him out for bullying. "Look at the mama's boy with no mama," he said. Thomas, stunned, walked away silently. Franco thought momentarily that he had succeeded in raising his social stock at the expense of a small, underdeveloped boy. But he had misjudged the situation. Thomas's three friends immediately jumped on Franco and beat him up, demonstrating the principle that the group only lets you bully certain children. Justin could bully Tony on the bus, but Franco was told quite clearly that he must not bully Thomas. Bullies are allowed to do the dirty work of the group, picking on rejected kids. They are stopped from bullying just anyone.

A successful bully has to read the crowd to do its bidding. If he consistently or occasionally acts out the group's aggressive impulses toward some rejected child, he will be rewarded with leadership status, albeit a status that adults will not honor, and internal satisfaction.

Olweus concluded from his research that the bully with low self-esteem is a myth. He found that children who bully feel good about themselves and their level of aggression. And why shouldn't they? The group has silently approved of their aggression. That is why they are not eager for adult help with their so-called insecurity problem. Whenever a negative leader boy is sent to me for counseling, he is baffled by why adults think he needs it. He sees their sending him to therapy as a way of breaking his power because they fear him. After all, he has found a way to be powerful in the group. He's at the top of his game, even if he is nowhere near the top of his life.

This refusal to see the need for counseling doesn't mean therapy isn't needed. Margie, the troubled and charismatic seventh grade girl, needed intervention. An eighth grade boy who is harassing boys or girls needs intervention, disciplinary consequences, and personal consequences to increase his awareness of and empathy for others. (Often such a boy has a father behind him who encourages his aggression. "Yeah, I know the teachers don't like it," the father will tell me, "but he'll be successful in business." Or a girl will have a mother who is a social queen in town and wants her daughter to be feared, just like she is.)

Hazing

All human beings have a deep need for acceptance by the group and a deep need for sacred ritual. So it is small wonder that we combine these two needs into rituals of group acceptance. We have a profound need for these rituals. They connect us to one another and to our spiritual life. Ceremonies such as christenings, weddings, and funerals help us mark the beginning of life, the end of life, and all the transitions in between. Graduation ceremonies tell us that we have finished our work and can now join the ranks of educated men and women. Ritual comforts us in times of anxiety and moments of change, reminding us of what endures. Ritual also tells us who has rank and seniority, who is worthy, and who wields power. Initiation ceremonies tell us who has earned the right to sit with the elect.

When I went to pick up my daughter after a month at a sports camp, the younger junior varsity girls all wore white shirts and the varsity girls wore tie-dyed shirts with the slogan "Spirit" on them. The counselors wore dark purple T-shirts. I am certain that the same kind of differentiation was being played out in the clothing of campers and counselors all over the nation. The younger girls were saying to themselves, "Someday I'll wear the tie-dyed shirt." The older girls were thinking, "If I work hard, someday I'll be a Division I college athlete like my counselor."

Children yearn for ceremonies that mark their progress through childhood and adolescence, and they are drawn to rituals that celebrate their growth and development. They also yearn to see their leaders, both adults and peers, sitting in front of them wearing the robes of power that they have earned by virtue of their age and struggle and knowledge of the mysteries of life. Those in the audience get to imagine that they will sit in those seats of power one day.

Children long to be initiated into the secrets and privileges of older children and of adults. In most cultures throughout the world initiation ceremonies have played an important part in the lives of young people, particularly as they make the transition from childhood to adulthood. In our culture, we adults work hard to meet the needs of children for ceremony, staging elaborate birthday parties and other rites of passage.

However, it is also the case that children like to design their own tests and competitions. They seek out situations of power where they can exert control and award their own medals to peers and to younger kids. "Can you run as fast as me?" a boy yells to his friends, challenging them to take him on. "We don't want you," says the girl leader of the sixth grade clique. "You're not like us," she declares. "Yes, I am," pleads the supplicant. "Let me show you. Please give me a chance." The willingness of the newcomer to be tested, and the group's feeling that membership is worth fighting for, creates the conditions for a test, a challenge.

This inherent need on the part of children to be initiated and to initiate one another leads to that distorted form of initiation we call hazing. I believe that the impulse behind hazing is the same as the impulse behind more positive forms of group initiation: to create a group worth being a part of, and to create a test that will challenge the newcomer and prove him or her worthy of being a member of the group. But there is one central difference between a rite of initiation and the experience of hazing. Hazing involves intentional humiliation of the individual; initiation never does. That is why, in my view, fraternity initiations often sink to the level of hazing. They are designed to make the initiate look stupid, foolish, and often even degraded.

I heard recently from an Ivy League college fraternity that new brothers had to appear naked in front of the assembled members with a marshmallow between the cheeks of their buttocks. The initiates had to prove their worth simply by allowing themselves to be exposed and humiliated in this way. (Never mind the homoerotic undertones.)

In other fraternitites the brothers are physically hurt. President

George W. Bush was once asked whether the initiation at his Yale club, Skull and Bones, had involved being marked on the lower back with a small branding iron. He wouldn't acknowledge the rituals he endured. He did add, however, "There was no harm done, either physical or psychological. Besides, it wasn't anything compared to what Texas fraternities do to their pledges. They use cattle prods on them." In this one exchange we can see layer upon layer of inclusion and exclusion, "us" versus "them," in versus out.

Seventy-nine percent of high school varsity and college athletes in the United States report that they have been hazed by their teammates. The most recent arrivals on the varsity soccer and football squads at one boys' school appeared one September morning with their heads shaved. It was a requirement for new members of the varsity teams, imposed by the older team members. The new players look funny and their individuality is stripped away, but everyone in the school communities notices them. They are the new heroes, the new gladiators. And they don't complain, because complaining, of course, marks you as an ungrateful outsider, refusing the glory of admission to the group. That's why adults get so confused about whether hazing is constructive, destructive, or neutral.

Studies of elementary school children in the Marquesas Islands show that they haze younger children, testing them with teasing until they prove themselves worthy of the group's respect. By enduring the hazing without being crushed, they prove they want to be a member of the group. It is no different here in the United States. The goal of hazing is to extract proof of loyalty and commitment. Complaining, quitting, or— worst of all—reporting excesses of hazing to the authorities is proof that a person does not want to be a member of the in-group badly enough and is therefore unworthy. In contrast, the rare child who responds to hazing with humor is quickly assimilated by the group. He or she has passed the test.

Hazing can allow individuals who tend toward sadism free rein for their behavior. In every incident of hazing where I have interviewed participants, someone always mentions the guy who gets out of hand. "We mostly just give little pats with the paddle, and we can tell how much a person can take," a fraternity brother will say. "But Rusty always nails each kid as hard as he can, especially any kid he thinks hasn't respected him enough."

This business of hazing, of allowing children to create their own tests for their peers, is a treacherous one. The impulse is natural and human and understandable. But the results are sometimes tragic. A young man at MIT died from alcohol poisoning after chugalugging too many drinks at his fraternity initiation. New members of the ice hockey team at the University of Vermont were required, as part of their initiation by their teammates, to wear women's underwear. Later each young man was made to crawl naked on the floor holding on to the genitals of the man before him in a line called an "elephant walk." This behavior went on for twenty years before someone felt traumatized by it and filed suit against the university. All team members lied to investigators from the office of the university's general counsel. This led the president of the university to cancel the remainder of the season, a drastic step in hockey-loving northern New England.

The players lied to protect their right to continue hazing practices into the future without the interference of university administrators. Young people do not welcome the intervention of adults in their hazing practices. Yet the University of Vermont example illustrates one aspect of hazing. It continued year after year with the silence—or, worse yet, the silent approval—of coaches who knew something about what was going on. In my opinion, peer hazing almost always has the silent, complicit support of adults who believe that the behavior is an important part of molding a group or a team.

I read recently that a college coach, a woman, had taken her women's soccer team out to some remote area where the new team members were initiated by being made to perform fellatio on bananas. As the father of a girl athlete, my heart sank. Here was a woman coach encouraging girls to carry out the style of hazing that has been traditional for boys' teams.

When you hear that women are doing things that men have long done, it throws these practices into a worse light. Of course it is just as unacceptable for boys to impose this on one another, but seeing it happen with girls wakes us up a little to the brutality of practices we have come to accept as part of being male in our culture. Crawling on the floor holding another man's genitals or performing oral sex on a banana has nothing to do with team building or athletics and everything to do with humiliation.

The problem with hazing is that once team members have been through such an ordeal, they defend it. Many adults think that the privilege of hazing junior members is a well-deserved reward for the senior members of the organization who have paid their dues. They see it as an important tradition that needs to be preserved. At times adults are simply fatalistic, imagining that it is impossible to stop kids from hazing one another. In turn, young people share that belief. Hazing is what kids do to each other, they protest; "it's just the way kids are." That is why it's impossible to eliminate long-standing hazing practices among young people without the moral support of the adults in the community.

Three years ago, Richard Hamilton, the new headmaster of Elm Grove School, a boarding school in New Jersey, asked for help getting rid of some hazing traditions. Knowing how hard kids fight to hold on to their rituals, and knowing that some members of the adult community might still believe in the traditions he was attacking, I approached the problem with some misgivings. Hamilton had taken the courageous stand that certain traditional hazing rituals, practiced by seniors on new students over many years, had to stop. He had begun with the most revered of these. Traditionally, for the entire fall freshman girls had to wear red scarves around their necks and boys had to wear blue blazers emblazoned with the school crest, a gaudy if traditional coat of arms. If any upperclassman found a new student without the scarf or the jacket, the older student could hand out a punishment to him or her. Usually the penalties were mildly humiliating, like being forced to sing in front of everyone in the dining hall. But occasionally the punishments were abusive and sadistic. Most members of the community saw these as isolated incidents. But were the cruel examples really unrelated to the milder public humiliations? Hamilton didn't think so, and by the time I arrived at the school, he had done away with the scarves and blazers.

Why had he done it? He told me that he believed the scarves and blazers were psychologically painful. He did not want to welcome new students to a community by subjecting them to arbitrary rules that made them anxious (one girl lay awake at night in fear that she would forget her red scarf) or could put them in the position of being humiliated by other students.

Hamilton wanted to put an end to the punishments that were meted out to younger students who violated the traditional senior prerogatives by walking down the "senior hall" or being found in a certain common area claimed by seniors. One new student who had walked down the senior hall had been blindfolded and tied up. Then he had been punched by a group of boys. Although the new student was not physically harmed, it became a major issue on campus because it was reported to the authorities. Another student, who violated the seniors' rules by repeatedly invading their common area, was awakened in the middle of the night, dragged out of bed and paddled with a traditional paddle passed down from one senior class to the next for many years.

Hamilton wanted me to run a training session for the student leaders and so, with Larry Cohen, I put together a full-day training experience focusing on the junior class, the up-and-coming leaders of the school. The night before we were to meet with students, I spoke to the faculty about the human desire for initiation. I asked the teachers to remember those moments when they had first felt as if they had truly made the transition from boy to man or girl to woman. For most women that moment was a ritual, either the cultural ritual of being given away by their fathers at the wedding ceremony or the biological ritual of giving birth. For the men, many of the experiences involved proving their masculinity by drinking excessively or undertaking a reckless act. We then talked about hazing and initiation. Many men spoke of their experiences with fraternity or military initiations and emphasized the importance of such rituals in their lives. In the middle of the discussion I thought of a question that might separate out the different experiences of initiation and hazing: "If you had a child, either son or daughter, how much of what you went through would you like to see him or her endure?" One man raised his hand. "About 50 percent," he said. Many nodded in agreement.

So are hazing practices bad or good? These dedicated teachers could report the excesses and the pain of hazing, yet they did not want to eliminate it entirely. They could see its value, yet they not want their children to endure the worst of what they had endured. This response, I believe, reflects the depth of our need for rituals, connection, and acceptance. However, I left the dinner feeling that the faculty, despite the expressed fear of losing some of the school's traditional identity, would support the elimination of the hazing traditions.

The junior class leaders were another matter. The ferocity of their loyalty to the idea of being able to require obedience of the younger students took me by surprise. I had heard this kind of conservatism before among high school students. They experienced any change in the tradition as a usurpation of their power. As students just about to ascend to the status of seniors, they were protective of their "rights." (Students never want traditions changed before they graduate and will fight any that are proposed, leading to my observation that all children are Republicans.) The juniors were unable to take the perspective of younger students and felt they had earned the right to enforce penalties on them. Indeed, in interviews later they expressed the view that they wouldn't have any status as seniors unless they were able to haze the younger kids. What is the advantage of being older if you don't have power over others?

In an effort to help the students appreciate the point of view of younger kids, I showed them a brief clip from the movie *Lucas*, a Disney film about a small, intellectual ninth grade boy who falls in love with a tenth grade girl only to be rejected by her. Aware that she is in love with the football captain, he goes out for football in an effort—a patently ridiculous effort—to impress her. The problem is that he is physically small and has not reached puberty. Nevertheless, he has to shower with the older boys. When he walks into the shower for the first time, an older boy immediately starts to tease him about his small penis, asking him if he uses a thimble for a jockstrap.

Lucas is not devastated; indeed he comes up with a humorous and intellectual retort, telling the older boy that the only reason he has a large penis is because the sight of other boys in the shower excites him. This comment enrages the older boy and his friends. They drag Lucas out of the shower and onto a training table, where they smear liniment on his genitals and throw him out of the locker room door wearing just a towel. He is in physical pain and becomes a source of ridicule for all of the students outside—including the girl he wanted so badly to impress.

The movie plays this scene for comedy, but many adults, especially women, cannot watch it without feeling shock and outrage. Some find it unrealistic, but I have heard many, many reports of varsity teams smearing liniment onto the privates of low-status team members.

From the adult point of view, it is self-evident that the incident in the shower begins with the older boy tormenting the smaller boy. But I couldn't get these high school juniors to focus on that part. What the boys said was "He shouldn't have talked back to varsity athletes," or "He asked for it." When I appealed to the girls for some compassion for Lucas, they declined to give an opinion. "It's a boy thing," they said, licensing their male classmates to discipline their own gender in their own way. If there were students in the group who identified with Lucas and disapproved of what the big boys in the movie did, they did not feel free to say so in the meeting.

Why didn't these intelligent, well-educated high school juniors speak out against the hazing of Lucas? Why did they hold so tightly to their right to inflict pain on others?

Perhaps these juniors really could not empathize with the terror in the eyes of younger children because they did not yet have the capacity to do so. There is recent, preliminary neurological research that suggests that adolescents cannot read facial expressions—especially fear—as accurately as adults can. An inability to read pain in the faces of others might account for their casual attitude toward Lucas's pain in the movie or toward the fear experienced by their schoolmate who was tied up and punched. They would say things like "He wasn't really hurt," or "He was a popular kid. The kids who did that to him liked him; they didn't hit him that hard," or "He broke the rules to bring attention to himself." I believe some of the juniors were rationalizing the pain of students who had been hazed. Yet the utter sincerity of those who simply could not see the pain suggested to me that they really weren't mature enough yet. Or perhaps the students hadn't reached the stage of moral development that allowed them to understand the equal rights of older and younger children. Indeed, in the minds of the students we interviewed in private, newcomers and younger students did not seem entitled to the same moral respect as the older students.

Perhaps there was a certain loyalty to the school that caused these students not to want to change their tradtions. The students liked their school and were proud of it. They may have been reluctant to say something disrespectful of the institution that they were about to lead as seniors—especially to outsiders like Larry and me. No one who morally disapproved of hazing was prepared to tell a psychologist that cruel things had happened in the school and might continue to happen in the future. Possibly no one was willing to contradict the majority in public.

Later, in private interviews with the students, one senior identified the moral issues involved in hazing and said he was happy to see the school rid itself of its hazing traditions. I asked him how he had come to be such a moral thinker. He gave credit to his religion and his father.

All of these reasons—institutional loyalty, lack of brain development, insufficient moral development, misguided adherence to tradition, and group cohesion—help explain why good kids from loving families want to maintain cruel hazing traditions. (Perhaps it goes without saying that those most fiercely opposed to dropping the tradition of scarves and blazers were alumni.)

For me, however, there is one central reason why kids are so cruel to other children and want to reserve the right to be so. It is because all children experiment with power and find it exciting. Children and teenagers experiment with everything in life—with competition, attractiveness, sexuality, athleticism, and academic prowess. Since they try out everything on one another, why wouldn't they try out cruelty and power? The experience of hurting the feelings of another child and feeling the thrill of one's own power is absolutely universal. The experience of discovering that the group has the power to really inflict harm may be guilt-inducing but it is also exciting. And the group's way of diffusing responsibility—"Everyone was doing it"—lessens the burden of guilt or moral culpability.

Adult human beings do not give up power easily. Dictators will do almost anything to hold on to power. The same is true of children. Though hurting others may get them in trouble and cause them guilt, it gives them a feeling of "bigness" that they cannot achieve in any other way. Popular kids love the power that being popular gives them; the powerful clique likes to flex its muscles; seniors like to haze freshmen. These impulses are human and understandable. They can also be destructive, even dangerous for the children who are rejected, hazed, humiliated, or—tragically—encouraged to be reckless with their lives.

I called Richard Hamilton as I was writing this chapter and asked how it was going. The scarves and blazers are gone, he told me. But he gave me the impression that although he has won this battle, the peace remains uneasy. Hamilton is a headmaster who loves his school and thinks it is a warm and friendly place. But he is baffled by the tenacity kids demonstrate in trying to hold on to their hazing rituals. They're still mourning the traditions that put down younger students.

"The older students are always asking, 'How do I get underclassmen to respect me?'" reported Hamilton. The change in policy has made students stop and think. "There is certainly wariness. The kids don't want to get in trouble on this, and I am glad of that," Hamilton told me. "But they want to be sure that the underclassmen know their place. It's especially tough when you are dealing with the crème de la crème of your students. Good kids do mean things. I wonder, do they ever outgrow it?"

Chapter Seven

Still Standing:
How Kids Manage Conflict,
Betrayal, and Reconciliation

One day in fifth grade Larry's daughter, Emma, told him that she had had "some trouble" with her friend Tricia. First Tricia thought Emma was talking about her, then Emma thought Tricia was talking about her. They made up and then fought again and then finally made up again. Mara, the peacekeeper, kept saying, "It's just a misunderstanding." They ignored her and told her to go away. At the end, when they realized it had been a misunderstanding, Emma and Tricia went to Mara and asked, "How did you know?"

Mara said, "I always say that."

Everyone has his or her own perch from which to observe people and draw conclusions about the nature of human life. Mine overlooks the schoolyard, and from that vantage point I am always watching children fighting it out and working it out. Some days the spectacle is horrifying; watching schoolchildren—both boys and girls—can be like watching gladiators. The previous chapter documented the damage that the strong can do to the weak, the harm that the group can do to a vulnerable individual. Without a doubt, children can hurt one another terribly. However, to conclude that kids live in a dog-eat-dog world and there is no hope for them would be incomplete and cynical. Most days, watching children is an inspiring occupation, because they have the innate ability to cooperate and to heal one another's wounds. They engage in a conflict, they feel the pain of it, and they immediately work at it until it is resolved. They don't throw their friends away after a fight. It was just a misunderstanding. Like Mara, they knew it all along.

During the course of a school day there are hundreds of tense moments between children. The running inner dialogue of a hypothetical fourth grade girl might go something like this: "Does Amanda like my shirt? It's just like hers. Did I say the wrong thing? Did I hurt Amanda's feelings? Is she mad at me now? How can I make it up to her?" These sentiments will be intermixed with a darker set of emotions, especially after Amanda did much better than Stephanie on the math test: "Amanda's bugging me. She thinks she's so smart. I'd rather sit with Ginny. If I do sit with Ginny, Amanda will be mad. I don't care. She's always trying to be first in everything. I hope Ginny invites me for a sleepover and I hope Amanda hears about it." Moments later she will be sitting with Amanda at lunch and they will be laughing together about how dumb the science teacher was—she couldn't get the experiment to work and she couldn't get the boys to stop making noise. What a loser!

Have I exaggerated the inner world of the fourth grade girl? I don't think so. She shifts swiftly from wishing to be loved to competing with and wanting to hurt her friend and then back to a sense of alliance and shared humor, all in the space of a couple of hours. Research tells us that early adolescents have higher highs and lower lows than adults; they feel things more keenly than we do. Still, adults also experience conflicting impulses toward people. We can want to murder someone who cuts us off in morning traffic; we are monumentally irritated by the inept service person at Starbucks; moments later we sweetly greet the receptionist at work. We might feel annoyed when we see our boss looking anxious, want to reassure her, then settle down to work with her in a problem-solving fashion and come away feeling admiration for her professional skills.

All human beings display conflicting desires, drives, and needs. All the great psychological or psychoanalytic theorists—Sigmund Freud, Alfred Adler, Abraham Maslow, and many others—have attempted to categorize and prioritize these needs in order to explain the drives under-lying human complexity. I have been influenced by all of them. However, without delving too deeply into theory and for the sake of simplicity, I am going to describe every child as wanting three different things in life: *connection*, *recognition*, and *power*. The very fact of wanting these three vital things in life inevitably puts us into conflict with ourselves and with our friends. There is no escape from conflict because all human beings want contradictory things. Here is how these three desires play out.

First, every child has a profound need for close *connection*, first in the early attachment to her parents and later in relationships with other adults and children. As we learned earlier, for most children friendships are the continuation of that early mother-child sociability. There is a pro-found need to feel connected to another person and special in his or her eyes. All children bring that neediness into their friendships and their group life. Over and over groups of middle school children define friend-ship for me: "Someone you can really trust . . . someone who likes you for you . . . someone who doesn't care if you're cool . . . someone who is easy to be with." In other words, someone to connect with. This search for the intimate, reliable connection is the basis of friendship. The need for affiliation is the basis of cooperation, collaboration, and generosity of spirit among children.

At the same time all children want to compete and feel successful in some arena that will bring them *recognition*. Recently a fifth grade class in Ohio informed me that "no one plays Pokémon anymore," and one boy unhappily observed, "Yeah, everyone says that, but a lot of kids still like to play at home." Clearly he was one of those kids, and clearly it was his fervent wish that Pokémon would somehow become cool again. I re-turned home from my trip there to find my son, Will, struggling with the same problem at his school. Almost overnight Pokémon—Will's favorite activity—had dropped in status. That was a big loss for him, both inter-nally and externally, encompassing a loss of status and a loss of a sense of self-worth. Will told me that he wants the other boys in school to see him as the best at something. He had considered himself best at Pokémon and catching all the characters had given him enormous personal satisfaction. Now that the game has fallen out of favor, he is looking for a new source of recognition from the group and from himself. The desire to achieve is, I believe, intrinsic to human beings and is the wellspring of motivation. Yet for most of us it is also linked to what others in our group value. For example, most of us wouldn't spend the time to master an instrument that no one wanted to hear us play. I once heard an interview with Bobby Riggs, famous for the Battle of the Sexes tennis match against Billie Jean King, in which he said that as a boy he was determined to achieve recognition, so he secretly practiced dribbling a basketball up the stairs in his house blindfolded. He then bet his friends that they couldn't do it, and showed off his superior talent. I suspect that recognition was more important to him than connection.

Finally, all humans crave some feeling of *power* and even dominance. There are many different ways to achieve that feeling of power, whether by wrestling, successfully skipping a stone across the top of the water, gossiping, having the best-looking pair of jeans, or having a navel ring. Typically, the types of power one seeks are shaped by gender. Boys seek a feeling of power through physical dominance. I have known many boys who wanted to wrestle their fathers in adolescence. Even after it becomes clear that it no longer makes sense for the middle-aged man to wrestle his son (because the father has a bad back, or is out of shape and they both know that) the son may insist on it. The son needs the feeling of challenging a powerful male. A daughter may need to put her mother down, acting contemptuous or patronizing. "Mom, you don't know anything about what's happening at school. Why do you talk about it as if you do?" Or, "Mom, no one wears that anymore!" The daughter, too, gets a feeling of superiority, even at the cost of hurting someone she loves. Her desire for power momentarily wins out over her need for connection and affection.

Children universally seek situations where they feel power, both at home and in the presence of other children. The patronizing remark that the girl made to her mother could just as easily have been about a girl at school. In the movie *Clueless*, when the brand-new girl is brought to P.E. class at Bronson High School dressed in baggy jeans, one of the fashionably dressed cool girls says, "She could be a farmer in those clothes." The high-status girl takes a shot at the new girl in the first moments after her arrival. She asserts her power immediately and takes great satisfaction in doing so publicly.

If you accept my premise that all people are driven by these three needs—connection, recognition, and power—then it is not difficult to understand why children are in conflict much of the time, particularly in their social lives. From the moment a child joins a classroom situation, he is likely to want and need the same things that his friends want, at the same moment. Let's take the simplest of examples from kindergarten life: lining up at the door to go to recess. I don't know how many readers have watched the scramble of children trying to be first in line, willing to push others out of the way to get there (power). Have you seen the future politicians who go to the teacher before the lineup to ask whether they can be first in line (recognition)? Some pairs will head for the door together, not caring where they are in line as long as they are next to each other (connection). From the adult point of view the problem is that if the teacher doesn't regulate the first-in-line selection process, the class becomes chaotic. From the child's point of view, the rush for power can damage friendships. If you see the faces of the children who are not caught up in the rush to be first in line, they often look dismayed. Their faces seem to say, "How could our lovely group disintegrate like this? Why are my friends doing this? And why does my friend want so badly to be ahead of me? Doesn't he know that it is hurting my feelings?"

Because kids are in the grip of different needs at different moments, they may offend their friends. A child who boasts, for example, may impress his friends at one moment, because they are receptive to his bid for attention, and irritate everyone at another time. All children have to learn how to manage their own individual neediness and greediness while maintaining a relationship with another. Friends have to learn how to do this; members of a clique have to learn this as well. If you do not learn how to regulate your own drives for power and recognition when they conflict with those of other people, you will end up hurting your friends' feelings again and again, and eventually they will drop you. But you can't give up your drives for recognition and power completely, or else you will be treated like a doormat. The task for every child is to learn self-regulation and self-control so that he or she can maintain a social life. Years ago I had a patient, a brilliant boy—almost certainly a genius—who always wanted his four-year-old companions to play computer games with him. They could not because they were not able to keep up with him intellectually. They chose to play simpler, more age-appropriate games. He would, in an effort to motivate them, deride their choices: "I don't want to do that. That's stupid. My game is better." He was a powerful personality and his attacks made them cry. They would want to go home and he was left friendless. His desire to be powerful in the relationship left him alone. He had to be coached to set aside his interests in order to keep a friend. He had to be taught to share.

Conflicts over the basic needs of the individual arise in pairs of friends, in trios (where power plays are legendary), in the relation of an individual to a group, and in the dynamics of the group itself, especially in cliques. In the following sections, I am going to look at examples of conflict in many different friendship situations. Though we will see friendships that end because of competitive pressure, we will also see friendships that endure because the need to be with one another outweighs the hurt. I want you to consider this fact: While conflict is inevitable in friendship, friends also have the ability to resolve their troubles. They have the capacity to tolerate each other's needs and to resolve differences. As Frans de Waal writes, "Fires start, but fires go out. . . . We know a great deal about the causes of hostile behavior in both animals and humans. . . . Yet we know little of the way conflicts are avoided—or how, when they do occur, relationships are afterward repaired and normalized." In his wonderful book *Peacemaking Among Primates*, Frans de Waal makes the case that for all primates, humans included, "making peace is as natural as making war."

Conflict in a Pair of Friends

A couple of years ago, Larry, his wife, and his daughter, Emma, had just arrived in the Boston area. Larry and his wife were concerned that Emma wouldn't know anyone in kindergarten, so they called one of the families from the class list published by the school. That was how Emma and Gillian met. They remember their first play date, but they think they became best friends just because they liked each other. They've forgotten the parental intervention that provided each with a friendly face on the first day of school. Emma and Gillian were best friends all that year and in first grade as well. The teachers deliberately separated them in second grade, in order to help the two of them widen their social circles. At first Gillian had a difficult time making new friends, and Emma had a hard time with Gillian having new friends. There were some big fights along the way, some hurt feelings about who sat with whom at lunch and about "talking about each other." They worked these issues out, the girls kept their friendship and were reunited in third grade, only to be swept up into the dramatic competition of two other girls who each wanted to be the class queen bee. The struggle over status pulled all of the girls in the class into a maelstrom of rivalries, alliances, and power plays. There was lots of "You can't be friends with her if you are friends with me" and "We're having a contest to see who has more friends, so you have to be my friend, not hers." Neither Emma nor Gillian were directly involved in the struggle, but the different approaches each took to the conflict strained their friendship.

In fourth grade, the two girls had very little to do with each other, at least at school. Nevertheless, the families remained close throughout the year, and Emma and Gillian continued to sleep over at one another's house. They struggled with what it meant that they had been best friends and were now just friends, with different social agendas at school. They each spread their wings some—reaching out to other girls, not inviting the other to things, in a way that was alternately good for the one girl but ruffled the other one's feathers. At the time of this writing, both have other best friends in fifth grade but consider themselves good friends. And indeed they are.

At several points in their lives however, this friendship might have been lost. Did it stay alive because the parents remained friends? Probably. Did the friendship endure because the two girls worked at it? Certainly. How did Emma and Gillian know to work at a relationship? Who taught them? Though the parents of each girl made observations from time to time or gave advice, for the most part the two girls taught one another how to hold on to the friendship. They both made mistakes and learned from competitiveness. They learned how to manage a relationship over the years.

How does Emma think about the history of her relationship with Gillian? She gives a fairly simple chronology: "Me and Gillian were best friends in kindergarten. Then in first grade we were still best friends but we found a couple of new friends. In second grade we were in different classes and it took a little while to make new friends, but we were still good friends with each other. In third grade we were in the same class but we weren't best friends anymore because we had each found so many other friends, but we were still friends. In fourth grade we were in different classes. We were still friends but not really good friends. In fifth grade we're still friends. We sleep over at each other's house all the time. But at school in a crowd we aren't really together."

When Emma's father asked her about the changes in their relationship and how those changes play out in the present school situation, Emma reported: "At recess I play soccer but she doesn't play soccer—it's not like she's my best friend and we do everything together like in kindergarten." Emma thinks of the changes as having come about because of changes in her and her friend's choices of sports and interests. She does not even mention the power of the group to shape her friendship choices or her athletic interests.

Emma's father then tried to articulate the reality of Emma and Gillian's relationship for her: "If someone saw you and Gillian at school, they would never guess that you have known each other really well for five years, that you sleep over at each other's house all the time, that you are close friends. But if someone saw the two of you at our house or at her house, they would see instantly that you are great friends, that you know each other really well, that you really enjoy playing together."

Even though she is articulate about this friendship, Emma, like most children, often overlooks the subtle social forces that operate between friends. Looking back on kindergarten, she thinks that it was shared interests that brought them together rather than familiarity. Now, five years later, she thinks it is divergent interests that keep them apart rather than different ways of fitting into the broader social groupings in school.

Whenever I speak about childhood friendships and social cruelty, someone in the audience always asks me to recommend a curriculum that will help children understand friendship. I never know what to say, because I want to support the idea of schools helping kids with their social development. However, deep down I have to admit that a curriculum can't really teach children all they need to master. The best practice for friendship is having a friend and working it out. That's what Emma and Gillian did. That's what most kids do. The counselor-led groups are there for children who cannot get into the game or who are so confused by the complex currents that they start to panic.

Problems in Trios

When two children are friends, the very fact of their friendship serves as a magnet that attracts a third person. Very often the two friends want to share their love and their fun with another person. They may also want to have an audience to admire their friendship. (Haven't you ever wanted to show off a good relationship?) That is okay as long as the new one is content to respect and admire the original two. However, when there are three people involved in any situation the late arrival will eventually want full status. And inevitably each pair in the trio will discuss the absent third member. Or, if one child is annoying in some way, her friend may turn to their other friend to complain about her, and the two friends will form an alliance based on their mutual distaste for the annoying habits of the other child. Suddenly the trio breaks down into one tightly bonded pair of children plus one on the outside. All three kids must then struggle to make it a trio again.

When my daughter, Joanna, was between fifth and sixth grades, she had begun to cement her friendship with Miranda, a girl in the neighborhood. Because they did not go to school together, and did not share the same classmates and teachers, their friendship was based on geography, mutual liking, and play. All that July they were swimming companions, spending hours together in the water, laughing and playing. They truly enjoyed one another. Theresa and I were also invested in the friendship. We respected Miranda's mother, Carol, and we simply loved seeing the two girls together.

However, both girls admired a third girl in the neighborhood named Celia. Celia was just a few months older than Joanna and ten months older than Miranda, but she was a grade ahead of them both. She is a beautiful girl, very tall and fashion conscious, and has always been socially skilled. In our small neighborhood she is the height of sophistication and both Joanna and Miranda looked up to her. She and Joanna had been playmates—one might call them summer buddies—since babyhood. Though never close in the winter, Joanna and Celia had traditionally always found some playtime in the summer. That summer was no exception. Though Joanna and Celia hardly saw one another during the school year, Joanna invited Celia to play with Miranda and her on a number of occasions in late July. It is likely that Joanna felt like the social center of the trio for a period of time. She had made it happen. During the last two weeks of July and the first two weeks of August there was a neighborhood trio that was really an uneasy combination of three separate pairs: the old, unstable friendship (Joanna and Celia), the new, tight friendship (Joanna and Miranda), and the new possibility (Miranda and Celia).

At the beginning of August Miranda came to believe that she was left out of some secret that Joanna and Celia had together. Her response to feeling excluded was to make a bid to have a special friendship with Celia separate from her relationship with Joanna. On occasion she and Celia would get together and not invite Joanna to join them. I remember seeing Joanna sitting on the steps of our house, watching Celia and Miranda go into Celia's house with a rented movie for the evening. Joanna was incredibly hurt.

For a period of time that summer the trio was also based on a shared baby-sitting job in the neighborhood. A young family with a new baby had moved into a house on the street next to us. Initially Celia's older sister, Katherine, was the number one baby-sitter for baby Andrew. Then, as the mother began to go back to work on a part-time basis, she hired Celia, then Joanna, and finally Miranda to help her out. Celia had got the job through her sister, and then Joanna got the job from her position as next-door neighbor and friend of Celia. Later Joanna introduced Miranda to the family, and she was hired also. The sisters considered the job to be theirs. Nevertheless, Joanna felt it was her first big employment break and was very excited and proud to be working regularly.

We soon noticed that whenever there was extra baby-sitting to be had, it went to Miranda. Joanna felt confused and excluded but didn't feel free to express this to Miranda. We could not at first figure out what was happening. It seemed unfair to us that a neighborhood job was unwittingly adding to the conflict in the trio. Gradually Joanna was squeezed out of the trio, the baby-sitting, and the friendship. She was hurt and furious. She expected Miranda to apologize. Joanna and Miranda stopped speaking to one another. They avoided one another. But as hard as Joanna tried to separate herself from the source of her pain in our small neighborhood, she was almost daily an eyewitness to the growing relationship between Celia and Miranda.

It was an agonizing time. My wife, Theresa, and Miranda's mother, Carol, talked about what was going on. Both were sad to see the friendship between Joanna and Miranda falter, but Carol was naturally obliged to support Miranda's feelings of hurt that she had been initially excluded. Miranda clearly wanted to win Celia's friendship and was succeeding—even though she knew it put her friendship with Joanna at risk. We made a pact with Miranda's mother not to get involved as parents. We agreed not to take sides, not to engage in reproaches. It was a wise decision.

The three girls played out the drama. I remember once standing in the driveway with Joanna and spotting Carol's car. Joanna saw it as well and registered that Miranda was in the front seat. As Carol drove by, Miranda looked away to avoid making eye contact with Joanna. She need not have worried about that. Joanna physically turned her back to Miranda. Carol and I smiled and waved at one another, straining to be adult, trying not to be pulled into the anger, hurt, and confusion of the two girls.

How did this drama end? Well, in September school began and Miranda moved to a new house several blocks away from us. Celia returned to her school, her grade, and her group of friends on the other side of town. She stopped courting Miranda. Miranda was extremely upset. After a two-week period of grieving she called Joanna. Joanna was delighted to hear from her. There were no reproaches, no postmortems. They were immediately friends again. I have a photograph of the two of them from that September. The photo documents two slender girls, one just twelve and the other eleven, wearing one-piece bathing suits. They have stuffed balloons into the tops of their suits, giving each of them a size 46D chest. They are facing each other, laughing and smiling, modeling their outrageous profiles. Girls on the cusp of being women. Friends again.

Over and over again in children's friendships, the need for connection triumphs over the inevitable conflicts that arise from competition and the need for recognition—but often not until there has been a great deal of suffering all around. If the need for power and recognition in one friend becomes too great, it may trigger a reaction in the other. When conflicts arise between two individuals, one or the other may be tempted to speak to a third person about the conflict. This strategy, which family therapists call triangulation, is a universal temptation. Instead of speaking directly to the person who has offended us, we discuss our friendship problems with the new person. It works as a short-term solution by bleeding off some of the angry energy one friend feels; however, it means that the original dispute may never be talked out. It may be talked *about* without ever being resolved. Typically, the end of a friendship comes in the form of a third person.

Here is Steve's description of his relationship years ago with David, how he ran for political office, and how a third boy entered the scene, leading to the loss of his friendship with David.

"I have been going to the same beach town for about twelve years now," he told me. "There were these two houses for sale, about eight houses apart. One had a pool and the other didn't. They were similar houses, and I remember going to this one house and my parents looking at it, and then we went to the house with the pool, and we crossed paths with these people who had a kid about my age. My mother liked the house with the pool; the other family bought the house down the street. That's how we clicked, me and this kid; his name was David. I'd always been friends with him, we'd always had this great time together. We did summer things, like go to the beach and out in a sailboat.

"One year, I ran for a junior event at this yacht club in our town. There's a commodore, a vice commodore, a secretary, a treasurer. I ran for vice commodore my first year, and I pulled everyone I knew in to vote. I even found people who weren't going to be in town for the election and did absentee ballots. I was only twelve at the time!

"Around then David met a friend, a guy named Luke. I did not like Luke. He was twelve too and he was into drugs. I said, 'David, I don't like him. You do whatever you do with him, and you and I will just hang around.' And I said 'David, you're going to come out and vote for me, right?' He said, 'Yeah, yeah, sure.' So I went down to take a last look at the ballot to see who's going to be in there. And *David* had put his name in against me for vice commodore. I know Luke put him up to it, because I never really liked Luke. I did win, though. I won overwhelmingly.

"That kind of ruined the friendship because my parents had a victory party that night. I brought all my friends together but David. We had a big pizza party. We came back home and I saw these two kids walking down the street all dressed in black, and I pull up to the house and my mother goes, 'Someone egged the house!' I said 'That's not egg, that's paint ball.' I remembered going over to David's house and seeing a paint ball gun in his mother's room because his mother wouldn't let him have it.

"So Luke and David paint-balled my house. They ran off behind a house in the dark. And that was the end of it. It was a bump in the road of friendship. Now when I look back I think, 'It might've been worth it, it might not have.'"

Steve does not evidence a lot of insight into how his political ambition and his desire to control things—that is, to try to pick David's other friends for him—might have jeopardized his friendship. He assumed that David would want to campaign for him. Perhaps David might have wanted to do so at the start, but his own competitive feelings left him open to persuasion by Luke. Was the loss of David's friendship just a bad thing that happened in Steve's life? He refers to it as a "little bump" in the road of friendship but then goes on to wistfully say this about winning an election but losing a friendship: "It might have been worth it, it might not have." It is clear, however, that he realizes he paid a price with the loss of his friend. Losing a friend is one of the most powerful experiences in childhood and it is likely to lead to insight and change. In Steve's case I'm hoping it made him both a more skillful friend and a more adroit politician.

Two Friends and Their Relationship to the Group

Anyone who has stepped into a middle school knows how quickly that experience can take you back to your own feelings from school—especially the painful ones. In one of my recent discussions with middle school children, I told them that when I was in seventh grade I was an un-successful athlete, afraid of having someone throw a baseball anywhere near me. My two closest friends, however, were both very coordinated boys and were part of the most popular group in school, which included most of the excellent athletes in the class. There were times, I told the students, when my best friends excluded me from the popular group, when they seemed reluctant even to acknowledge my existence during the school day, but would still play with me on weekends. "Why," I asked the kids, "would my best friends leave me out during the school day? Why wouldn't they tell me the secret initials of their group or show me the secret handshake?" Many of the students tried in an earnest and concrete way to explain to me why I was left out. They took my ques-tions as evidence that I was still confused about what had happened to me. "I don't want to insult you," one boy said, "but if you weren't popu-lar, you know, your friends couldn't hang with you during the school day. I mean, they just can't, 'cause, you know, the other popular kids wouldn't like it." The tone of his voice and those of the several girls who followed him and tried to clarify the matter for me suggested that this state of affairs was (possibly) regrettable but (definitely) not negotiable. It is just the way things were back when I was a kid, and it is the way things still are now. It was not the fault of the popular kids that they excluded. It is what you have to do if you are a member of a popular group.

An eighth grade girl, Liz, told me that she had had a friend, Mandy, for many years. As they approached middle school it became evident that she had been accepted by the popular kids but Mandy had not. Liz was aware of the situation but tried to keep the reality of it out of her mind. The coolest girls were not happy with her attempt to hold her worlds together to maintain a friendship that didn't fit the rigid rules of popular society. She described a time when the most popular girl in sixth grade demanded that she rank all the other girls in the class on paper. The carrot and the stick were implicit: If she didn't rank them, she would lose points. If she did a good job, she would gain points. Above all, where would she rank Mandy? Low, according to the truth of social status, or high, according to the loyalty of their friendship? So Liz did the best thing she could think of, giving Mandy a ranking near the middle of the class. The queen bee was full of contempt when she saw the score that Liz had given her friend. "That's not right," she declared. At that point in the telling of the story Liz began to become vague about what happened to her friendship with Mandy. Her discomfort was such that I chose not to ask her the question I wanted to ask: "Did you drop Mandy in order to keep your standing with the popular kids?" I intuited the answer. The group had succeeded in devaluing Mandy in Liz's eyes, or at least it had been able to put Liz in enough conflict that her friendship with Mandy made her uncomfortable. Often that is all it takes, and the Mandys of the world ease out of the friendship to avoid an outright rejection.

Much of the cruelty that is attributed to cliques has to do with the pressure that a group implicitly or explicitly puts on kids to abandon their friends. As a member of the eighth grade group that Catherine got to know said, "If you stick up for someone, they look at you like you have ten heads."

We would like to see children—especially those with a basic level of acceptance—say no to cliques when they demand that a child abandon a friend as the price of admission. But the dilemma is not an easy one, as the need for power and recognition competes with the need for connection. To have to sacrifice friendship in order to join a clique is a price that many children find extremely painful. It forces them to betray not only their friends but their best selves as well. How many of us remember participating in a group that made us feel morally ugly? How many of us remember joining in the gossip about a friend and feeling guilty all the while? How many of us said things about a dear friend in order to curry favor with the popular clique and then felt sick afterward? Such is the power of groups and the neediness of individuals.

Cliques

Cliques are the inevitable and natural convergence of the forces I talked about in Chapters 5 and 6: diffusion of moral responsibility, in versus out, up versus down. Children silently sort themselves into the catagories of popular, accepted, and rejected and then gather themselves into groups according to their social status. The popular children stick with the popular children, the accepted with the accepted, and so on. Birds of a feather flock together. "We" are different from "them."

If it is natural for human beings to cohere in groups that share their identity (the sociological perspective), then they will also seek out friends who share their social identity. African-American students will sit together in the cafeteria; the Asian-American students will seek each other out and compare the rules in their homes with those of the African-Americans and the Euro-Americans. Everyone will talk about "us" and "them."

As children move from the world of their families to the world of peers, they stop for a while in a middle world of cliques and narrowly defined social groups. Although this is a natural impulse, many children suffer as a result—especially those who want desperately to be included and instead are cruelly excluded. There is another kind of suffering, not as intense perhaps, where the person is accepted but is always on her toes, always fearing rejection. In an even more subtle form the child becomes preoccupied with looks, appearance, fashion, money, status—whatever the markings are for membership in that clique—and forgets about everything else, including grades, family, and friends.

Cliques start as short-lived clubs in kindergarten and first grade and begin to take definite shape in fourth and fifth grade. They can be cruel from the outset, like an I-hate-Heather club, or they can just be a gang of kids who like to hang out together. They peak in power in middle school—sixth, seventh, and eighth grades. Only the most popular clique tries to keep itself together in high school. Most other kids settle into small groups of friends and the more democratic and accessible interest-based groups to be found in high school. Though cliques can trigger real suffering and can splinter a class, it is important, I believe, not to villainize cliques. They are simply the inevitable consequence of the universal human drive for inclusion and group cohesion. To attack cliques is to attack all of our children, because almost all kids want to be part of a clique in middle school. They are interested in how leaders emerge, how they wield power, and why children feel different when they are part of cliques. Children are intensely interested in the codes of behavior that cliques require. I would say that exactly the same impulse that drives people to be interested in political campaigns, in the practice of law, or in being a member of Congress is at work in the minds of middle schoolers who join cliques. They do not see themselves as evil, and they are not.

Here is how one group of girls who spoke to Catherine described the cliques in their school and the formation of their group. There is really nothing more a psychologist can add to their description.

Catherine: Are there cliques at your school?

Girls: Yes. Definitely.

Catherine: Tell me about them. What kinds are there?

Angie: We have different groups. Some people are the popular people, some people are—

Kim: Really smart or—

Angie: No, they usually have smart and mixed.

Becky: There's the popular clique, the semipopular clique, the smart clique. We're the athletic clique.

Kiley: Then there's an off-clique.

Catherine: Yeah, the kids who aren't in any clique.

Angie: There is a trendy clique too.

Kim: There's a druggy clique and—

Becky: We've got it all.

Angie: You were talking about competition between the cliques. I think in a way there is. Some of the other cliques don't like our clique at all.

Becky: We were just talking about that. They stereotype us, saying, "Oh, they're snobby."

Catherine: What do they stereotype about you?

Becky: That we're rich and get everything we want. It's not true at all.

Kim: Some groups all want to look exactly alike. They all comb their hair the same way. They all wear exactly the same clothes. The same style of clothes from the same stores and everything.

Catherine: You don't do that?

Angie: Every once in a while . . . Once I went to a party. I had on blue jeans and a black turtleneck, and my best friend, her name is Kara, was there. We hadn't seen each other for three months. And she was wearing blue jeans and a black turtleneck and so was I. It was so cool.

Catherine: Do you have individual friends in the cool group?

Kim: It's a competition between our two groups because they get mad when we try to be nice to one of them, and they think we're taking their friends but we're really not. We just think they're nice so we want to hang out with them.

Kiley: We want to just hang out, but they think of people more as possessions than as friends.

Catherine: So you girls are more supportive of each other than the kids in the coolest clique?

Angie: I think we're more supportive.

Catherine: Did the cliques start in middle school?

Becky: Sixth grade.

Kim: Seventh grade.

Catherine: How can you tell who is in which clique? What do people do?

Girls: Lunch tables.

Catherine: Lunch tables?

Angie: Who sits with each other at lunch. And who's together at recess.

Becky: And who hangs out with who.

Catherine: Let's say you're not in the popular clique and you have a friend you've had for years, and she's in a different clique. Are you still friends with that person?

Girls: Yeah.

Catherine: But you don't hang out with them at school?

Angie: We'll talk in classes or something but we might not go to the movies with them.

Catherine: If I came to your school, do you think I'd be able to tell who was in which clique just by walking down the hall?

Girls: Yes.

Catherine: What about your group? What are you like?

Angie: I think we're all dedicated to each other. Some people, all they care about is school and their friends come last. I think our friends come first.

I think these girls bring vividly to mind the types of experiences that support—one might say rationalize—cliques. "We're us, they're them;" "we're different, they're cooler;" "we're caring and accepting, they're possessive;" "our group just likes to be together, their group is an exclusive clique." And above all, when children see themselves reflected in the clothes and attitudes of another person ("She was wearing jeans and a black turtleneck and so was I. It was so cool"), they feel affirmed in a way that no adult can make them feel.

It doesn't matter what the actual identifying marks of a group are. Cliques exist because at a time of shaky identity it is essential to feel part of a group. We gravitate toward people who are like us. And there is intense pleasure to be found there. As one girl Catherine interviewed says: "Every day is a new surprise when we see each other."

However, there are a few points I can relate from the research that the reader might not know from direct experience. Cliques are so important and universal that almost every child finds himself in a clique, even if it is the off-clique. The problem is that the children with better social skills tend to gravitate to the more popular cliques at the top, and the children with less skill find themselves in the low-status cliques. This is a case of the rich get richer and the poor get poorer.

Low-status cliques tend to become deviant. Once a boy has joined other unskilled boys under the tutelage of an aggressive leader, the clique can become increasingly lawless and delinquent. Smoking or promiscuous sexual behavior may become its norm.

Parents fear the power of cliques and wish their children weren't so influenced by them. Parents fear peer pressure. Kids fear being left all alone. They will gladly pay the price of doing whatever everyone else in the group is doing in order to have the security of acceptance in the group. The problem is simply this: As bad as it is to be part of a deviant clique, it is better than sitting by yourself at the lunch table. The other members of a clique all know this, because they fear sitting alone as much as anyone does. They have perfect empathy for the isolated and the lonely. Their knowledge of this universal child vulnerability, however, can lead some members of a clique to inflict a punishment on an individual that is, for the early adolescent, something akin to being tortured on the rack day after day.

When I interviewed Naomi, a teacher at a Jewish day school who was in her mid-twenties, she related: "My mother told me that during most of my seventh grade year she stayed home during lunch because she knew I would call. Her friends would invite her to do things, but she said no. She knew I'd be calling from school because I had no one to talk to at lunch. None of my old friends would sit with me or speak to me for months."

What had happened? "I had a fight with Marjorie, and before we could sort it out the group met and decided that it was my fault. I went into school one morning and found that they had all turned on me. No one would have anything to do with me." But this sudden excommunication by the group was not the end of it. "They began saying anti-Semitic things to me. My name is Goldman and they started to call me 'Goldjew.' People tried to help and eventually we made up in some formal way, but none of them were really ever my friends again after that. It all died a slow death. By high school we weren't friends. It influenced all the choices I made after that. When I went to college, I moved as far away from home as I could get. I dreaded going home. My need to run away from the hurt the group had inflicted on me caused me to make one bad choice after another.

"Over the years I said to myself that what happened in seventh grade could not have been responsible for the depression I had in high school and the drinking and the drugs I got involved in. It wasn't until years later that it clicked for me. Maybe what I went through then was responsible, at least partly, for what happened to me later. I felt I had a huge insight, and that was a help. The group can be that important to kids. And rejection can drive them into depression."

Cliques are not inherently bad. However, they do have the power to inflict this kind of trauma on an individual. No single child is psychologically equipped to handle this kind of group rejection. No child—and not many adults for that matter—is capable of defending herself against hate.

Because cliques engage in groupthink, because they bring out conformist behavior in children who are, developmentally speaking, at their most conformist age and are not capable of a level of moral reflection that will free them from it, they can engage in cruel acts over many months. They can reject, exclude, and punish. They can become anti-Semitic not out of ideology but just as a tool of group exclusion and cohesion. The rejection of Naomi by all of the members of her clique and her subsequent troubled adolescence is a testament to that fact.

The Primate Capacity for Healing and Reconciliation

We must always remember that human beings have a capacity for reconciliation that is every bit as strong as the human appetite for aggression. So it is with chimpanzees, with whom we share an extraordinarily large percentage of our DNA, and other primates as well. Frans de Waal writes: "Violence is not the normal state of this ape's [the chimp's] social life. It is there as an undercurrent, a constant threat, but chimpanzees keep their heads above the surface 99 percent of the time." It could be said that 99 percent of a school day is made up of cooperative acts. Children are nicer to one another more times than they are cruel. If you stand in a school cafeteria, most kids are talking and laughing with a friend. It is not as if they haven't had aggressive thoughts or feelings toward one another; they have. But they have found a way to get past the conflict. They seek constantly to be reconciled with one another despite their differences.

The ways in which humans reconcile with one another are strikingly similar to those used by other primates. All primates have a huge repertoire for appeasing, reassuring, apologizing, and seeking favor with others. Two rhesus monkeys that have fought will not explicitly apologize, but one combatant will walk slowly by his former foe so closely that their hair will be touching. If no new hostility breaks out, soon the tension between them begins to dissipate. Bonobos use sex to calm one another after a conflict. Dominant chimps seek harmony and so do submissive members of the troop. A submissive chimp may put his hand into the mouth of a dominant male as if to say, "I trust you to be calm. I acknowledge your power." Male chimps seek reconciliation more than female chimps, even when you control for their greater level of aggression. (Females are more selective in their forgiveness. They forgive members of their families but hold grudges against outsiders.)

De Waal describes the great parallels between chimp reconciliation and that of humans, most notably the role of kissing. "Humans make up in a hundred different ways: breaking tensions with a joke, gently touching the other's arm or hand, apologizing, sending flowers, making love, preparing the other's preferred meal, and so on. Nonetheless, the kiss is the conciliatory gesture par excellence."

If a sixth grade girl starts to cry, her friends will gather around her and console her. They will hug her and pat her hair. Every time I meet with high school students in a girls' school, there are always three or four pairs of girls leaning or lying on one another, grooming one another's hair. When a member of my daughter's soccer team comes off the field and returns to the bench she is welcomed back with pats and arm touches. Though boys in U.S. culture are not as free to hug or kiss one another as are girls, boys do an enormous amount of patting, especially in tense situations, such as in competitive sports. Boys who are teammates defuse the tension by touching one another in ways that are more intimate than usual. The pat on the butt is one of these obvious encouraging and reassuring gestures. (Boys are not generally quite as intimate as male gorillas are in the calming techniques they use. Male gorillas will sometimes grab hold of one another's testicles when things get tense. The message is clear: "Let's all calm down here so nobody gets hurt.")

Whenever we think about controlling cliques or dealing with group power, we must acknowledge again that the power of the group cuts both ways. Children have the power to hurt and the power to heal. If you watch girls in cliques, they spend most of their time supporting, calming, and tending one another. If you watch the faces of boys in a group, much of the time they are smiling, laughing, and reassuring one another. A classic boy maneuver is to appear to take offense at some small thing. A boy might square off against another boy in a fists-up position as if to fight, then suddenly smile and laugh in an I-was-just-kidding manner. He might throw a punch in a harmless, slow-motion sort of way. The message is clear: "I could have been aggressive but I choose to be friendly. You are my friend."

In one striking story de Waal describes two male chimps who engaged in a similar piece of theater in order to reconcile their differences:"Yeroen [the dominant male chimp] . . . would feign interest in a small object to break the tension and attract his adversary. He would suddenly discover something in the grass and hoot loudly, looking in all directions. A number of chimpanzees, including his adversary, would rush to the spot. Soon the others would lose interest and leave, while the two male rivals would stay. They would make excited sounds as they sniffed and handled the discovery, focusing all their attention on it. While doing so, their heads and shoulders would touch. After a few minutes the two would calm down and start grooming each other. The object, which I was never able to identify, would be forgotten."

When I talked with Penny, a teacher in Minnesota, about this chimpanzee reconciliation behavior she was taken aback. "That reminds me of a falling-out I had with a friend in high school," she said. "Rona and I were attached at the hip. We had just gotten our licenses, and we took turns driving each other to and from school every day, even though it was only a few blocks away. We were both in the drama club. We were pretty much inseparable. But once, during a party, I made a play for the popular crowd in our class. Up until that time, we had both been outsiders, secure in our friendship since neither of us made the A-list of parties or lunchtime seating preferences. But at that party I saw an opportunity to get in good with the cool kids and I took it."

Penny described how she turned away from her friend to participate in a game of Twister, which Rona considered hopelessly childish. Penny probably would have thought so too if it had been just her and Rona talking together about what they liked and what they didn't like. But at this party the cool people were playing Twister, so Twister was cool. Tangled up with the cool kids, Penny fell over, right at Rona's feet. It was too much: "She was disgusted with me." For the rest of the semester Penny found another way to get to school and she and Rona passed each other coolly in the hall, avoiding each other's eyes, not speaking.

"Then we were cast as college roommates in *Take Her, She's Mine*. Our characters were best friends, so we had to act like best friends. We had to sing a folk song, whisper to each other, be animated." Penny laughs. "After that, it was pretty hard to stay mad at each other. It was just like those chimps you describe. First we were pretending; then, through the singing and the laughter onstage, our real feelings for each other resurfaced."

Chapter Eight

The Rules of the Gender Game: Biology and Friendship

A few years ago my son, Will, came home from first grade with a very
long face.

"What's up, Will?" I asked.

"I can't play with girls anymore," he announced.

"Why not?" I asked.

" 'Cause Ethan says so."

"Is he the only one who believes that?"

"No. Jimmy says so too."

"Can you ever play with girls?" I asked, thinking with regret of his various nice friends who happened to belong to the other gender.

"No, never."

"Never?"

There was a pause.

"Well, maybe if Ethan and Jimmy are sick," Will said.

This poignant little story illustrates a moment that arrives in the lives of all children. Early in elementary school kids discover that there are rules about how the gender you belong to is supposed to behave. Those rules strictly govern your dealings with members of the other gender. Violation of these rules results in teasing, rejection, gossip, and other punishments. One of the most powerful and consistent rules about gender is to spend most of one's time and energy in single-sex groups. This division into two groups starts in preschool or kindergarten and lasts at least until the beginning of adolescence. There are exceptions to this separation, of course, including games of boys chasing the girls, crushes, teasing, and genuine friendships across gender lines. But the segregation of the two sexes is a fact in the lives of most children.

When Will reluctantly accepted the loss of half his class as potential friends and playmates, he wasn't just obeying an abstract social force that segregates classrooms by gender. He was also responding to powerful social dynamics. Why did Ethan and Jimmy get to set the rules of how the boys in that classroom would behave toward girls? Were the girls making their own rules about boys at the same time, and having their own separate "elections" about who gets to be the boss?

Gender Segregation and the Cootie Factor

In her authoritative book *The Two Sexes: Growing Up Apart, Coming Together*, psychologist Eleanor E. Maccoby explores the group lives of children. She observes that this powerful tendency for children to separate themselves by gender and to play more compatibly with friends of the same sex occurs across cultures and in nonindustrialized as well as industrialized societies. All over the world, kids begin to gravitate to their own gender for companionship as early as age three, and the tendency progressively strengthens as they grow older, becoming quite strong by middle childhood.

Besides playing separately, boys and girls also play differently. Girls tend to spend more time on relationships and intimacy, while boys orient themselves to physical achievement, sports, and instrumental tasks such as building things. As Larry Cohen says in his book *Playful Parenting*, boys more often roughhouse, while girls more often play house.

Reviewing decades of research on sex differences, Maccoby concludes that biological differences in behavior are quite small, but these small differences become magnified because of the segregation of boys and girls into separate groups. In other words, there is a spiraling effect: Segregated play increases gender differences, and gender differences reinforce the segregation. Along the way, the other gender is considered not only different but inferior. We might call it the "cootie factor."

I was invited to a school in Washington, D.C., to help the teachers there figure out how to reconnect the boys and girls in a fourth grade class who were becoming increasingly isolated from each other. Their warfare confused and saddened the teachers, who had a genuine commitment to gender equity. They wanted their students to understand and affirm each other. But the kids had a different agenda.

We sat in a circle on a rug on the classroom floor, with the fourth graders sitting boy-girl, boy-girl, an order enforced by the teacher for the purpose of this discussion. I asked them why they had separated themselves from one another so dramatically. One tiny girl, sitting up straight so that she wouldn't bump into the two large boys on either side of her, said matter-of-factly, "We found out that boys have cooties!"

There was a chorus of assent from the other girls.

"Girls have cooties too!" the boys yelled, not to be outdone.

Once this critical discovery has been made, it becomes a way to enforce the gender separation and to affirm the superiority of one's own gender. In a way, gender becomes the child's first "home team" to root for, and the other gender is an appropriate target for put-downs. Of course, some children lead the way in this more-or-less friendly rivalry, while others, as we saw with Will, have to be dragged into line.

If children are asked to explain the nature of these cooties that infect the other gender, they usually describe the different ways that boys and girls play, interact, and behave. Boys and girls are social in different ways. When the boys run into conflict, they often push and shove to resolution. When girls disagree, they'll usually try to compromise.

Adults often underestimate the extent of gender segregation, because children are forced to mix at school and in other settings. But sometimes even in mixed play there are actually two different games going on at the same time, one for girls and one for boys. Larry watched a mixed group of second and third graders playing a ball game and observed that the boys played in an every-man-for-himself manner while the girls tried to set up alliances and teams. When no girls were on the field, a boy made a rule: no teams. As girls rotated in, they respected the rule until that boy was gone. Then they began making teams again. Meanwhile, one girl acted "girly," flipping her hair from side to side, giggling, and pretending she could barely hit the ball. She was clearly playing a different kind of game. But at their stage of development the boys didn't even notice. They were much more interested in the ball game. (Does that sound familiar?)

Conventional wisdom says that boys are more aggressive and more violent in their interactions with one another than girls are. However, the gender difference in aggressiveness is not as pronounced as we used to believe. It resides not so much in behavior as it does in the definition of aggression. Recent studies show that girls can be aggressive too if we understand "aggression" to include harsh words or the silent treatment as well as physical expressions of aggression. Social scientists call hurtful words "relational aggression" and believe that this is as painful to its victims as physical blows—and may be more lasting in its effects.

Many teachers and parents bemoan the fact that gender dynamics at school are hardly different from what they were forty years ago. The captain of the football team still goes to the prom with the head cheerleader. The girls still play dumb and place more emphasis on appearance than homework, while the boys strut their stuff and outdo each other with stupid bravado and antisocial behavior to impress the girls. Things haven't changed in forty years? Try forty thousand! Children's socialization into sex roles must have been adaptive at some point in the human race's hunter-gatherer past—but that was long before schools or playgrounds. Most jobs today don't involve male hunting or female gathering skills. But if we look at the different ways that boys and girls tend to play and the criteria they use for determining popularity, we see remnants of that distant era.

To learn what it means to be a boy or a girl, your child looks not only to you but also to the larger culture and especially to peers. Beginning in early childhood, that usually means choosing to spend most of the time with groups of one's own gender. Within these single-sex groups, they learn the rules of being male and female. They also develop dominance hierarchies and fight out the popularity wars. They coalesce into a kind of study group to figure out who's boss, to determine what's socially appropriate and what is not, and to practice the behaviors that characterize their gender. Just to make sure there is no confusion, they exaggerate the differences and ostracize anyone who blurs the lines.

Even schools and parents who make a special effort to go against old-fashioned sex roles find themselves swimming upstream against a strong current. Maybe it's because the whole idea of belonging to a gender is new to them, but young children tend to exaggerate these stereotyped gender differences, even in families that are more progressive. So the sons of Quaker pacifists chew their peanut butter sandwiches into gun shapes, since they aren't allowed toy guns, while the daughters of committed feminists become obsessed with Barbies and fashion and makeup.

Alpha Males, Queen Bees, and the Nature of Popularity

At a high school in a small midwestern town, kids congregate in a narrow hallway between classes. They sit on the floor, lining up along the walls. When they stick their legs out, there is barely room to pass. The boys jostle and trip each other, laughing as they block access to the lockers. It's relatively good-humored, although the possibility for the jostling and joshing to escalate into physical intimidation lurks just below the surface. Then the double doors at the end of the hallway swing open and a pair of tall, muscular, physically mature basketball players saunters into the hallway. The other students immediately pull their knees up, making room for the athletes to pass without interference. Girls who had been giving as good as they got in the repartee in the hall fall silent. The alpha males are passing, and the queen bees stop to notice.

Because the rules of gender and popularity are so reminiscent of animal behavior, it has become common to refer to boy leaders as "alpha males" and girl leaders as "queen bees." These terms are apt metaphors, as any close look at a group of middle schoolers will reveal. Like top dogs, boys will even mark their territory by urinating (or more commonly by graffiti or vandalism). Top-ranking girls, ruling absolutely like queen bees, flit from group to group, spreading nectar or stinging as the situation demands.

But who gets to be the alpha and who gets to be the queen? As I suggested when I used the terms hunters and gatherers, the criteria for choosing popular peers hasn't changed much in human history. Boys continue to be valued for traits and achievements that signal success at hunting and fighting against the neighboring cave. Girls are valued for their appearance and their sociability. These traits are clearly indicators for success at childbearing and maintaining a home. Is it a coincidence that the biggest, most athletic boys and the most attractive, most social girls are overrepresented in the popular crowd of virtually every school? Of course it can't be a coincidence, though students—and even adults— usually insist that it is.

Powerful, popular boys—like the ones Will felt he had to listen to about girls being off-limits—tend to be the most traditionally masculine of their peers. Socially powerful, popular girls tend to be the most feminine. Likewise, the least popular children are those who stray from the age-old "ideals" of their gender. Who gets teased the most in school? Incompetent or effeminate boys, unattractive or aggressive girls. Although this behavior peaks in middle school, it starts much earlier. A few years ago Larry asked two six-year-olds, his daughter and her friend, what makes a child popular. Emma said, "Being nice, having a lot of good ideas, being smart." Peter said, "Shooting missiles."

Researchers studying preschoolers and elementary school students have observed that boys try to establish their dominance as soon as they meet a new boy or enter a new group. In preschool, this might mean grabbing a toy from another boy just to see how he reacts. An elementary school boy asserts himself by being terrific at sports, by arguing forcefully about the rules of the game, or by verbal put-downs. Once the alpha boy is in place, the other boys in his group don't usually challenge him unless they see a sign of weakness. But they turn around and fight with one another over second place, third place, and so on, quickly creating a dominance hierarchy. In many groups of boys, each one can tell you— with an astonishing degree of agreement—who could beat up whom. Other groups are more "civilized," basing their hierarchy on athletic prowess rather than outright fighting. But the effect is the same. Boys manage their lives in these groups by recognizing their place in the group and maintaining it.

If you spend a recess period observing a playground, you quickly see that there are dominant, physically adept, and socially powerful boys—the alpha males. There are also queen bees—socially gifted, pretty girls who typically gather a court of supportive, less confident girls around them. The boys are accorded their status based on their potential for physical domination, even if they don't act on their power. Girls gather their power not only through physical attractiveness or talent, but also through the ability to establish and manage relationships with others. This physical and social jousting begins in nursery school, intensifies in elementary school, becomes rigidly codified by middle school, and begins to loosen its grip in high school or college.

Physical prowess, especially when it is expressed in athletic stardom, remains powerful in high school. So do physical appearance and other outward signs of status. Earlier I quoted Emma as saying that the recipe for popularity is to "be nice." That is just the beginning. One eighth grade girl, asked how girls get to be popular, replied, "By being dumb." In a popularity move that exasperates adults, some girls hide their uncool intelligence.

As children move away from the worst battles of the popularity wars, they leave behind what I call the primitive Darwinism of middle school, where size matters. Muscle size, breast size, and wallet size give way to characteristics such as leadership ability, character, and charisma. But this primitive basis for popularity does not disappear entirely, as we can see from looking at popular magazines. However, while we may admire Brad Pitt and Julia Roberts, we don't elect them president.

I imagine you were as dismayed as I was to hear the eighth grader above say that being dumb was a requirement for being popular. I asked a group of senior girls at the same school about this comment, and one girl said, "We still have our popular kids, but they aren't our leaders." The leaders are good students, good athletes, and active in extracurricular activities, not just focused on status, appearance, and cliques. In high school this divergence of popularity and leadership may mean that the most popular girls may paradoxically no longer be the most liked, or even broadly liked at all. They may remain highly visible and wield considerable social power, but usually in a more narrow range of influence. As things develop, however, this social status may come at a high price: If her peers see the popular girl as stuck-up or as too powerful, she may be toppled off her pedestal.

The accusation of being stuck-up is a potentially damaging one for girls, and though it is usually aimed at popular girls who reject offers of friendship, the insult may also be aimed at shy girls, whose social fears are misinterpreted as snobbery, increasing their isolation. Avoidance of being seen as stuck-up encourages girls to live out stereotypes of niceness, phoniness, and decreased achievement as they attempt to minimize inequality and not to surpass friends. A woman in her forties described her friends turning on her in eighth grade, saying she was stuck-up. This remark devastated her at the time. She says now that it has taken her thirty years to accept the assertiveness that her eighth grade peers interpreted as being "stuck-up."

Girls, though generally better than boys at intimacy, often feel pressure to focus on attractiveness, status, and male attention, which interferes both with their ability to maintain good friendships and with their school achievement. One teenage girl I heard about had been at the top of the heap in eighth grade—athletic, talented, and sociable. In high school, with its increased social and emotional pressures, she suffered what her teacher described as "female adolescent collapse," spending more and more time socializing instead of studying, becoming preoccupied with appearance and male attention, devaluing school, and not being able to participate in athletics because of poor grades. All this led to a downward spiral of school failure.

The fear of being left alone can be a source of pressure and anxiety for girls even when they are very young. A second grade teacher described girls getting to school early to anxiously line up "recess dates" before class began. The boys, she said, scratched their heads in bewilderment at this intensity; they just played with whoever was around.

So boys' famous insensitivity has some unexpected benefits. Because the whole issue of status and dominance is less emotional for boys, they are less likely than girls to suffer a fall from being "too popular." However, because of rigid sex roles, popularity affects boys' friendships negatively as well. It is quite common for the most popular boy in a school to come to the school psychologist or guidance counselor, saying he has no one to talk to. He has to maintain his cool pose, not revealing to any other boys that he has worries or troubles.

Also, some boys who seemingly have it all suffer from the overwhelming expectations on them to be alpha males. One popular and successful boy, who, according to his teacher, could easily have been student council president and/or captain of the football team, is now in detox. The pressure he felt to measure up to his high-powered father and to the expectations of his peers led him to give up trying. His reason? Better not to try than to try and fail when the stakes are so high.

Maintaining status is a delicate balancing act and a child's body does not always cooperate. Boys who physically mature early are more likely to be athletes and school leaders. Those who had been popular up until fifth or sixth grade may fall by the wayside if they get their growth spurt late. The opposite is true for girls; those who physically mature early are teased and often have lower self-esteem. Girls who develop breasts early must cope with the objectification and sexualization of their bodies. A college student, in therapy for a severe eating disorder, reflected this difficulty. When asked if she was popular in high school, she couldn't really say, since she experienced people's reactions to her developing body as a complex mix of rejection and acceptance. Meanwhile, late-developing girls are teased for not having breasts. Developing late means not being "useful," either for childbearing or as a sexual object.

In recent years sexual activity has changed as a factor in popularity. No longer an automatic basis for social exclusion of girls from the "nice" crowd, sexual activity can either enhance or decrease a girl's status, depending on the what, where, how, and who of the situation. Some adolescent girls have an extremely difficult time navigating the shoals of sexual expectations. A ninth grade teacher described a girl in his class who alternated between wearing baggy clothes and spandex, between trying to disappear into the floor and strutting her stuff in front of the boys, as her grades and interest in school declined precipitously.

Alpha males rely on physical prowess, but queen bees don't require physical domination or direct confrontation to establish their superiority. In her book *The Difference Between Boys and Girls*, science writer Susan Gilbert cites an elegant study in which researchers observed two groups, one of four girls and one of four boys. The children tried to watch a movie that was threaded so that it required several people to operate it but only one could see it at a time. A leader emerged in each group who quickly managed to get the others to do most of the work. The alpha boy used physical tactics to establish dominance, shoving other boys away from the machine. The dominant girl, on the other hand, sweet-talked her companions into believing that she needed to see the movie more than they did.

Educators and parents (and students themselves) often bemoan the fact that elections for everything from student council to cheerleader to homecoming court are "just popularity contests." This phrase reflects the awareness that popularity does not rely too heavily on the cerebral cortex but is instead controlled by more primitive parts of the brain. Unconscious appraisals of physical attractiveness, for example, have a much greater role in our reactions to people than most of us would like to admit. Furthermore, the surface factors that are considered attractive are often stand-ins for those perennial hunter-gatherer favorites: strength and competence in men, childbearing and child-rearing ability in women.

But popularity isn't automatic just because a child has certain characteristics. So how do these leaders emerge? When I spoke at a California school I had an opportunity to find out. During my speech I talked about how popular children sometimes put down other kids, establishing their dominance by teasing. It turns out that a fifth grade class took offense at my remarks. They felt I had attacked popular kids, and asked to see me. So I visited their classroom.

"It seems like you think all the popular kids are bad, and it's not like that," a student said. "We didn't ask to be popular! It's just us and our friends."

"It's hard to be popular," another student added. "Sometimes kids come up to you and say they wish they were like you, and you don't know what to say."

I asked the students how they know they're popular and what makes them that way.

"In this class it's like we have a king and a queen," one boy said. "There's the court and the commoners."

"Which are you?" I asked.

"Oh, I'm a commoner," he said. It didn't seem to bother him.

"How do people get to be king or queen?" I asked.

"Let's ask Tim!"

"Why Tim?"

"Because he just got here this year, and he's the king."

I walked over to Tim and asked him how it had happened.

"I don't know," he said. "A couple of people like me. . . ."

You probably won't be surprised to hear that Tim is a fine student and a young Adonis, California blond, graceful, and athletic. Even as a newcomer he's an alpha male—and the rest of his class is very matter-of-fact about it.

Sometimes, though, the top position can be complicated. A third grader in a Maryland public school calmly told me that she is the most popular girl in her class. "What's that like?" I asked her. "Well, it's okay, I guess." she said. "But everybody's always fighting over me. It seems like I never have any time for myself. And I have to be nice to everybody all the time, and they all want to talk to me at once." This child's sister, her fraternal twin, is in another section of the third grade and does not share her twin's high status. "I'm not the most popular girl in three-B," she says. "Stacey is. I think she's kind of mean. And anyway, I have a best friend." This girl's comfort with her status in the middle of the fray comes from the reassurance and pleasure her close friendship provides, while her sister's high status comes at a price in terms of friendships and privacy.

A seven-year-old also explained to me that being a queen bee has its downside. "It's true, I think I'm a little popular," Marnie told me. "I don't try to be. But all the girls go mad about me. They all want to be friends with me." She went on to describe how her classmates fought over which one of them was going to stand next to her in line. "I left the line so no one could be next to me," she recalled ruefully.

Marnie's compassionate solution to her dilemma defused the bad feelings that social power can engender. But she is right to worry about the potential dangers of being too popular. Part of popularity, as these young girls already know, means saying no to many overtures of friendship and alliance. Too many of these rejections, and a girl can be seen as stuck-up and snobby. She may even come to relish the position of deciding who is in favor and who is not. The rest of the group can get together and dethrone the queen, especially if another powerful leader emerges or joins the class. Once deposed, former queen bees are often subjected to cruel reprisals from former victims. In fact, adults often condone the vengeful abuse against the onetime queen, feeling that she deserves it as punishment for her earlier tyranny. Indiana University sociologist Donna Eder calls this phenomenon the "cycle of popularity."

Popularity can indeed become a source of social power that is wielded with viciousness. A guidance counselor at a middle school recalls her toughest challenge. The trouble started with two groups of seventh grade girls.

"The groups had had a history of difficulties getting along and being exclusionary toward one another," the counselor notes. "I had done friendship groups with those kids in the fifth grade, mixing up the kids for fun activities. We had done a ton of problem solving over the years with whoever was involved in a particular conflict."

Then a very powerful girl moved into the peer group in the seventh grade. This new girl became the ringleader of one group's animosity toward the other group and especially toward one girl who had switched groups. That girl became a scapegoat and was deeply marred by the experience.

"What was so striking was that I was unable to intervene in any effective way," the counselor says, the pain of the memory obvious on her face. "I tried meeting with the two girls, I tried meeting with all the girls. I tried enlisting their parents' support. I had the principal of the school meet with the girls, and the principal and I together met with the girls. We had a mediator from the high school come. But nothing would stop the exclusionary behavior and the real cruelty that went on from one group to the other.

"No matter what strategy we used it didn't make a difference. Nothing helped. It reached a head when the principal and I were going to meet with the mothers and the girls together. But the girls didn't want that, so the meeting never happened. After this, the aggression and the exclusion stuff stopped, at least on the surface, but it didn't really go away underneath.

"I lost relationships with kids who didn't feel that I supported them properly, and that was hard. But at the end of eighth grade, when all the departing kids were signing yearbooks, kids who had been participating in the behavior wrote to me, 'You were right all along and I couldn't tell you and I was so angry at you but you were right, that was a really awful thing that I had done.' "

What is striking about this incident, which several years later has not lost any of its power for the guidance counselor, is the intense degree of the ringleader's social sway over her peers. Even major interventions by adults were not enough to change how her followers behaved. Only later, as they moved out of the school year, were they able to get enough distance from their leader to acknowledge their own cruelty.

I have focused on girls so far, but a leader's cruelty can be especially hard on a lower-rung boy. Ray, a smart, nonathletic boy, was a close friend of a boy named Sam who was very active in sports. Ray preferred reading and drawing cartoons. When they were alone together, these two eight-year-olds did very well. They would compromise, sometimes playing sports, sometimes drawing or watching cartoons.

Ray and Sam had been friends since preschool. Their moms had become friends too. Then day camp began. Ray and Sam had attended the camp together for several years, and both had loved it in spite of their different interests. But the previous summer there had been a new camper, a very tough ten-year-old boy named Mike. He was great at sports, and the other boys at camp idolized him. Under Mike's dominance the boys played only basketball, and they played it seriously, following NBA rules. Basketball was a sport Ray didn't play well, and he'd never really learned the rules.

At first the other boys didn't let Ray play at all, and he came home each day in tears. Ray's mom dubbed the ballplayers the "Sportos" and became very angry about them. Day after day they tormented Ray. Told by the counselors that they had to let him play, they gave Ray a position as a sub but never let him on the court. They told him that if he walked away to play on a nearby climbing structure while he was waiting to play, he was off the team, so he felt obliged to hang around on the sidelines doing nothing. Finally they made him their water boy, allowing him to fetch their water bottles when they were thirsty. His alternative was to play with the girls, which might have been fine if they had wanted to draw or do art projects, Ray's specialty. But this group of girls wanted to sit around and comb their dolls' hair for hours. On the days Mike didn't appear, other games were played, and Ray was able to realign himself with his friend Sam. But when Mike came back, the Sportos headed for the basketball court and Ray was left out again.

What made Ray's mom most upset about all this was that her son's oldest friend, Sam, joined in the exclusion. Her hurt feelings extended to her relationship with Sam's mom, which became extremely strained. The power of a single ten-year-old alpha male to wreak havoc in other lives extended to adults as well as to his peers.

The unwritten and ever-changing rules of group life can dominate the lives of children. The complications of establishing one's place in the social life of school, camp, or neighborhood are practically a full-time job. This may be especially true for girls, who spend hours analyzing and discussing the hierarchies of their groups and what's cool or not cool to do, say, wear, watch on TV, or listen to on their personal CD players.

At least through middle school, it's the alpha males and queen bees who take care of setting fashion trends in everything from book bags to slang. But which comes first? Do popular kids make a certain style popular, or are they more in tune with the larger culture, predicting where other kids will want to follow? Or as Eleanor Maccoby speculates in *The Two Sexes*, "Is it the case that the children who become style-setters in the group are the ones who have been socialized so the interaction style they display fits best with some underlying disposition that most members of a certain sex share? Or fits best with stereotypes, widely held in a culture, as to what modes of behavior are sex-appropriate?" These are questions that social scientists, educators, therapists, and parents grapple with every day.

To adults, the question of who's in, who's out, what's cool, what's uncool, and how you tell is one of the eternal mysteries. "Why on earth do you pull your hair into that tight ponytail?" a mom asks her daughter, whose forehead is pulled taut by her punishing hairdo. "We *all* wear our hair this way," the daughter moans. Her mom insists that she release her shoulder-length curls. "You look so much prettier that way," her mom says. The daughter leaves the house that way, but by the time she's at the bus stop, her hair is right back in its ponytail. That's the way the *popular* girls wear it. (Apparently this mother has forgotten the dead-white lipstick she used to apply on the school bus when she was safely out of her mother's sight.)

As I travel the country I hear literally hundreds of stories about kids' conformity to the popularity and gender rules established by socially dominant group leaders. To adults these rules may seem meaningless, even arbitrary. But that is the point. After all, when others follow your arbitrary rules, you know your authority is being recognized. If your rules are cruel and still being obeyed ("Nobody talk to Susie" or "Everybody tackle Joey"), then you really know your leadership is working.

Sometimes the rules are enforced not by one person but by the entire subculture of which the child wants desperately to be a part. One mother told me that her son refused to go to school until she had bought him exactly the right baggy, below-the-knee shorts to wear. He had seen the other middle-school-age kids at the mall; he recognized their uniform and knew he needed it before he got to school. To turn up in something else would be to risk the greatest horror of school life: humiliation, cluelessness, being uncool.

The Tools of Dominance

Within groups, teasing and other dominance behavior—whether gentle or not so gentle—are used to establish and reinforce the hierarchy. Between groups of boys and girls, teasing is a way to communicate. But whether the repartee is intra- or intergroup, boys and girls are teased for being different, especially for being different from the norms of their own gender. There ought to be an unlimited number of acceptable ways to be male or female, but society's rigid sex roles narrow these down to a few stereotypes. The language of insults aimed at children gets much of its power from these stereotypes. Think of the variety of insults directed at girls, and notice how many are variants of the same few "failures": *stuck-up*, *bitchy*, *flat-chested*, *fatty*, *ugly*, and *slut*. What do those insults have in common? They are violations of proper female behavior or appearance. Meanwhile, insults directed at boys are variants of *girl*, *sissy*, *fag*, *baby*, *crybaby*, *mamma's boy*, *nerd*, *retard*, *spaz*, *fatty*, and *shrimp*. These insults clearly punish children for diverging from how their gender is supposed to be—attractive and sociable for girls, physically competent, aggressive, stoic, and independent for boys.

The methods boys and girls use to taunt other members of their own gender differ as well. Girls favor excluding, snubbing, backbiting, and gossiping; boys favor physical and verbal aggression. These different techniques bring us back to the time of the hunter-gatherers. Boys are asserting their superiority on the hunting grounds and battlefields, while girls are asserting their superiority in the world of interpersonal relations. But don't think that boys are mean and girls are nice. As one teacher said, "Boys may punch each other, but girls are crueler. Girls make snide remarks to their friends about other girls, remarks that could be overheard if you were paying close attention. And of course the targets of these remarks are paying very close attention."

Dominant girls exercise a subtle form of power. Carole Beal of the University of Massachusetts observed that when an elementary or middle school girl is upset with another girl, she doesn't confront her directly with her feelings. Rather, she passes criticisms via other girls without identifying herself as the source of the criticism, as in "I heard that she did that and that's really bad." Eventually the word gets back to the miscreant girl, but no relationships are openly damaged. This is a useful strategy, since girls form small social groups and have much at stake when they criticize, and risk alienating, a friend.

Emma has observed this indirect technique in action. Larry asked her how things were going socially in school, and Emma said, "When Alison and Tina have a fight, each one goes to a different lunch table. The people at Tina's table all say, 'Alison's so sensitive, she always does that.' The people at Alison's table all say mean things about Tina. Whoever's not there they say mean things about."

Adults respond differently to boys' and girls' intragender teasing. The behavior that cements a boy's position as alpha male—shoving, verbal put-downs, physical fights—tends to be noticed and disciplined by adults. Popular girls' behavior—exclusion, backbiting, bitchiness—is often unseen or ignored by adults. When it is noticed, adults tend to do what the girls do: talk and gossip about it with other parents, avoiding direct confrontation.

Research shows that words can be just as harmful as physical blows. Not only that, the pain words cause seems to have a longer shelf life than physical pain. Unless a boy was beaten up regularly, I am much more likely to hear women in therapy talk about the scars of backbiting than to hear men talk about the physical struggles for dominance. Not only that, but as dominance struggles go on in girl groups, differences persist rather than being settled once and for all. This may explain why 95 percent of popularity problems that come to the attention of school administrators concern girls. (This could be a result as well of girls' willingness to talk about their troubles, while boys' stoicism keeps them from showing up in the counselor's office.) In fact, when boys do report extreme examples of teasing or bullying, they often retract their statements later, when their initial upset over the abuse gives way to fear of retaliation for breaking the code of silence.

Let's turn now from teasing within each gender to teasing between the genders. In some ways this kind of teasing is more complicated, because it reinforces the gender separation while at the same time serving as a point of contact between the genders. This goes on from elementary through middle school. Emma, remembering kindergarten from the vantage point of fourth grade, said, "The boys would chase the girls. That was all we'd do at recess. Then some girls would chase the boys. Soon all the girls were chasing the boys and the boys made it really easy for the girls to catch them. So the girls didn't really get to show they could catch the boys. So they stopped, and everyone got really bored. We started thinking up new games to play." (Larry notes how the boys "let" themselves get caught so as not to open themselves up to the humiliation of *really* being caught by the girls. Girls are at least as strong and fast as boys at age five, but the boys are dedicated to preserving the myth of male physical superiority. It wouldn't do to let the gatherers catch the hunters!)

A tightly knit group of eighth grade girls from a public school north of Boston has maintained a coalition with each other since elementary school, particularly since sixth grade. Their connection is based on their shared interest in sports. These ten girls are a powerful bunch: popular, smart, and competent. They come from well-off families and are physically attractive and highly visible at school. And boys tease them.

"Sometimes, they won't let go of something and they'll just keep making fun of someone for one thing. Like they'll say things about the shirt you're wearing or something," says Molly, the queen bee girl, who always speaks first for this group.

"And it gets old," says her friend Beth.

"It tends to hurt a little more every time," Molly adds. "I think boys make fun of people a little bit more than girls do."

"They hurt girls' feelings," puts in Tara.

"They always think the girls know it's jokingly," says Molly. "But sometimes they'll go a little bit too far. They don't think."

Catherine asked the girls why the boys do this.

"Because they think they're funny," says Beth.

"To show off," Tara says.

"So all the other boys will laugh," Molly continues. "They each want to be the macho man."

(Interestingly, some of the same boys who mercilessly tease these girls during the school day are benign friends when they hang around together on weekends. Away from school, the rules of engagement in the gender wars are temporarily suspended.)

Despite their complaints, these girls probably aren't missing the fact that they are teased precisely because they are popular. Boys tease high-status girls in a very different way than low-status girls, and the same goes for girls teasing boys. Boy-girl teasing helps identify the parameters of the split between the genders. If one member of the group isn't following the program, he will quickly learn how.

At a suburban public school, a nice, conscientious, somewhat over-protected boy arrived in fourth grade at midyear—a tough time to figure out the hierarchies of established groups. It took a while for Ronnie to make friends because his parents, who had emigrated from Indonesia to the United States, did not know about setting up play dates for him. Not being especially athletic or aggressive, he wasn't able to connect right away with boys who might have taken him in and helped him establish a place in the group. But after a period of loneliness for Ronnie, a pair of boys in his class set out to teach him the rules. To be in with the boy group, Ronnie had to learn to put down girls. The teacher overheard the two boys asking Ronnie which of the girls in their class he would diss, as in disrespect.

"Uh . . . Laura, Julie, and Shannon," Ronnie answered.

"Laura's good," his coach told him, meaning that Laura was an appropriate candidate for teasing. "Julie's okay. I think you have the concept."

Since that "lesson," the teacher reports, Ronnie has "gotten the concept" and has been teasing girls along with the rest of the boys in the class. The teacher had bittersweet feelings telling this story. Ronnie had been such a sweet boy, not engaging in all that boy-girl teasing. Now he wasn't so sweet, but he was part of the gang—and that is important too.

Beyond the Popularity Wars

Strict gender segregation makes it difficult, if not impossible, to sustain cross-gender friendships in elementary and middle school. When my son made his decision to avoid playing with girls at school, he was bowing to the will of the more socially powerful boys in his class. He admired those boys and wanted to ally himself with them. They didn't have to threaten Will with violence or torment him for being a sissy. For Will, those boys had legitimate authority. They were the top dogs, so they established the rules. The chance to join up with them—to partake of their status—made Will willing to forgo his comfortable friendships with girls. Yet his affection for his female friends left him painfully aware of what he was giving up in exchange for acceptance into the boy "club." His glimmer of hope was that when those important boys weren't on the scene he could revert to his original friendly feelings for girls.

When your children come home and declare that girls—or boys—have become the enemy, it can be helpful to remember that the way a child behaves at school, under the sway of socially powerful kids, may not reflect his or her deepest feelings. The pain caused by the emotional split between accepted behavior in the group and private behavior at home or in the neighborhood can be memorable. A first grade teacher at a public school outside Boston recalls that her most socially painful moment as a child came when she had to pretend that her very best friend, a boy, wasn't really her friend at all. They went underground with their friendship, and it was very hard on them both.

But one of the most reassuring facts about children's social pain is that it tends to get better over time. It may take a while, but most children find in due course that their unique abilities and qualities are valued by someone, even if they were dismissed or rejected by the dominant hierarchy. The primitive Darwinism of middle school fizzles out. Why? Because hunters and gatherers don't go to college. Through most of human evolution and cultural development, skills such as scholarship, literacy, or mathematics didn't have any relevance to survival or to sex appeal. But now these skills matter. So boys who study a lot, get very good grades, and are dismissed as nerds in high school are admired in college. High-achieving girls who are seen as unfeminine in high school are honored in college. Not that this primitive Darwinism disappears entirely—take a look at sororities and fraternities, or at any prime-time evening of television.

In the new information age, geekdom may well qualify as a survival skill that has the social power of traditional hunter-gatherer traits. A recent *New York Times Magazine* cover story profiled gifted science students at Midwood High School in Brooklyn, who are positioned for huge success in the dot-com universe. Far from being outcasts, these students "move comfortably in the newly respectable mainstream, where being scientifically astute has a certain cachet," writes Stephen S. Hall.

However, popularity remains connected to visibility, and many schools offer very limited opportunities for visibility. Often schools un-wittingly reinforce the pattern of the most visible activities being the most strongly gendered. Male athletic contests are still central school or town events in many places. Although national women's soccer and basketball teams are changing this dynamic, girls' teams still often have to take second place on the fields or practice at odd hours. In the docu-mentary *A Hero for Daisy*, the championship Yale women's crew team recalls how they had to sit on the bus freezing while the boys used the boathouse showers to warm up after being on the river at dawn.

Gender roles as they are practiced in schools across the country and around the world are not just outdated, they are neolithic. In today's world they are oppressive and inconsistent with our goals and ideals for young people. The effects of these roles on popularity and friendship are hard on everyone but especially so on those who don't fit in. These roles undermine community and undermine achievement by claiming so much attention, both from popular students who need to maintain their status and from unpopular ones who strive to attain status or nurse the wounds of falling short.

But things can change. Sociologist Donna Eder found that extracur-ricular participation was critically important in who became and re-mained popular in middle school and high school. Eder and others have found that the increased range of activities available in high school lessens the damaging effects of social exclusion experienced in middle school, suggesting that it would be helpful to widen the range of activi-ties and in general expand opportunities for visibility within the school while deemphasizing those that promote stereotypical gender roles (such as boys' competitive athletics and girls' cheerleading). One school in Vermont requires students to work on a farm that is part of the campus. Boys as well as girls get a chance to nurture by raising animals. Girls as well as boys get a chance to be physically strong by mucking out stalls, thus helping all of them push against the hunter-gatherer tide.

No school entirely transcends the biology of our evolutionary past. Some schools accept the status quo as inevitable or even desirable, pro-moting football as the ultimate school activity and choosing a homecom-ing queen based on beauty. Others try to ban bullying or exclusion or sexual harassment, saying they "do not occur in our school because we do not allow them." Most schools are in the middle, however, fighting back but discouraged. Naturally it is hard to turn back thousands of years of evolution. But we can try.

Children may feel that the separation of girls and boys is immutable and will last forever. As adults, we know that the day arrives when previously reviled boys begin to look better to the girls who have scorned them as stupid and mean. And the girls begin to look pretty good to the boys, too.

Catherine remembers her experience of being teased by boys in eighth grade. She was a newcomer to a class that had been together since fifth grade. She was the only girl in the class who wore an undershirt instead of a bra, which the boys noticed. She wore the wrong clothes and had the wrong hairstyle. She had no alliances in the class. She was no likely candidate for hunter-gatherer success. So the boys picked on her cruelly, opening their lockers and loudly pretending to vomit when she walked by.

But by tenth grade things changed. In the less-codified social world of high school, Catherine managed to gain status from her drama club appearances and having some poetry published. (She also admits ruefully that she finally figured out the dress code.) The ringleader of the vomiting boys asked her to a tenth-grade dance. It gave her pleasure to turn him down. But it felt even better to know that her status had changed. She had moved from the world of cooties to the world of romance.

Chapter Nine

From Cooties to Dating

It's prom night, and most of the students from Chapel Hill–Chauncy Hall School in Waltham, Massachusetts, have gathered in a small ballroom at the local Westin Hotel. A few have brought dates from other schools, but most have paired up with classmates, arrived in groups, or showed up on their own. Catherine and her husband, who heads this small high school, are chaperoning the event for the fourth year in a row.

To attend the prom, you don't have to bring a date. You don't even have to be a junior or senior. Unlike the days when we baby boomer adults were attending proms, every kid who buys a ticket is welcome.

Catherine noticed something about the prom this year. The seniors, students she has known since they were freshmen, mostly have paired up. In their tuxedos and ball gowns, these pairs of boys and girls converse easily and fluently with each other. There's no awkwardness on the dance floor, even during slow songs. The older kids navigate the buffet dinner with aplomb and sit in small groups at the draped tables, chatting with each other like forty-year-olds at a dinner party. Their social confidence is palpable.

The behavior of the younger attendees is a different story. Apart from a few ninth and tenth grade girls who have boyfriends in the upper classes, most of these younger students travel in groups rather than pairs. Though they are dressed in formal attire like their older schoolmates, they aren't nearly as relaxed or confident on the dance floor, in the buffet line, or at the tables. They got to prom night on time, chauffeured by their moms and dads. The older kids, meanwhile, sauntered in fashionably late, having arrived in their own cars or in rented stretch limos.

During the party, the youngest boys especially stand out. They are distinctly smaller than the junior and senior boys—and smaller than many of the girls. They spend most of their time hovering around the perimeter of the room. They also hang out at the DJ's table, checking out the CDs, teasing each other, and occasionally flashing glances at the girls who are dancing in groups on the floor. Clusters of girls, meanwhile, move back and forth to the women's room like so many glittering shoals of fish.

These young people live in a small, intimate community that prides itself on how supportive and caring its students are with one another. And so they are! At school, even the youngest of these adolescent boys and girls know each other well and are comfortable in their school setting. But in the fishbowl of the prom, the pressure of knowing how to ask a girl to dance, or whether or not to put *both* arms around her waist during a slow dance, is making the younger boys pretty nervous.

As she watches this scene, Catherine remembers that the polished, poised senior boys relaxing at the tables with their girlfriends were the very ones bumping one another anxiously and clumsily at the edge of the dance floor only three short years ago. But look at them now! They could be actors in a Noel Coward play. They have successfully navigated the passage from the harbor of single-sex group life through the choppy currents of coed group socializing and on into the more settled waters of dating in pairs.

A large study of tenth and eleventh graders from two suburban school districts in western New York showed that adolescent dating patterns undergo considerable flux over time, reflecting gradual increases in romantic involvement. The researchers who conducted the study found that for most students there is an orderly, gradual progression from no dating to casual relationships and eventually steadier connections, just as Catherine saw in action at four years of Chapel Hill–Chauncy Hall proms.

From Détente to Dating

As we observed in Chapter 8, boys and girls separate into distinct groups in elementary school. For most children, members of the opposite sex become "the other" and are to be avoided. This desire to stay away from one another can be pretty powerful. One study asked children to approach unfamiliar children and measured how close they got before they stopped. The researchers found that a child as young as three would stop farther away when the unfamiliar child was of the other sex.

But there are areas in which boys' and girls' territories overlap. The result is an ambiguous border zone. These meetings often have an aggressive edge to them, as the intensity of the repulsion/attraction dynamic heats up. (You can almost hear kids thinking, "Yes, girls have cooties. But Annie is awfully cute," or "Yes, boys have cooties. But Jack can be really sweet when he wants to be.") Boys and girls play at being enemies even as they are fascinated by one another. Some kids get this sooner than others do, understanding that the game has shifted from really not liking each other to pretending not to like each other.

The boy-girl dance of approach and retreat starts early. A teacher in an afterschool program told me, "Every year around the end of September we have to have a talk with the kindergarten kids about no kissing. There are two kinds of kissing that spring up around the same time—mutual and chasing. Mutual kissing is a form of sexual exploration, usually initiated by one or two more-advanced kindergartners. Chasing games that include kissing are usually done in groups—and it is the girls who initiate the kissing. At this age, boys are starting to be more athletically confident, so they can chase the girls. But the girls are more socially confident, so if they turn it into kissing, they end up chasing the boys."

Boy/girl chasing happens on every playground. I watched a group of second graders playing around a large climbing structure at an urban elementary school. They screamed and ran and tagged each other. Most of the girls were inside the structure; the boys were outside. The object of the game was for the boys to capture the girls and put them in "jail." The rules allow a girl to be released from jail only when one particular boy reaches through the bars and tags her. That boy is the king of the playground, the alpha male. During the game, he chooses the popular girls— the prettiest and most conventionally girly ones—to release from jail. The most popular girl, the queen bee, gets out first. Then, in turn, most of the other girls are released, chased around the playground, tagged, and recaptured by the other boys. Although the girls are clearly competent and athletic and could easily escape from jail on their own, they stay put once they're caught, giggling and feigning helplessness.

This game expresses many of the dynamics of gender and group life, including within-group hierarchy and the magnetic force of intergroup attraction and repulsion. Strict gender roles are in play too, as the boys act fierce and the girls act weak. This stereotyped behavior may well be a way for children to cope with the stress and uncertainty of the ambiguous border zone between young boys and young girls.

So boys and girls play their separate parts yet make forays toward each other. I watched another playground game, this one among students at a suburban Catholic high school, where the kids wear uniforms. A group of seventh grade boys were playing a game of capture the flag. The girls stood on the sidelines, pretending lack of interest but actually watching every move. The "flag" the boys used was the plaid uniform skirt of one of the most popular girls in the class. During the game she was hunkered down in the girls' room in her gym shorts, waiting for the return of her tattered skirt. I imagine she will wear it as a badge of her attractiveness throughout the semester. In her torn skirt, she is a visibly cool girl. After all, the boys wanted *her* skirt. The less popular girls will have to be content with neat, ironed kilts. There's a powerful undercurrent of sexual interest and selection in this game.

Through middle school, ritualized games like these evolve into mixed-group socializing. Boy-girl groups of kids head to the mall for movies and pizza, attend games together, or have parties at someone's house. This group socializing, and the increased ease with the other sex that comes with it, sets the stage for closer relationships—for dating— between boys and girls in high school.

West, a ninth-grader at a public high school in rural New England, has experienced this firsthand. A rising tenth grader, fifteen-year-old West hasn't picked up the phone to call a girl and ask her out—yet. So far his interactions with girls have come about more casually. But he says he has had "a couple of girlfriends."

I asked West how he has connected with girls when he doesn't take the initiative. "Stuff spreads in school," he says. "One of their friends will come up to you and say, 'So-and-so likes you.' They give you her phone number. It takes a little while to get started. Things sort of evolve."

When he has gone out with girls, West has socialized in groups or in a pair with another couple. What do they do?

"Movies are very big," he says. "There are dances that the high school has, but not a lot of people actually go to the dances unless it's the prom. Kids go to parties instead, at people's houses. At the parties there's a lot of standing around and listening to music."

West, who's involved in several sports and serves on the student council, says he isn't looking to pair off with a single girlfriend and start what he calls "real dating" in tenth grade. "I don't pursue girls," he says. "I don't think about it a whole lot. I'm going to wait and see what happens."

West's experience is pretty typical for a male in middle adolescence. At that stage, the lines between friend, crush, and boyfriend or girlfriend are blurry. Boys and girls tend to date in groups. In fact, in middle adolescence, having a boyfriend or a girlfriend can be considered an extension of the peer group. Everyone knows who's going with whom, even if those who are going together have a pretty casual connection. Even though West talks about having girlfriends, these relationships are clearly group events rather than a real pairing off. The group orchestrates the arrangement and comments at length on every move. The group as a whole is moving hesitantly into more mature romantic behavior—usually with the girls in the lead.

Within their groups, boys talk about girls, and girls certainly talk about boys. But single-sex groups may not be the best place to learn the scripts of dating and romance. You're supposed to be learning about the other sex, but you're just as likely to be picking up misinformation about it. Not only that, you're reinforcing behavior that sets boys and girls apart from each other. The psychologist Eleanor Maccoby observed that the segregated play of childhood leads to distinctive interactive styles and that these styles are carried over into adolescence. The girls' interactive style involves talking, while the boys spend more time doing.

According to the research, girls become interested sooner in crossing gender lines for relationships, both platonic and otherwise. Often their interest leads them to pick up the phone and call the boys they like. (Girls also indulge in long, detailed conversations with their female friends about how and when to call a boy. Teenage advice books provide instructions for making these calls and what to talk about. These days, e-mail and instant messages prove useful for getting in touch with boys too.)

The calls can make many boys nervous. A recent Penn State study indicates that boys are more vulnerable in dating situations than previously thought, since they find themselves in relationships before they're fully equipped to handle them. As we've seen, boys bring fewer intimacy skills into the dating arena. Yet the boys in the study reported being "in love" more often than girls and had a harder time bouncing back from these brief, intense experiences. (Being "in love" at this stage can be pretty indirect. There may be no physical contact or spoken declarations. But the feelings are real and very powerful.) Not only are young adolescent boys behind on the physical and cognitive development front at this age, they feel less confidence in their skills because they have less practice in sharing intimate information. No wonder so many eighth grade girls tell me that they're looking forward to high school so they can meet some "real guys." Boys, meanwhile, may be relieved to find that girls will actually listen to their thoughts, fears, and dreams without belittling or teasing them the way their male friends might.

Even in ninth grade, girls have little time for their male classmates. You're more likely to see them hanging around the edges of the groups of junior and senior boys, asking for help with math homework (an age-old ploy) and generally making themselves visible. Meanwhile, the older girls are either paired off with the more popular senior boys or have older boyfriends, away at college, to brag about.

When girls are not spending time with upperclassmen, they can act as coaches to help their boy peers make the transition into the mature world of boyfriends and girlfriends. Fourteen-year-old Marty's story captures that, as well as the very real division he feels inside himself as he tries to balance the world of boy rambunctiousness with the emotional depth and self-disclosure of romance.

"At school a girl told me how to get a girlfriend," says Marty. "Don't wear red! I have this one red shirt and she says I look pale in it. And wear cologne. That gets expensive! I wear cologne, but not every day." He goes on to explain why he seeks out this kind of advice from female pals.

"I have a reputation for being kind of crazy. I play all the time, so no one thinks I'm being serious even when I am. But I have a serious side, a romantic side. When I tell girls what I'm like as a boyfriend they laugh and say, 'Can I be your girlfriend?' But they don't really believe me. They might believe that I'd give a present or spend money on a girl, but not that I like to take walks or have candlelit dinners. No one believes me except Betsy. She says to girls, 'Marty is a human being with thoughts and feelings,' and they're like, 'Yeah, right, don't make me laugh.' " Marty is in the process of making the journey to more intimate attachments. But he's finding out the road can be bumpy.

Why are girls the ones making phone calls and delivering the "Susie likes you" messages in the school hallway? Because the average fourteen-year-old girl knows she can carry on a conversation and establish a relationship—and she enjoys practicing her social skills. Boys aren't so sure about their skills—although once contact is made they're willing to give it a try.

If you have a young adolescent in your household, you know that their romances tend to be numerous, intense, and short. (You may sometimes think that the primary function of these romances is to give kids something to dissect in their endless phone and e-mail communications after school.) The romances may be fleeting, but the contact is frequent. Boyfriends and girlfriends see each other or talk on the phone almost daily—and the average length of the phone calls is sixty minutes.

As boys spend more time with girls and begin to have one-on-one relationships with them, their other-sex relationships may become closer than same-sex friendships. Girlfriends prompt boyfriends to be intimate. Boys still feel most comfortable in their boy culture, but girl culture has its attractions too. As fourteen-year-old Jason put it: "Guys are much more fun to hang out with. You can do crazy things with them. But girls are much better to talk to on the phone. You can't talk to a guy on the phone at all."

Young adolescents who have not yet made real-life connections with the other sex spend a lot of time thinking about romantic attachments. Megan, an attractive and somewhat shy fourteen-year-old, was devastated for a couple of days when actors Brad Pitt and Jennifer Aniston married. Megan had been nursing an intense crush on the handsome actor since sixth grade. She carried his picture with her and imagined herself having long, loving conversations with him.

"I mean, I knew I wasn't ever going to really meet him," Megan says. "But this means I *really* will never meet him."

Crushes are a healthy developmental stage that allows children and teenagers to experiment with various feelings without the pitfalls of romance with actual human beings. It's the ultimate safe sex. Crushes on unattainable figures avoid the complications of more overt sexual experimentation that is part of the tension of dating, whether in groups or in pairs. Having crushes helps cement same-sex friendship too. Friends, especially girls, will spend hours discussing the ups and downs of each other's romances, even if they are imaginary ones like Megan's. These conversations are a safe outlet for expressing and exploring the powerful emotions that come with romance.

Why do young people tend to experiment first with purely mental romance? Because sex and romance are so intense, so emotionally charged, so confusing. Crushes simplify it by making it one-way. Imagination does the rest.

However, a fantasy is perfect, while real people aren't. This can cause complications. A real person may not behave the way you thought he or she would. Noelle asked one of the most popular junior boys at her Florida high school to a Sadie Hawkins dance, the only event of the year to which girls invite boys. Paul was two years older than Noelle and a football player—quite a catch. Noelle had had a crush on him all year, and he had said hi to her in the hall once. She and her friends analyzed that "hi" for days, teasing out its every nuance. "Call him, call him, I *know* he likes you," they urged. Spurred on by her friends, Noelle called Paul, who had recently and publicly broken up with Shannon.

Paul was a well-mannered boy who didn't know how to say no when Noelle asked him to the dance, especially with his mom standing near the phone. So they attended together. But Paul had no intention of dancing with a puny ninth grader in front of all his friends. Once in the gym, Paul went right over to his old girlfriend Shannon and asked her to dance. They stuck together all night—literally, during the slow dances. For an interminable two hours Noelle sat on the bleachers trying to look casual. This wasn't what she had had in mind for the evening at all.

Negotiating the World of Romance and Sexuality

In calling Paul, Noelle had been pushed by her friends into the risky act of calling a high-status boy. In a similar way, a group can push designated members toward testing the waters at each stage of romantic and sexual experimentation. Research shows that contact with the other sex and dating appears to emerge most often within a group context of friends and peers. After all, someone has to be sent to look over the hill into the unknown territory ahead and send back dispatches about what teenage romance and physical contact are all about.

Remember those alpha males and queen bees? Often the dominant boys and girls—who tend to be more emotionally and physically mature—are the candidates elected to enter the terra incognita of romance and dating. (Research reports that in the early stages partners are selected on "stimulus characteristics," which is social-science-speak for good looks. Ask a young adolescent, "How did you pick your boyfriend/girlfriend?" and you're likely to hear, "He/she's cute." In later adolescence, however, common interests and values and interpersonal compatibility become important reasons to pair off.)

The group silently elects these attractive pairs of candidates and pushes them forward as advance scouts. As surrogates, they are licensed by the group to try out this sex business first. They're the bold explorers—and the group is deeply invested in their discoveries.

Have you ever watched a nature documentary of penguins crowded together on an ice floe? I recently watched a film of these comical birds pressing closer and closer together, vibrating with what seemed like fear and anticipation as they approached the edge of the ice. They were so crowded because they weren't sure whether it was safe to hop into the frigid water (there might be polar bears). The penguins reminded me of a bunch of teenagers massed together to push a designated pair among them into the stormy seas of sex and romance. Eventually one or two penguins lose their footing on the ice cliff and plunge into the sea. The others peer intently down into the water, waiting to see if the pair bobs back up.

Eventually virtually every adolescent will make the leap from gender segregation to dating, romance, and sexuality. (Gay and lesbian teenagers shift from palling around with same-sex friends to dating same-sex partners at this stage too.) There are profound differences in when and how this happens, based on differences in family values, ethnic and religious traditions, and the cultures of their particular school and peer group.

A thoughtful young actor I know spoke with me about his memories of making the shift from dating and sexual experimentation to romance and its serious sexual involvement.

"The first time I had a fool-around girlfriend was in eighth grade," he remembers. "The first time I had a real *serious* fool-around girlfriend was in ninth grade."

"What were people doing in ninth grade?" I asked.

"There was a kind of a split. There were a whole bunch of ninth graders who were still waiting to kiss their first boy or girl. And there were some kids, like my friend Frank, who were reporting having had sex in eighth grade. There were groups formed around that commonality. The sex-having people hung around the other sex-having people and the never-been-kissed people hung around with or dated the other never-been-kissed people."

"Did you feel you had to have more experience to qualify for the group you were in?" I asked.

"I was a pretty confident ninth grader. In ninth grade I dated a tenth grade girl who was far ahead of me. She dragged me kicking and scream-ing . . . or kicking and enjoying myself. She took her shirt off. She in-vited herself into my room. She is probably the first person who ever talked dirty to me. That was huge. The first person who ever told me what she wanted to do. Mostly kiss. She was a big kisser. She wanted to have me alone."

I wondered if my actor friend had moved through his sexual discov-eries alone or if he had talked about them with anyone.

"I had an older sister whom I was quite frank with. A lot of vicarious experience came from that. I certainly had enough information. My sister told me that she'd had sex and it was only fun with people you were in love with. The first time I had the chance to have sex—it was the summer after tenth grade—I called my sister and asked, "What do I do?' She asked, 'Are you in love with her?' I said 'Yes.' She said, 'Well, wear a condom and have fun.'

"My girlfriend and I had oral sex first. She proposed it and I thought it was just fine. She was the first person I ever tried to have sex with, but it was unsuccessful. The equipment didn't fit. Oral sex was safer.

"It was in the summer at my house. Our unsuccessful attempt at intercourse came the next day and the discomfort from that . . . it sort of took the fun out of it. It made us both pretty uncomfortable. I didn't talk to anybody about the failure. Not for a long time."

"Were you one of the popular kids? Did having sex enhance that?"

"Being able to talk about sex was definitely a hallmark of popularity. Because it was such a huge issue. It was the big social and political issue of the day. Sex was the issue in ninth grade. But I think pretty strongly that talking about sex and having sex were two different issues in ninth grade. There were a lot of big fish stories and bragging."

This young man spent his junior year of high school in England. There his sex life continued. He and a girl he met there became very close in the intimate setting of a small farm, where a group of students were living with minimal supervision.

"She really wanted to have sex," he recalls. "Physically it wasn't a big deal because she'd done it before. She was wonderful and instructive. We left the lights on and laughed and had a goofy experience. We felt really strongly about each other. I felt like she was the person I wanted to have sex with the first time. We could talk about fears and condoms. We went to the pharmacy together to buy condoms. We had a very close relationship before we had sex. Our relationship was very public."

"Were you the king and queen of the group?" I wondered.

"Yeah . . . because of the seriousness of what we were doing."

Sexual feelings and curiosity are universal. And all parents, whether they admit it or not, worry about what their adolescent children are up to. They know that their children are struggling to interpret and respond to the complex social and sexual situations they find themselves in. Whether we like it or not, our children will likely be in situations that involve group pressure, alcohol and drug use, or intense, fast-moving emotional relationships they may not be prepared to handle. It's a different world out there than it was when we parents were bragging about getting to second base at a make-out party. Our generation spawned and has supported a media and TV world soaked in sexual imagery and gorgeous, seminude bodies. Casual sex is portrayed as not only acceptable but almost mandatory. Lately the Internet has complicated these matters even more. Moreover, teenagers spend far more time unsupervised than they did when we were young.

Biology plays a role, as well. Girls are developing almost two years earlier than they did thirty years ago. Boys too are developing a couple of years earlier. This early onset of puberty for all children puts pressure on these teens to act like adults before they are emotionally or cognitively ready.

When do these young people "do it"? The average age of first intercourse has been falling in this country for twenty years. It is now midway through the sixteenth year.

This generation of teenagers—boys and girls—have flipped our generation's order of things. They tend to try oral sex before they have intercourse. But even if they aren't having oral sex or intercourse, young teenagers engage in some pretty intimate sexual behavior. The Sexuality Information and Education Council of the United States (SIECUS) reports that:

- 73 percent of girls and 66 percent of boys thirteen and younger have been kissed
- 20 percent of thirteen-year-old boys have touched a girl's breasts
- 25 percent of thirteen-year-old girls have had their breasts touched
- 23 percent of boys and 18 percent of girls age thirteen and younger have fondled someone's genitals

The realities of teenage sexual behavior may give a parent pause, especially in a world in which kids can contract a fatal illness from having unprotected sex. SIECUS reports that one-quarter of all high school graduates in this country leave school with some variety of sexually transmitted disease. We can be thankful most of these diseases are less serious than AIDS, but they are still serious enough to affect fertility and sexuality later in life.

As parents, we have an absolute obligation to teach our children the importance of protected sex no matter how we feel about our kids' sexual activity. To give them anything less is to put their lives at risk. We also must teach them the basics of emotionally safe sex, that is, the importance of an intimate, loving relationship as a context for sexuality.

"My Girlfriend Knows the Real Me": The Value of Committed Relationships for Adolescents

As children grow into adolescence they move through progressively more complex levels of relationship. At each stage they bring along the skills and lessons they have learned at the previous stage. Not only that, they bring along their needs, met or unmet, and their social styles, whether hesitant or competent or somewhere in between. And at different stages they bring these factors into play with different people.

Harry Stack Sullivan charted shifts in the primacy of relationships through childhood to adulthood. He said that our attachments shift from mothers during infancy to family members during early childhood, chums and friends in middle childhood and early adolescence, and finally romantic partners during late adolescence. Establishing these romantic relationships is a central developmental experience, and during adolescence individuals develop the capacity to fall in love.

Like adolescent friendships, romantic attachments are a training ground for developing social and communication skills, including negotiation, self-disclosure, and intimacy. Intimacy means being able to sustain an openness that reveals thoughts and feelings; loyalty involves a commitment to shared attitudes and values. The psychologist Willard Hartup adds additional qualities to the mix: reciprocity, commitment, and equality. When these forces are in balance, love can bloom.

Nevertheless, it can be hard to watch your son or daughter fall in love. Not only does it bring back memories of your own early romantic feelings and their attendant heartbreaks, it is a clear sign that your child is moving away from your family to form intimate alliances elsewhere.

Parents often feel jealous of their children's romantic partners in a way that they usually don't feel about their children's close friends. That jealousy can take the form of attempted seduction of a daughter's boyfriend (remember Mrs. Robinson?), repression (never allowing teenagers to go out), or attempts to undermine the relationship (as Romeo and Juliet's parents found out, this last option can backfire). But parents should take heart from the fact that these early romantic experiences will play a critical role in your child's journey to competent adulthood.

Psychologist Brett Laursen has studied patterns of closeness within adolescent relationships. Laursen found that among rural New England high school students with a median age of seventeen, overall relationship closeness was highest with romantic partners. Friends come next on the list, followed by mothers, then fathers. Siblings are lowest. Romantic partners also ranked highest on specific attributes that make up closeness, such as how often the members of the pair saw one another and how strong their influence was upon one another. Laursen also looked at the frequency of contact between girlfriends and boyfriends. The students reported that they spent an average of fifty minutes more in daily social activity with their romantic partner than with the next closest person in their lives.

Intimacy between young people becomes possible as the result of the physical, cognitive, and social changes experienced in adolescence. These advances allow adolescents to establish and maintain more mature relations and reach more advanced levels of empathy and responsiveness to someone else's experiences. All of this happens at a time when increased independence offers kids greater opportunities to be alone with their romantic partners. We already know that friends provide adolescents with companionship, shared activities, and opportunities for self-disclosure. Romantic partners also offer all this—plus the physical rewards and increased status associated with sexual activity and being one of the lead penguins (as long as there are no polar bears).

In late adolescence, feelings of intimacy emerge as central to romantic relationships. This intimacy is in many ways a grown-up version of attachment, with added layers of sensuality. Remember that mom on the plane that we met in Chapter 2? She patted, stroked, and soothed her baby throughout the flight. Boyfriends and girlfriends can play similar comforting, reassuring, even calming roles for each other. Often these functions are expressed through cuddling and smoothing and stroking—even cooing and baby talk.

Young love is a way to reexperience the pleasures of early attachment and childhood innocence that may have been lying dormant for a while. Think of the way teenagers regress during courtship. You see them on the swings, at playgrounds, "holding hands and skimming stones," as Elton John's song "Crocodile Rock" puts it, using baby nicknames, and exchanging stuffed animals as tokens of affection.

A baby's attachment history is to a large extent the template for his or her later romantic relationships. Romantic relationships throw into relief young people's relative neediness, their tendency to reject others before they are rejected, their need for reassurance, their ability to feel loved, and their ability to hold the other in mind while believing that the other holds them in mind. (Ryan, an eighteen-year-old who is quite jealous of his girlfriend when she is paying attention to other people, says, "I want to know that she would notice if I got up and left!")

Romantic attachment can also be a chance to redo things, to get a fresh start and have needs met that weren't met before—especially for affection, physical contact, feeling loved and valued, giving love to others and having it accepted. It can be hard to get started in a healthy romantic relationship if these early needs were not met. But if the romance works out, it can be a second chance. And for many, many boys, having a girlfriend means finally being able to talk to someone about their emotions.

The social skills it takes to maintain same-sex friendships are further developed in romantic relationships. Openness to one another's thoughts and feelings characterize these connections. "When I started going out with Simon, I finally felt that someone was seeing the real me," Gretchen, a senior in high school, told me. "I can tell him anything and he can tell me anything. We trust each other."

When an older adolescent relationship is going well, the pair is a delight to behold. Last summer on a plane I sat beside a couple of recent high-school graduates from Ohio. Isabel and Darco were on their way home from visiting her parents in Maine, a last vacation before each went off to a different college. I asked this obviously happy pair about their relationship. And they were eager to talk.

Isabel: It started at the beginning of senior year. We just became better friends; I don't remember the moment exactly.

Darco: It was just when we realized it.

Isabel: We became best friends when we started dating.

Darco: We were in separate spheres, separate classes. I don't know, I guess I had always been attracted to her.

Isabel: I wasn't always attracted to you. (She laughs)

Darco: I know you weren't.

Isabel: But he's a guy. Guys' attraction is different. Guys are generally more lusty. They look at many girls that way.

Darco: That's true. But when I was with the guys I would mention her name. And I thought maybe something would happen senior year.

I asked them who had initiated their relationship.

Isabel: We went to this party and he and I stayed up all night talking and we went out to this lake and watched the sun come up. But nothing happened. Nothing physical happened, it was just talking.

Darco: And then of course our friends saw that we were up all night and they asked, "What's going on?"

Isabel: Neither of us is the type to be very bold too quickly.

Darco: So I told the person who asked me, "Yeah, I like her." And it got back to her. And then someone told me that Isabel was interested in me, so I felt more confident.

Isabel: My friends were very nosy about it. They were kind of into it. One friend would always say, "Darco is so good-looking."

Darco: Her friends didn't sway me. I already knew that I liked Isabel a lot, but it was kind of encouraging. It was her friend pushing me in this direction. There are hardly any people in the senior class who have had a relationship as long as we have.

I told Isabel and Darco that the average duration of a serious relationship in adolescence is four months. Isabel laughed and said, "Well, the average relationship for middle school is one week!"

Young people like Darco and Isabel, who are able to maintain steady relationships, are entering a stage that social scientists call "maturing out," a period characterized by increasing disengagement from the broader peer subculture. In this couple's case, that disengagement rests in the fact that Darco was a member of the cool crowd and Isabel wasn't. By senior year Darco was more interested in forging a bond with Isabel than he was with staying in with his cool friends. He was making a choice based on his own feelings rather than the norms of his group.

"Is Darco popular?" I asked.

Isabel: I really think he's—I have to be totally honest here—in the top 10 percent. He's athletic too.

Darco: She's different. She's very independent. She's not afraid to do her own thing. In our school there were these groups of girls who dressed the same way. Isabel wasn't part of that.

Isabel: I do dress differently, but I'm not trying to make a radical statement, I'm just trying to be myself.

Darco: At the end of the year the senior class elected us Most Unlikely Couple.

I asked Darco and Isabel, who had been in the same class since eighth grade, if they had noticed each other early on. Darco's memory of meeting Isabel at a party was vivid.

Darco: I have one memory from the beginning of eighth grade. There were two people from my school who lived on a cul-de-sac. They had a tent and the whole grade was invited. I had never talked with Isabel before but I asked her to dance and I still have a mental picture of the background, what was behind her, the house behind her, the tent pole. I remember what color shirt she was wearing. That wasn't the first time I had seen her, but it was the first time I had talked with her.

Isabel: I was so happy that he asked me to dance. I was just standing there all by myself. I've never told you this, Darco. (She laughs) I remember thinking you were nice, but my first impression was the gel you had in your hair. I remember seeing it there.

Isabel and Darco are heading to different colleges in different states. They will be a time zone apart, too, she in the East and he in the Midwest. Their romantic connection may endure in college, it may evolve into a friendship, or it may end. As I spoke to them, it was clear that they had been thinking about their parting. And it wasn't easy. I asked them about the prospect of separation. "It can be pretty harsh, being in different colleges," I said.

Isabel: Yeah. That's why we're talking about it tomorrow. (Long pause) We're talking about it tomorrow. We waited to talk about it until tomorrow.

Darco: (Sadly) Yeah, we're talking about it tomorrow. She leaves for college next week. . . .

Conflict and change characterize all human interactions. But for young people in the throes of their first serious romance, change can be especially threatening. That's what Darco and Isabel were trying so poignantly to postpone. But change happens.

What happens to the close friendships of adolescence when couples begin to pair off? During late adolescence, intimacy with same-sex friends declines, while with other-sex friends and romantic partners it increases steadily. In fact, research shows that steady romantic relationships are associated with increased discord in close friendships. A boyfriend or girlfriend frequently usurps a best friend as the closest relationship, and that can be difficult. And even though good friendships are resilient, it can be hard to compete with the intensity of a relationship that includes sexual feelings and romantic intimacy.

Here's another dialogue, this time between two same-sex friends, Josh and Anthony. They had been best friends all through high school and had to deal with a romantic involvement by one of them during their senior year.

Josh: Unfortunately, well, not unfortunately for me, unfortunately for Anthony because he hates my girlfriend, at the end of last year I was introduced to Julia.

Anthony: Hate is a very strong word. I don't hate her.

Josh: Anyway, I met Julia last year and we were going out for quite some time. We're still going out, we've been going out now for almost a year. We have a great relationship. Anthony and I, we still do all the same things we do, it's just that I'm not as available. He might call occasionally and I'm not always home, and different things like that, and I've been very careful not to spend too much time with Julia, but it takes up more of my time. And Anthony wasn't exactly fond of her. She wasn't exactly the clean-cut kind of girl that he would have liked to see me go out with, or that he would have chosen for himself. I said to Anthony and Julia separately, 'You guys really just have to be able to make this work between the two of you. You haven't always seen eye to eye.'

Anthony: We were lab partners in chemistry, Julia and I, and we worked out fine.

Josh: Then something happened. The two of them, they started to get on each other's case. We went out to dinner together, the three of us, and it wasn't pretty. And it hasn't been pretty ever since. And I would have liked for this not to happen, but it did happen. I'm just going to have to sort of balance myself out.

Balancing the demands of romance, home, school, sexuality, and friendship can be overwhelming even for the most mature adolescents. Sometimes the romance is the thing that has to give.

During the production of her senior-year school play, Dana, the star, entered into an all-consuming romance with James, her male counterpart in the show. The two were together late into each evening for rehearsals and spent weekends together watching plays on videos or going to live theater in the city. A few times, when their parents were out of the house, they almost had sex. When they weren't together, they were sending e-mails, writing love letters, or talking on the phone. They were madly in love, both onstage and off.

Then the play closed. James started his winter sports season, with its long practices and hours spent on the bus going to away games. James also rediscovered the easygoing fun of hanging out with his male friends. Before long he told Dana that he "needed some space." And that was that.

Dana's winter was spent recovering from this heartbreak, which at the time seemed fatal. Her parents despaired. Dana wept for hours every night when she wasn't on the phone with Molly, her best friend. (While Dana was part of a steady couple, Molly had been left out in the cold. Following the breakup, the friends had reconnected.) But even through her tears, Dana admits now that she was relieved to be freed from the pressure to have sex that had been building in her relationship with James.

Adolescents learn from bitter experience that sex can't be played as a casual game. In fact, it's often what brings them into therapy. They find out that the heart and the body are connected. The heart follows the body even when you try to keep them separate. And hearts can break.

For many teenagers, confusing, humiliating, or painful sexual experiences lead them to want to have a fully loving relationship instead of one that feels exploitative or too casual. A girl I saw in therapy wanted to "revirginize" herself after an unsatisfying sexual relationship. I believe strongly that this impulse toward reserving sex for a committed, trusting relationship can be as true for boys as it is for girls.

Teenagers do not know—and their TV shows and rock videos don't tell them—that good sex takes a depth of intimacy and maturity. We need to let kids know that the most gratifying and meaningful sex is to be found in committed, loving partnerships characterized by equality and open communication. We must guide the children we love toward the kind of trusting and passionate relationships that make us grown-up human beings feel lucky to be alive.

Chapter Ten

Crossing the Lines of Difference

Trinh has always been Trinh; she's never been "Trinh my Vietnamese friend."

—Maeve O'Neill, nineteen

When Catherine was in grad school, she spent time volunteering in the playroom connected to the orthopedic ward of Children's Hospital in Washington, D.C. What she saw there amazed her.

"Some of the kids on that floor were recovering from major surgeries or accidents; some were undergoing chemotherapy as well as surgery. Many of them were very ill. They came to the playroom lugging IV poles or strapped in traction in rolling hospital beds. But no matter how sick they were, they all wanted the same thing: to connect with other kids."

Catherine remembers watching the children, who ranged in age from six to twelve, playing with each other. They played with dolls and G.I. Joes, with stuffed animals and board games. They didn't run around, but they played. And they appeared astonishingly indifferent to each other's disabilities and physical differences, to the baldness of chemotherapy or the disfigurement from accidents. They didn't care about that stuff. They wanted to play and they wanted to make friends.

This is not to say that the children in the playroom lacked empathy. In fact, Catherine thought, their empathy was so profound that they were able to treat each other simply as children rather than as symptoms or scars. Not only that, but being together allowed them to forget, for the time they were in the playroom, how different they were from each other and from the well children they had left behind at home and at school.

In fact, to connect with others, particularly others who may not look or act like us, requires empathy. We need to understand that other people are separate from us, that they have their own feelings, but that we can relate to those feelings. And at the same time we have to find the points of connection, the ways that they are human beings just like us. As the saying goes, if there is one thing all people have in common, it is that we are each unique. Psychologist M. L. Hoffman proposed that the capacity to experience empathy develops in tandem with the development of a sense of others. When that happens, a child is able to recognize that something—good or bad—is happening not to oneself but to someone else. At first the other person's distress feels like our distress too. That's why babies in nurseries all start to cry when one of them begins wailing. But by age two or three, children perceive that others have feelings and perceptions that differ from their own. That leads to a more sophisticated form of empathy. At first they may try to help by doing something that they know makes the other person feel good, such as offering a bottle or a toy to a distressed child—or to a distressed adult. As they grow older they begin to recognize that the other's needs may not be the same as their own and thus may require a different solution. Hoffman says that older children experience feelings of compassion, along with a conscious desire to help, because they feel sorry for the sufferer, not simply because they want to relieve their own distress.

As you have read this book, you have come with me into some pretty dark places in the lives of children. We have seen how children can hurt, exclude, and marginalize each other, even over a simple difference like the wrong hairstyle, living in the wrong part of town, or throwing a ball the wrong way. In spite of those dark forces, which are very real, I believe that children—well or sick, physically able or physically challenged, straight or gay, male or female, of whatever race or culture—share a fundamental quality. That quality is the drive to connect with other human beings in positive, nurturing ways. A lot of things can get in the way, as we have seen. Yet those fundamental connections can be made, and the vast majority of kids do make them. They connect in spite of differences in health, sexual orientation, race and culture, and levels of poverty or wealth.

The ability to cross these lines of difference depends on seeing, feeling, and seeking to understand otherness as well as on recognizing and embracing similarity. As adults, we usually find it heartwarming to see different sorts of children effortlessly making friends with each other. And we are often impressed when we see them make an effort to forge and maintain friendships that take a bit more work, when they overcome differences that could get in the way. But we shouldn't get carried away and think of these children as saints or of these friendships as little miracles. When a disabled child and an able-bodied child are friends, they are just friends, with the same conflicts and reconciliations, the same give-and-take, as any other friendship. The same goes for children who cross racial, ethnic, or class lines to make a lasting bond. It is a wonderful thing to see and a positive thing to encourage, but children tend to have a healthy matter-of-fact attitude about such friendships, as Catherine saw at Children's Hospital.

Among groups, differences can easily lead to polarization, or exclusion of anyone who doesn't fit the mold of the dominant group. On the other hand, there are strong forces of acceptance, tolerance, and inclusion in groups. There is also another factor in groups—the desire to establish identity by being with people who are similar to oneself. The ins and outs, ups and downs of friendships and group acceptance across lines of difference are a product of these competing factors. For a metaphor of how these factors operate, look at a medieval city. There were high walls to keep outsiders out and bridges to let outsiders in. Within the city, there were marketplaces where everyone gathered and other places for specific groups to gather—churches, synagogues, guild halls, palaces, and so on.

The same play of forces can be seen in any school today. Ray Rist observed this balance that kids achieve between crossing lines and sticking together in his book *Desegregated Schools*. In a chapter about social and race relations at an elementary school in North Carolina, Rist observed patterns of informal segregation (the black kids sitting together at their own lunch table). At certain times the focus was on identity—"Which group do I belong to?" However, the rest of the time, kids practiced what Rist calls "political cooperation," a conscious deemphasizing of difference and conflict. This cooperation allowed harmony to be maintained between groups. At those times the focus was on building bridges—on asking "How are you like me?" Rist called this "social mechanics."

From social mechanics can come an atmosphere that allows the formation of personal ties. If social mechanics are based on minimizing differences (the old melting-pot idea, or the all-inclusive marketplace of medieval cities), the next stage is based on noticing and celebrating differences. As one mother put it, talking about being a black family in a predominantly white school: "I don't want to be melted in a pot. How about if we think of it as a tossed salad instead, where every different ingredient is savored for itself and the unique flavor it brings?"

In our current society, with diversity a fact of life, we can't be content with just avoiding the worst types of conflict. We have to foster real bridge making. In his book *Children's Friendships in Culturally Diverse Classrooms*, professor of education James G. Deegan explores ways to facilitate children's friendships in culturally diverse settings. Among his suggestions are:

- Support different kinds of friendship by talking with children about differences.
- Actively listen to more than one side of a story.
- Model that there is more than one "right" cultural practice.
- Make connections between children's everyday experiences and broader social issues and concerns.
- Challenge seen and heard instances of stereotyping as they occur.
- Avoid derogatory discussions of race, gender, class, or any other areas of difference.
- Fight against the trend to sacrifice differences for commonalities.
- Build communities.

The balance between identity and friendship isn't always easy. Larry met for a semester with a group of eighth graders in a K-8 public school outside Boston. They were a mixed group in terms of race and class, and

Larry was struck by how well these kids had managed to maintain close friendships across these lines. But when they talked about the impending move to high school, there were major differences. The white middle-class kids were looking forward to high school, academically and socially. The black kids and the white working-class kids had mixed feelings about the transition. For them high school meant an end to the one big happy family they had experienced in their grammar school. Because these students were a minority, they spent some time hanging out within their groups, building identity, and part of the time with the majority kids, building bridges. In high school, though, as they had heard from older siblings and friends, the black kids hung out with the black kids, the Asian kids with the Asian kids, and so on. There were big enough groups in each of these categories that identity politics often took precedence over friendship. Friendships across these lines weren't impossible, but they were much harder. The children most affected by this, the ones who were going to face losing their grammar school buddies, were much more aware of the dilemma.

In this global world and our multicultural country, the ability to cross the lines of difference is a skill we all need. No one says it's easy. It's not. We can learn to respect difference and turn to it as a source of strength. Let me tell you a few stories about young people who have successfully crossed the lines of difference. They have a lot to teach us adults.

Catherine's niece, Maeve O'Neill, is a sophomore at the University of Virginia. Maeve has a best friend who is Vietnamese. Catherine asked Maeve about their connection:

Catherine: When did you and Trinh become friends?
Maeve: We met when we were both eleven years old and starting sixth grade.
Catherine: Did you spend time at one another's house?
Maeve: Trinh and I lived at each other's house throughout middle school and high school. Trinh's parents didn't care if I called late or stopped by unannounced. She was equally welcome in my house; my parents even call her my sister. I think that her family and culture may put more emphasis on formal family gatherings than mine does. But I'm more than welcome at dinners and holiday gatherings with Trinh's family.

Catherine: Did you ever talk about your differences of race and culture?

Maeve: Yes, but it's never really been an issue with either of us. When we were both applying to colleges, we talked about how she felt more of an obligation than I did to stay close to home, especially since she is an only child. We've also talked about the fact that her parents would probably want her to marry someone who is Vietnamese, but I don't think that's going to happen. We've also always joked about how I have to wait years for her to finish eating because she has to finish everything on her plate. In her culture it's seen as disrespectful to waste things like food. Americans don't associate any guilt with buying something, throwing it away, and then buying more.

Catherine: Have you stayed close all these years?

Maeve: Trinh and I have been friends for a little more than eight years now. We've gone through middle school and high school together and now we're both at UVA. We've played on the same soccer team, worked together, and of course just hung out. I think there are some people that you will just always have some sort of a bond with even if you don't keep in touch as much as you used to. We live closer to each other now than we ever have, but I haven't seen her in a couple of weeks, since we've both been so busy with classes, jobs, and other activities. But that doesn't change our relationship at all. We've shared so many experiences over the years that I don't think there's any way that we wouldn't still be close.

Catherine: Is your friendship with Trinh different from your relationships with others because she is from another country originally?

Maeve: Not at all. Living in northern Virginia, especially in Arlington County, has blessed me with probably the most diverse group of friends you could imagine. Trinh and I both have friends from all ethnic, cultural, and religious backgrounds. Trinh has always been Trinh; she's never been "Trinh, my Vietnamese friend."

Catherine: What did you notice when you were in school about friendships between kids who are different from each other? Did your school encourage those friendships?

Maeve: I'm lucky to have grown up in such a diverse community and to have so many different friends. I think kids in elementary school may notice differences between races, but unless otherwise told, they don't associate those differences with any negative connotations or stereotypes. I remember a teacher in elementary school complimenting me on my cheekbones and "Native American features," and I didn't have a clue what she was talking about! I think kids realize these differences as they get older, and then their views of other races are based primarily on their parents' beliefs. Then those views often change the more you interact with people through high school and college.

Catherine: Do you think you and Trinh will stay friends?

Maeve: Definitely. By the time we leave UVA I will have known Trinh for more than half my life. She knows more about me than most people ever will and I about her. We may lose touch as we go off into the world but we'll never not be friends.

Maeve's easygoing approach to the diversity of her family, which is biracial, and her school environment reminded me of the casual way in which a group of high school boys from my neighborhood approached a relationship with their friend Eric. After a spinal injury, Eric was left a paraplegic. Eric's school struggled to accommodate his needs. His family, friends, and schoolmates all went the extra mile to make things accessible for Eric. His gym teacher got him involved in a wheelchair tennis program. His parents bought him a specially equipped van so he could drive once he was old enough. His friends included him in all their activities. I don't think they thought they were being noble. "He's the same person he was before," one told me.

Eric's senior high graduation was held off campus, on a stage that was not wheelchair accessible. When his name was called, there was an awkward pause. But one of his friends, a young man who partnered with him on the tennis court, matter-of-factly swept Eric up in his arms and carried him onto the stage to accept his diploma.

This matter-of-factness around difference can be surprising to adults. At some school proms heterosexual couples nonchalantly share the floor with gay couples (not all schools have yet achieved this level of acceptance). Maeve described how she and Trinh and their friends loaded up their plates with food at a potluck post graduation party put on by all the parents at their Virginia public school. They mingled in a crowd that represented some twenty different nations and as many languages. A visiting adult remarked, "This place sounds like the UN." The kids' response: "What's the big deal? This is our life. This is normal."

Because people can be rejected so cruelly for being different, because differences are sometimes automatically considered to be abnormal, this idea of the normality of difference is very powerful. I learned this lesson once again when Christine, the daughter of a friend, was hospitalized in Boston for chemotherapy. "Her friends were incredible when she was sick and recovering," my friend recalls. "The first time she went back to school after she had lost her hair, she came in wearing a hat. Her whole fifth-grade class came to school that day wearing hats. Everyone else in the school was asking them why they were wearing hats and they said, 'Oh, we're in the hat club. We just like wearing hats.' No one said what it was for, and it made Christine feel welcomed without being singled out as different."

It turned out that one or two friends had started a phone chain the night before Christine returned to school to make sure her classmates turned up in hats. "One friend came to the hospital the day she had to have surgery and put on a hospital gown," Christine's mom remembers. "Her friend had put on the gown just to be funny and to be in solidarity with Christine. But then the nurses said that Christine would have to take off her shirt for the procedure because it was too tight. I could see that this upset Christine, but I didn't know what to do about it. Her friend piped up, 'Could she wear this one?' pointing to her own oversized shirt. The nurses said sure, and they traded. We always joked about this afterward, saying, 'She would give you the shirt off her back,' because her friend literally did that."

Christine's mom was impressed by the other girls' lack of embarrassment at her daughter's baldness after chemo and at their creative solution to making her feel normal and one of the crowd. But not wearing a hat was fine too. "After that first day, she felt so supported by her friends that she wouldn't rush to put a hat on when a friend came over. Christine felt comfortable, and so did her friends," her mom recalls. "Her friends were very nonjudgmental."

Christine is now well again, I am glad to say. One of the things that strikes me about her very moving story is how compassionately Christine's friends supported her, communicating their feelings through a language that all middle school girls speak fluently: "clothsese." The compassionate use of the clothese language is all the more striking because we know how mean children can be about not owning or wearing the right clothes.

But kids have deep, deep reservoirs of compassion. They can be graceful and kind with others. They can make a difference in other children's lives. Larry tells this story about one of his nieces: "She did something I thought was incredible," he says. Because things had been divisive in her classroom, with lots of teasing and clique rivalries, Larry's niece's teacher said that everybody in the class had to write something good about another girl in the class. The teacher handed out little papers, each of which had a girl's name written on it. They were supposed to go home and write nice things about the girl whose name they pulled. "Apparently there was one girl in the class who was very overweight and everyone teased her," Larry says. "No one wanted to get her name. My niece saw that the girl who got her name just dropped it in the trash. She didn't even care if anyone saw her. My niece went over to the trash can and took the paper out." She came home and told her mom about finding the name in the trash. She didn't especially like this girl either, but she knew she'd be terribly upset if no one wrote anything about her. "Her mom asked her what she thought she should do," Larry recalls.

"I think I should write something about her," she said. She ended up writing about the girl whose name she'd drawn and then the rejected girl too.

When Larry's sister told him that story, she said it reminded her of a time in her own school days. A classmate came to school in little white ankle socks at a time when the other girls had moved on to more sophisticated footwear. "Everyone made fun of her and I told them to stop it," Larry's sister recalled. "The other girls marched over to me and said to me, 'We're not going to be your friend unless you drop her.' And I said, 'No way I'm dropping her!' " By taking a stand, she was able to keep her new and her old friends—although her admiration of her old friends was diminshed.

I think it's important to share these stories with our children, the times we stuck up for someone or broke an unwritten rule in the name of friendship. Our children will also benefit if we explain our remorse about the times we acted cruelly—not to suggest that it is okay, but to convey that we eventually learned that it wasn't harmless fun. If we hold ourselves up as perfect beings who never said an unkind word, our children aren't going to be able to come to us with their moral dilemmas about being pressured to turn against someone different in order to be accepted by the group.

Adults can have a tremendous impact on children's social comfort with difference. In our neighborhood in Arlington, Massachusetts, we have a neighbor whose house is a welcoming place for everyone, kids included. My neighbor is from Holland, and she entertains people from all over the world. When my children spend time at her house, they hear people speaking different languages. They see people of different colors. These neighbors are adults who stand out because they embrace difference. They have made this a neighborhood where everyone is welcome—and they have made an effort to make sure it is. These adults model the fact that it's not enough to just not hate; you have to make an extra effort to include everyone.

This came home to me quite dramatically at a recent parent meeting I attended. The moms and dads gathered their chairs in a circle. One foreign-born mother, from the Philippines, came in a bit late and sat down in a chair outside the circle. Another mother urged her to pull her chair up. "No, no," the Filipina mother said. "It's not important. It doesn't matter."

"It does matter," the first mom said firmly as she stood to widen the circle and welcome the newcomer in.

Children deserve to live in a world that widens the circle to welcome everyone in. That's why I believe in speaking openly about gay and lesbian young people even though it still makes many adults uncomfortable. As a society, we have become more adept at talking about sexual orientation. But gay, lesbian, bisexual, and transgendered young people continue to suffer terribly. The Gay, Lesbian, Straight Education Network (GLSEN), an organization that works to end antigay bias in schools, conducted a nationwide survey in 1999 to ask gay, lesbian, bisexual, and transgender students about their lives in school. Ninety-one percent of those surveyed reported that they heard homophobic comments regularly, 69 percent had experienced verbal harassment, and 24 percent had suffered physical harassment. Clearly we need to learn to reach out to these students in our neighborhoods and schools.

Gay and lesbian children are five times more likely to report skipping school because of feeling more unsafe than straight kids are. They are twice as likely to consider suicide and four times as likely to actually attempt suicide. These children have to struggle to exist in a world that often feels totally hostile to them. Not only that, but they still have to manage the complex tasks of adolescence like their straight peers. Connecting with accepting adults and supportive friends can be lifesaving.

The support of a friend can literally save a child's life. One woman I met at a summer teaching seminar told me a story about running into a man she had gone to high school with. They had been good friends but had been out of touch for years. "After we caught up with each other's lives a little," she told me in amazement, "he told me I had made it possible for him to go on living while we were in high school. I was overwhelmed by that. I had no idea I was doing it!"

Her friend, it turned out, had known in high school that he was gay. Unable to face telling parents, teachers, and friends about his homosexuality, he became increasingly lonely and isolated. He contemplated suicide. He didn't tell the woman who told me this story, either. But years later he told her that his weekends spent hanging out with her buffered him from his worst feelings of rejection and despair. She accepted him as he was. She listened to him. She didn't need to make the friendship romantic or sexual, yet it was intimate and trusting. Herself a bit of an outcast, she too took great comfort from the relationship. In fact, she didn't put it together at the time, but she always liked that he didn't put the moves on her and that he really valued their friendship. Bolstered by this connection, he was able to wait it out until he could find a safe place to come out and make a life for himself without the emotional turmoil of constantly hiding his sexuality as a matter of survival.

"I had no idea he was gay at the time," the woman repeated. "I'm not sure I even knew what gay was. I knew I loved him, and I accepted his quirkiness. But I didn't know that he felt I was the only one who did."

Any parent of an adolescent knows the terrifying statistics on teenage suicide. And every therapist and school psychologist knows that many more children think about it, often seriously. I believe that many close friendships involve stories like this one—which only was told years later—of kids who are rescued from terminal despair by friends who cross the lines of difference, whatever they may be.

Today's teenagers live in a world in which homosexuality is far less hidden than it was twenty years ago. Only within the last couple of decades has homosexuality ceased to be regarded as a mental illness. But the costs are still enormously high for young people struggling not just with the onset of sexual feelings but with the onset of sexual feelings for their own sex. (On average, most homosexual boys know that they are gay by the age of twelve. Middle school or early adolescence is a natural time to begin to announce sexual identity. It is also a time when all adolescents tend to declare their autonomy and do things to outrage their parents.) Although we are more open and accepting of gay and lesbian people today, murderous homophobia remains, as the 1998 killing of college student Matthew Shepherd in Wyoming so tragically proved.

If you are the parent of a gay or lesbian child, you have a difficult road ahead. Your child will face prejudice, perhaps even prejudice from you. The reality of your child's life will be difficult. Try to cross the line of difference to hold and support your gay child.

When children do tease and torment a friend who is in some way different from them, they may come to regret it and even use it as a way to learn empathy instead. I was told the following anecdote by the father of a college student. It perfectly illustrates this kind of learning. The father was obviously proud of his son, his youngest child, and was very emotional as he told me this story. His son Jeremy was one of seven boys around the same age who grew up together in the same neighborhood. Jeremy was always picked on and teased. He struggled to maintain a place for himself in this gang of boys but never really made it. In high school Jeremy developed leukemia. The other boys rallied around him and showed him incredible kindness and devotion. Now they are all around nineteen, and Jeremy is in full remission and playing college football. Jeremy's father spent some time recently hanging out with his son and several of these boys during a college break, when they were all back in the old neighborhood. They talked openly about how they could now look back and see how important the whole experience was to them. I asked this father if Jeremy's friends had revised their history, forgetting their earlier cruelty (as often happens) and acting as if they had always been friends. The dad said no. "They speak very poignantly about how badly they used to treat him, and how his illness woke them up, " he says.

As adults, we need to help kids wake up to the feelings of others. In the next two chapters I will explore ways in which schools and families can combat social cruelty and support kindness and caring.

Chapter Eleven

What Schools Can Do

L ike all Americans, I am haunted by the horror that took place in Lit-
tleton, Colorado, in 1999. If I close my eyes, I can still see high
school students running in terror from a building where they should have
felt safe and joyous. I can still see the fresh-scrubbed, hopeful faces in
yearbook portraits of the dead children. And we lose other children to
violence every day in this country.

Unfortunately, the debates about childhood violence tend to be limited to punishments, media images, and access to guns. Another factor—
the role of social cruelty—is often overlooked. Rejection and alienation

can lead to suicide and/or revenge, as in Columbine. In fact, isolation, taunting, and exclusion are factors in most teen suicides. Intergroup rivalries can lead to lethal gang warfare. And the promise of group membership can lead to recklessness, as when college freshmen drink themselves to death in extreme hazing rituals. When we take a serious look at social cruelty, we have to acknowledge that its results can be fatal. Even on a lesser scale, the outcomes can be scarring. That's why it is so crucial for schools to take a moral stand—a stand against exclusion, scapegoating, bullying, destructive cliques, and other cruelties.

I know that I have said throughout this book that parents shouldn't be too worried about their kids, that most of what goes on between children is normal experimentation or a variation of deeply ingrained primate behavior. But there are situations that demand action. And every school has to take into account the potential for everyday teasing and bullying to turn into violence and emotional trauma.

If anything good has come from the tragedy of school shootings in this country, it is that we are beginning to understand that the emotional well-being of our children—indeed, their very lives—depends on the attention we pay to the social aspects of school. I know that the shootings, the hazing deaths, the suicides, and the lawsuits have galvanized many schools into action. They aren't always sure what to do, but they know that they can't keep sweeping these problems under the rug. The tragedies have helped schools see that security does not just mean locks, guards, and surveillance cameras. Real security is psychological and emotional. It means that every child feels safe and respected and able to focus on learning. It means adults in schools knowing at a basic level how each child is doing.

The shocking nature of the murder-suicides at Columbine has also brought the issue of school violence front and center in suburban America. We can't pretend anymore that it's an inner-city phenomenon, that it "isn't our problem." In other words, the dangers of social cruelty are not limited to a few "crazy" kids or a few dangerous neighborhoods. We *all* have to think about it.

In addition to providing basic safety, schools have to think about producing good citizens with leadership skills, empathy, and responsibility, not just people who can get a certain score on a standardized test. Anyway, you can't learn effectively if you're scared of being beaten up after school or if you are getting dirty looks all day from the in crowd.

Our children spend more than thirty hours a week in school for twelve or thirteen years of their lives. That's a huge amount of time—and it seems even longer for a child who is socially marginal, lonely, or victimized. A large body of research suggests that a good adjustment to school requires participation in friendship and acceptance by peers. Having a friend in the classroom makes school a more comfortable, less threatening environment. Studies show that children who are disliked are three times more likely to drop out of school before graduation (approximately 24 percent of rejected children drop out compared to 8 percent of other children). One study found that peer rejection was more likely to cause a child to leave school than academic struggles. Rejected children also tend to be absent from school more often. Many rejected children don't have positive relationships with teachers either. So these kids lack not only the opportunities for learning and companionship that come with friendship, but also basic adult support and kindness.

Teachers expect to deal with children's academic problems, such as math anxiety, reading difficulties, unfinished homework, and unread history assignments. But when I speak to groups of teachers, these are not the problems they want to talk about. Over and over, at all kinds of schools, they say their toughest situations are those involving social cruelty. Some teachers want these problems to go away so they can get back to teaching French or biology. Others want to reach out and help children with their social pain but aren't sure how. Either way, they recognize that the ups and downs and ins and outs of social life preoccupy many of their students and get in the way of learning.

Sometimes after a talk to teachers I hand out index cards and ask them to jot down the thorny social challenges they have faced in the classroom. They tell stories of scapegoating and exclusion. They describe parents who take sides in student conflicts. They worry about how slow things are to change. They wish they could do more to inspire kids to be kind. They wonder if young people and adults in schools can truly welcome diversity. They try to rid their classrooms of the word *hate*.

I am always struck when I do this exercise by how much teachers notice and how much they care. Teachers know intuitively that children who are suffering socially are endangered academically and emotionally. And they have a lot of energy for remediation and change. They want to make a difference. But their feelings of helplessness and hopelessness come through loud and clear.

Part of the problem is that there are hundreds, maybe thousands, of programs, curricula, books, and workshops out there about how to make schools safer and more nurturing places. There are conflict resolution courses, peer mediation programs, bully-prevention strategies, staff sensitivity workshops, and so on. With a quick Web search or trip to the library you can compile a long list of them. I am not going to attempt to evaluate these or make recommendations about which programs are best. After all, no two schools or school systems are alike. Rather than providing a laundry list of programs, I prefer to lay out some basic principles about what schools can do. I believe these principles will empower you to effectively choose from what's out there or help you create your own program to address social cruelty and the potential for violence in your school. To illustrate these principles, I will mention specific schools and what they have found successful, but don't let this limit your creativity and resourcefulness in applying these principles to your own school.

Create a Moral School

Our school systems, with large numbers of children and small numbers of adults, put children at social risk. It's as simple as that. Some children, when they go to school, enter a world in which they will be marginalized, tormented, and damaged. The powerful rules that govern group life, which I have discussed in this book, require adults in schools to take a stand against cruelty and exclusion. We need to make our schools—*all* schools, whether private or public; religious or secular; urban, suburban, or rural; large or small; rich or poor—safe places for children to be. We must create moral schools. It's a big job. And we have to do it.

I believe that a school must have an ethos and a moral code that stands against excessive exclusion and social cruelty. Will any school be able to stop exclusion entirely? No, certainly not. But it remains the number one social problem from pre-K through twelfth grade. I believe it is a moral problem.

Even though I am a psychologist, I can't help feeling that these issues must be addressed at a moral level, with clear standards of what is the right thing to do and high expectations about how people treat one another. We do have to help individual students with emotional disturbances, whether they are victims of cruelty or perpetrators, but we also have to think about the moral climate of the whole school.

As I travel the country talking about the lives of children, my path often crosses that of Professor Tom Lickona, educator and author of *Educating for Character: How Our Schools Can Teach Respect and Responsibility*. On one occasion I asked Tom to define a moral school. I was surprised at first by his answer: "A moral school is a school where people spend a lot of time discussing what a moral school is." But the more I thought about it, the more sense it made.

Tom means that if we all keep talking about how to be a moral school, our antennae will be up, constantly monitoring our behavior and that of the children we teach. We will pay attention to how we treat one another—not for the purpose of catching people in the act and deciding whom to punish and whom to praise, but for the purpose of making our moral standards clear. A list of written rules in a school handbook does not make the moral message clear. That can only happen through conversations, talking about what is okay and what isn't, and discussing how the school should respond to social situations. Please don't dismiss this idea as only *talking* and not *doing* anything. An ongoing conversation about values and moral principles will provide a solid basis for any specific actions that may be taken.

In her book *Practicing Virtues*, Kim Hays describes the startling discovery she made when she studied two completely different types of high schools: Quaker schools and military academies. She found that they actually had remarkable similarities. Even though they had dramatically different values—pacifism versus militarism, individuality versus group loyalty—they shared something much more important. Both types of schools lived their values every day, at every level of the school. The ideals of the school, the rules, the disciplinary measures, the policies—all were rooted in each school's core values. Many parents and teachers fear that a moral school has to embrace a particular moral perspective, but it doesn't have to be that way. Holding strong values and using those values to inform your decisions is what makes a moral school.

Include Everyone in the Conversation

If a moral school is one where people talk about what makes a moral school, then one key component of talking is to make sure that everyone is included in the conversation. Often schools implement a new program only to see it fizzle out or fail. I think that's because there wasn't enough talk first about what was needed and why. Or there might have been plenty of talk but only among certain members of the school community. Some schools shut out parents from such discussions, while others shut out the faculty. Most shut out the students.

When I ask schools what they have done in the areas of community building, bully prevention, or social cruelty, they often recite a list that sounds something like this: lectures by experts to the faculty and staff, assemblies for students where an administrator admonishes them about the rules, and a PTA meeting featuring a lecture to parents.

What's missing here? Listening to the faculty about what they see and what they think needs to be done. Listening to students about what they experience and what they think needs to be done. Listening to parents about what they think and feel about the topic.

So when educators ask me to talk *to* students in response to their cruelty or bad behavior, I always decline. If they ask me to "get them to be more responsible," I not only decline, I head for the hills. We know what doesn't work in schools: experts lecturing teachers, who in turn lecture to children. The Anti-Defamation League sponsored research that found exhortation to be the least effective method for changing prejudiced attitudes; in fact, it often produces a result opposite from the desired effect. The same is true for trying to change all types of cruelty and mean behavior. Simply telling kids to be nice to other kids isn't going to accomplish much. That's why I don't lecture kids. Instead I ask them questions and get a conversation going. Not only do they give my lecture for me, but they don't shut me out as just another clueless adult. They don't always say the right thing. In fact, they can be walking advertisements for insensitivity. But even so, it helps to get these thoughts and feelings out in the open to look at and talk about.

At Lincoln School, a K-8 school in Brookline, Massachusetts, the principal recognized that the usual menu of expert lectures and faculty in-service training was not doing the job. With the help of two psychologists, she organized a Teasing and Bullying Task Force of eighth graders. The group met ten times, talking about their own experiences, collecting information from their classmates and younger students, and talking about what changes they would like to see made in the school. This was the information that had been missing. For example, the students felt that the administration focused too much on the rare incidents of physical bullying—punching and shoving a smaller, weaker child—and not enough on the pervasive, subtler forms of social cruelty such as put-downs, talking about people behind their backs, and being left out of a group. The principal and the teachers were surprised to find out that the students felt that adults *care* very much about what goes on but *know* very little about what goes on. I was happy to learn that the students on the task force made the same recommendation that I often make to schools: Spend less time responding with punishment to individual situations and more time on understanding the underlying social dynamics in the school. An observation like this is always more powerful coming from individuals within a school than from an outsider like me.

Including everyone in the conversation is not always easy. Some people feel empowered to talk more openly and freely than others. And some topics are just plain hard to talk about, such as differences in race, class, and academic achievement. These topics are hard for adults to talk about, as well, but they are the hot-button issues behind a great deal of teasing, exclusion, and social cruelty. Schools need to foster safe, honest discussions about these topics among and between parents, faculty, and students.

Be Proactive

Last month I got two calls from two different schools. Even though both wanted me to come and consult with them about social cruelty on their campuses, the calls could not have been more different. In one the head of the school was in a panic because of an extreme incident of hazing on the varsity football team. Lawsuits had been threatened, the student body was in turmoil, the faculty was in an uproar, and the football team, its coach, and the alumni supporters were on the defensive. The second call was calmer. The head of this school had felt for some time that the social climate of the school was getting worse and worse, with more name-calling, more put-downs, more aggression, and more complaints from parents and teachers. Realizing that a case-by-case response to all of these little incidents wasn't very effective, she wanted to begin a school-wide initiative.

For me as a psychologist, both calls promised interesting work, but it is always easier—and more effective—to do preventive maintenance than to mop up after a disaster. Of course, there isn't always a clear line between these two situations. Many schools are able to use an embarrassing or dangerous incident as a wake-up call to do more about social cruelty on a deeper level.

When schools react to situations, it often ends up stirring up many bad feelings from everyone involved. On the other hand, when schools act proactively—putting programs, guidelines, and curricula into place before major trouble surfaces—then the groundwork is laid that will help when inevitable conflicts arise. One such program is the Council to Combat Teen Cruelty (CCTC). Founded by Dr. Debora Phillips, of the faculty at the College of Physicians and Surgeons, Columbia University, and Dr. Michael Rothman, of Harvard Medical School, this organization enlists the power of successful, socially competent kids to change the lives of marginalized kids in their schools.

Drs. Rothman and Phillips, who are siblings, saw the pain that middle-school children were experiencing, expressed in school shootings and deaths. "The cruelty of children to each other, the exclusion, the put-downs, the cliques, the intimidation, the taunting, and the lack of empathy and tolerance were exposed as open wounds," says Phillips. "We all felt surprised and helpless and wondered how to stop the bleeding."

To begin, CCTC worked with schools in New England to identify a council—one hundred high school students whom teachers, counselors, principals, and other school professionals considered creative, committed, and compassionate. The program pairs a teased, picked-on middle schooler, termed a "trainee," with a popular tenth or eleventh grade advisor from the council. Trainees and their guides spend intensive time together in the program over the summer. When they return to school, the trainees have their guides as buddies and supporters.

Besides coaching one particular child, the example set by the guides can influence teen culture, Dr. Rothman says, leading the pack in setting a new tone of empathy and acceptance. He hopes CCTC will create an atmosphere in schools in which "it's cool to appreciate difference and uncool to be cruel." CCTC hopes to expand its proactive model into public and private schools around the country. For example, a West Coast chapter, involving schools in San Diego, Los Angeles, and San Francisco, focuses on uniting student athletes with marginalized kids in its effort against teen cruelty.

Friendship groups are another example of a proactive response to creating an atmosphere of kindness and support. At Metairie Park Country Day School outside New Orleans, these groups are selected and put together by teachers and counselors to include a range of classmates who might not otherwise seek each other out. At first the groups are led by a school counselor who helps them see that they can make friends outside of their original clique or circle. But the groups are so effective that by third grade the kids voluntarily convene their groups to solve problems. "It is not uncommon," says Tissie Bean, lower school counselor, "to see a group of third graders walking toward the Pink House, where the groups gather, with their serious faces and their lunches, heading toward a meeting that *they* have called to discuss a friendship problem."

In 1987 educators at the Stone Center at Wellesley College developed Open Circle, a social competency program for elementary schools. Since its inception the program has trained more than 3,400 teachers in some 220 elementary schools in seventy-six communities in New England and New Jersey.

Open Circle includes a curriculum for teachers as well as a parent component, and provides lots of support for the teachers and the principal of schools that use it. The parent component is six sessions, two hours each, which are conducted by a psychologist and a learning consultant. The parents learn the practices that the school is using with the kids and find out how to apply the same skills in their parenting. Topics include problem solving, giving compliments, and good listening. A segment called "Solving People Problems" includes lessons on how to calm down, how to read other children's faces, and how to brainstorm solutions. The final segment, "Building Positive Relationships," includes leadership training and positive self-talk.

Open Circle is designed to develop a cooperative classroom community, so instead of the teacher listing the rules at the beginning of the year, in Open Circle the class decides the rules. "Therefore we are much more likely to follow them," says Linda Morin, a learning center teacher in the

Ridgewood, New Jersey, public schools, which use Open Circle. "A few teachers held out at first. But after the first year, when they saw the impact on other classrooms, most of these teachers asked to be trained. And school nurses in Open Circle schools have reported that they need fewer ice packs at recess, because the kids are not fighting as much."

One of the best things about Open Circle, Morin believes, is that it creates a shared language. In Open Circle schools students and staff know that a "listening look" is a facial expression that shows one is paying full attention.

Open Circle doesn't limit its focus to just bullies and victims. Starting with introspection and self-reflection, children learn to speak up for themselves and discover what they can handle for themselves and what requires a teacher's help. Instead of solving children's problems for them or sending them back to solve them on their own without skills, teachers ask, "Is this dangerous or destructive? If not, you have strategies to try to work this out by yourselves. If you have trouble, come back and I'll help."

The program has been effective, Morin says, citing a new child who joined a Ridgewood school in the middle of fifth grade. "He came to the principal and teacher after his first week and said this was the nicest, kindest place he had ever been to."

Creating thoughtful programs, teaching kids to use them, and then allowing them to work together to create a positive social environment— that's proactive.

Instill Ethical Standards

Exclusion and teasing are as inevitable as the tide. However, as Vivian Paley demonstrated in her beautiful little book *You Can't Say You Can't Play*, it is worthwhile swimming against that tide. One year Paley put up a sign in her kindergarten class that proclaimed, "You can't say you can't play." She had gotten to the point where she couldn't stand the amount of power that the high-status children exercised over others, even in kindergarten. She saw the hurt on those eager young faces when someone said, "You can't play with us." So she provided a moral code against which children could measure their behavior, a concrete ideal that she could point to and say, "How did we do today on *not* saying 'You can't play'?"

At first the sign and the guideline it stood for were greeted with disbelief. "What's the whole point of playing?" one student wailed. Over time, however, it became more or less second nature to most of the children.

Did Paley completely stop exclusion in kindergarten that year? No, not exactly. But every time a situation arose, she could ask the children whether their behavior lived up to her rules, and she generated a moral discussion as a result. She concluded that her rule was a "ladder out of the trap" they'd been in. It helped children get out of the habit of exclusion.

Any moral stand, any code of conduct, posted at the front of a classroom and pointed to as the basis for understanding and settling conflicts, helps children out of the trap of their own meanness. But it doesn't do that good work just by being written, or just by being the basis for punishments. It only works if it is used as a moral ideal, a standard to strive for as a class and as a community.

Paley believes deeply in the essential goodness of children. As an example, she tells the story of Teddy in her book *The Kindness of Children*. Teddy is a boy she met while visiting a preschool. During the morning she visited, children from a school for the severely disabled came to visit. Teddy rolled into the classroom in his wheelchair, limbs twitching. As Paley watched, the other children gently incorporated Teddy into their play. "I believe children are always on the edge of committing an act of kindness," Paley has said. A school that takes a strong moral stand can help children step over that edge to be kind.

Another example of using moral guidelines rather than specific regulations comes from a comprehensive antibullying program called Bully-Proofing Your School. The authors of that guide propose three basic planks to their antibullying platform. The first: "We will not bully other students." Second: "We will help others who are being bullied by speaking out and by getting adult help." Third: "We will use extra effort to include *all students* in activities at our school."

It is that last plank that is best, I think. It isn't enough just to make a rule against forbidden behaviors. To change a school culture and climate, you have to go the extra mile; you have to make the extra effort to reach out. It's a rule that can't really be enforced, and it isn't meant to be. It is meant to be a higher standard, an ideal.

Encourage Good Citizenship

The second plank of the antibullying platform I listed above—help other students who are being victimized rather than do nothing—is a key to good citizenship. Many of the best interventions against social cruelty focus extensively on the bystanders, the people who wouldn't initiate vicious teasing or violence and might not condone it but don't do anything to stop it either. They might be intimidated or afraid of becoming targets themselves, or they might get a vicarious thrill out of the show. No matter what, they can be encouraged to take an active role in maintaining respect and civility in a school. Together, these witnesses are much more powerful than any bully. But it usually takes some careful effort to get them to work together since there can be consequences for bystanders who speak up. Part of the power of any group is the way it punishes whistle-blowers, snitches, rats, narcs, or tattletales.

Some of the most intractable problems of exclusion I have seen in schools have involved children who stepped forward, spurred by their own conscience, and were ostracized for getting high-status people in trouble. Even the victims the whistle-blower was trying to help may turn against them. That's how powerful the group can be. A new group ethos of helping others, reaching out, and not tolerating aggression, must replace that blind loyalty and protection of the aggressors.

Creating an atmosphere that encourages kindness one to another should, and can, also support values that are fundamental to being members of the human family. I believe that good citizenship participates in the same principles that good friendship embodies: empathy, responsibility, sharing, self-sacrifice, self-disclosure, and faithfulness.

At a public middle school in Wayland, Massachusetts, an effective, school-wide program supports all these principles. The school organizes itself into teacher advisory groups (TAGs) consisting of a staff person and a small group of students. Each child participates in a TAG every week, and every teacher and administrator leads one. One week every group may discuss the same topic; other weeks a teacher may run her group according to what she thinks it needs. The TAG program teaches, models, and allows students to practice interacting with one another with respect and kindness. One student said of the program, "I wish we could talk with each other all the time like we do at TAG groups."

The goal of the TAG program is to build a cohesive community to reverse the tide of meanness and cruelty that can characterize relationships among middle schoolers. The skills and traits nurtured by the TAG program—listening, respect, openness, honesty, cooperation, interdependence, empathy, conscience, conviction—are the building blocks of emotional intelligence and of active participation in a community.

In addition, the Wayland school has chosen ideal "mentors" to embody the virtues they would like their children to leave middle school with. In sixth grade the kids take Henry David Thoreau as a mentor; in seventh grade it is the biologist Rachel Carson, author of *Silent Spring*. Eighth graders claim Dr. Martin Luther King Jr. as their mentor.

In his commencement address last year, Richard Schaye, Wayland's middle school principal, explained the importance of these mentors to the graduating class. I include his talk here almost in its entirety because it captures so well what I mean when I say that a moral school encourages good citizenship:

Three years ago you came to our school as energetic, somewhat frightened eleven-year-olds. You learned very quickly that our school had three role models that were chosen purposefully to serve as your guides through the middle school. We chose Henry David Thoreau because he didn't follow the crowd, but did what he thought was best. He had the courage of his own convictions and he found beauty in the solitude of a pond and the woods so very close to our school.

Rachel Carson taught us that science starts with good research. She demanded that we ask tough questions. Her concern for the environment is one of the reasons that we can drink our water and breathe our air—not exactly unimportant in our lives. It is also worth honoring the struggle she had as a woman scientist who was doubted just because she was a woman. Our graduate schools in the year 2000 are filled with bright and creative women because earlier generations of women were willing to persevere when society told them that they were not capable of being serious scientists or lawyers or doctors or president.

Martin Luther King taught us the hardest simple truth that I know: Either we are all free or none of us is free. Either we all have rights or none of us has rights. His message was inconvenient. It meant we had to give up our prejudice against people who looked different from ourselves. Free of prejudice means that people of different religions and people with no religion are all welcome at the table. Dr. King's message meant that we had to give up the last great prejudice, the one that says you're only human if you are heterosexual. If you have given up the worst insults about race; if you have stopped worrying about whether someone is Christian, or Jewish, or Hindu, or Muslim, or Buddhist, or Baha'i, or an atheist (all of whom are represented in this school) but you still call someone "gay" or worse, then you haven't passed our eighth grade test. Dr. King meant all people. The word *all* seems so simple, but each of us in this room today knows that it is not.

I spoke to Richard Schaye about how his school nurtures this kind of citizenship on a day-to-day basis. Since the TAG program is a fairly new, I asked him, "How can you tell it's working?"

"I think we have been successful for three reasons," he said. "First, it is now taken for granted by the entire faculty that we will meet with, talk with, and listen to our students every Wednesday for twenty-five minutes. This has become routine and basic, and that fact is wonderful. Second, once every few TAG meetings we gain an insight, learn a key fact, or solve an important problem that might be missed without a program that is now routine. Third, students treat TAG as routine too. It is routine that we talk with and listen to students. It sounds small, but it's actually a big deal."

"Do you think the students get it about the values of King, Carson, and Thoreau as antidotes to middle school trends toward conformity, exclusion, and self-centeredness?" I asked.

"I think we have been able to keep the values of our three mentors on the student radar screen," said Schaye. "We make slow progress regarding student behavior, but all of our students know that we value how well they treat each other. They expect me to talk about our mentors and I think they appreciate my graduation speech when they leave our school, which references the progress they have made in emotional development in their three years of middle school life. Many students have commented to us about how difficult the middle school years are. They also tell us that this school cared about every student and expected each student to become kinder as he or she got older. That is as important a goal of school as producing an accomplished academic individual."

Take a Systems Approach

In order to really tackle the problems of social cruelty and provide every student a safe learning environment, we have to take a systems approach rather than dealing with every incident on a case-by-case basis. The largest example of this system-wide approach that I know of was conducted in Sweden and Norway by Dan Olweus. After studying hundreds of thousands of schoolchildren, Olweus proposed interventions that were implemented first at the school level, then at the local level, and ultimately at the national level. The amount of bullying (his term for what I've been calling social cruelty) decreased dramatically and stayed down.

This approach included a questionnaire to parents, educators, and students; a school conference day to discuss the results of the survey; increased supervision at lunch and recess; construction of more-attractive school playgrounds; specified contact people at each school to report and discuss problems; small teacher groups focused on improving the social climate of the school; and parent education/support groups. At the classroom level, the intervention consisted of clear classroom rules, regular class meetings, role-playing, reading, cooperative learning, and class activities with a common goal. On the individual level, educators began a system of "serious talks" with bullies and victims, helped rejected children with their social skills without blaming them for being excluded, and organized neutral students to be activists against cruelty. Obviously a great deal of thought and planning and implementation goes into a comprehensive program like this, and that is part of why the results were so impressive.

In this country I've worked in schools that have instituted their own package of interventions, including conflict resolution curricula in the lower grades, peer mediation programs in the upper grades, PTA talks on the topic for parents, in-service training for staff, posters on the walls, and so on. In general, the schools make it priority one. I am not suggesting that every school adopt exactly this list. The key point is that eradicating exclusion takes more than just punishing the troublemakers, lecturing the student body, or changing the classroom assignment of a child who is struggling to be accepted by the group.

One innovative aspect to school-wide initiatives is parent support groups. In most schools clusters of parents get together and talk before and after school, on the playgrounds, at soccer games, and on the phone. That's fine—unless they are gossiping about the children and re-creating the cliques of the classroom on an adult level. But some schools have found that having more formal meetings for any parent to attend is helpful—not lectures by experts, but just a chance to get together to talk to each other. For example, in one school, sixth grade parents got together to talk about Halloween. How much independence were people allowing their eleven- and twelve-year-olds? Was every parent hearing "Everyone else is trick-or-treating with friends and no parents!" from their child? The group didn't make rules for every family to follow, but they came to a consensus about how much independence made sense for that age. Another useful aspect of parent groups is to get those parents who are more marginal in the school—minority parents, recent immigrants, non-English-speakers, less affluent parents—to be a more central part of the school. Of course, the children of these parents are often the same ones who are marginalized during the school day.

Though each school has to take its own unique approach to these problems, it helps to have moral leadership on a district, state, or national level. Theodore S. Sergi, commissioner of education in Connecticut, recognized this when he called for a statewide effort for violence prevention and school safety.

Sergi sees school safety as a responsibility of the entire community, not just educators. In an effort to get everyone involved and on board, Sergi asked for a statewide analysis of what works to keep schools safe for kids. The initiative includes school support groups, student mentoring, Parks and Recreation Department activities (after school and in the summer), counseling services, parenting programs, Scouting, and more. The Connecticut committee identified several areas that require attention:

- The need for broader programming for young teenagers
- The need for greater respect for differences between young and old
- The need for more parenting programs
- The need for specific activities during school vacations

Because I believe that safe human connection is the foundation of all learning and of all community building, I am encouraged to see safety of this kind addressed at a statewide level. Not only does an initiative like this get everyone involved, it demonstrates in a concrete way that we adults care and want to ensure that our children and teenagers don't get lost in loneliness, anger, isolation, and violence.

At this writing, the Connecticut schools are still evaluating their efforts. Meanwhile, on the other side of the country, psychologists Daniel J. Flannery, Ph.D., and Alexander T. Vazsonyi, Ph.D., along with several colleagues, have looked at the effects of a violence prevention and school safety program called PeaceBuilders. PeaceBuilders has been implemented in seven Pima County, Arizona, elementary schools and the researchers have concluded that two years of the school-wide, climate-changing program gave children greater social competence and more-positive behavior patterns.

PeaceBuilders teaches simple rules: praise people, avoid put-downs, seek wise people as advisors and friends, notice and correct hurts that have been inflicted, and right wrongs. These principles were taught to both teachers and students in an attempt to change the setting that triggers aggressive or hostile behavior and to provide role models for good social behavior. The researchers report that the program was "purposely woven into the school's everyday routine to make it a 'way of life,' not just a time- or subject-limited curriculum."

After beginning PeaceBuilders, teachers noted significant improvement in student social competence, rating students higher on factors such as empathy, cooperation, and sensitivity. PeaceBuilders differs from previous violence prevention programs, say the researchers, because it attempts to change the entire school climate rather than focusing on individual risk factors. In addition, the program is long-term and focuses on universal prevention beginning in kindergarten.

Harness the Power of Teachers

Even if you are a teacher whose school does not have the resources, leadership, or tradition to combat social cruelty on a system-wide basis, you can make a difference in your own classroom. You can work to establish the safety essential to learning, making your room a haven of acceptance and civility. And kids will recognize it; they always know which teachers create safe classrooms.

Research has shown that teachers who use cooperative and collaborative teaching methods, in which popular and unpopular children and their various talents are showcased to one another, and where children depend on one another, can make a real difference in improving the day-to-day life of relatively unpopular children. Sometimes it is the parents who resist such efforts more than the children. A mother once said to me, her voice full of a sense of injustice, "Dr. Thompson, the teachers at this school don't let children pick their lab partners!" Clearly she thought I was going to agree with her that this practice was terrible. My answer disappointed her. "Good for the teachers," I said.

A teacher needs to be in charge of the social groupings in her classroom; it cuts down on the social anxiety of the children. Some teachers use seat lotteries to regularly mix up the group; others shake it up through different activity groupings. In the classroom of such a teacher, an unpopular child will be less unpopular by the end of the year. The whole atmosphere of cliques and popularity wars can change, as a great teacher makes being in her class more wonderful than being in the coolest clique. On the other hand, in the classroom of a hierarchical teacher who creates a competitive, dog-eat-dog situation or who unwittingly colludes with the cliques in the class, the misery of an unpopular child will deepen throughout the year.

When a child is suffering from social isolation, a teacher can help by arranging for peer modeling. The more generous and socially capable children in the class might be able to take a child under their wing. That's the premise of big-brother and big-sister pairings in many schools. Peer counselors in high schools often serve this function. A teacher can also offer herself to a child as a private coach. She might say, "I see that things are sometimes tough for you socially. Would you mind if, when I notice that you are doing something particularly successful with your classmates, I point it out to you?" An encouraging and discreet coach, never a critic, can be enormously helpful to a socially unsuccessful child. Creating a prosocial school environment in these ways increases the frequency of children's positive behavior, develops their social skills, and may limit future aggression.

A teacher at a Kensington, Maryland, middle school found out that this kind of intervention can bring unexpected rewards. One of her fifth graders, a boy named Jake, was having trouble fitting in with a very verbal group in the class that was staging a puppet show. The class had a puppet theater, built by the teacher's husband, but it kept falling over. So she asked Jake to be the foreman on a construction project to fix the theater.

"He was wonderful," she recalls. "He chose different groups for different tasks regardless of their status, and *his* whole status changed. The class was very intellectual, and Jake was not. Before, he was always the last to be picked for committees—we have a lot of committees, and on each one there is always a facilitator, an artist, and a scribe. But the others saw he had a strength and started choosing him to be the artist and even the facilitator."

Through strategic classroom interventions like this one, which was really quite small, children's lives can be changed.

Work in Your Community for Smaller, More Caring Schools

I am someone who thinks that the big junior high school, a collection of fifteen hundred seventh and eighth graders, is a modern nightmare. It is surpassed as a bad idea only by high schools of two and three thousand children. It is a step in the right direction that around the country the old warehouse junior highs are giving way to more moderately sized middle schools, or K-8 schools that keep a family-like environment through middle school.

It is time for us to address the problems of huge high schools and the cruel social environment that can flourish in them. In schools of twenty-five hundred students, there are many kids at the bottom of the social ladder who feel rejected and humiliated. As extreme and disturbed as the Columbine shootings were, the suicidal revenge of two low-status boys directed against high-status athletes tells us something about the lives of boys in a big high school. It is extremely difficult for the adults to monitor the behavior of students in a big school; it is impossible for the teachers to feel accountable for creating a moral climate when there are so many people in a building. If I could design psychologically safe schools, every elementary school in the United States would go from kindergarten through grade eight and would be no larger than four hundred children. No high school would have more than eight hundred students. This is a tall order, but in the meantime, we can support the schools-within-schools trend—smaller, more manageable communities within larger institutions.

If I had to sum up my feelings about large versus small schools, I would say that every school needs to ensure that every child has one adult who looks him or her in the eye and shakes hands every day. That's a more effective security measure than any metal detector.

I have heard the arguments in favor of big schools: the broader range of course offerings, the economies of scale, and the savings on janitorial costs. I still strongly suspect that we favor these enormous high schools because we're not thinking about what children need. Instead we're thinking of things such as what powerful football teams such schools can produce. As long as we think of the competitive power a school might possess because of its size rather than what the daily social experience will be for the vast majority of children (most of them not football players) we are missing the boat. What all children want is a safe environment where they are known and appreciated. I do not believe it is possible to provide such an experience for enough children in gigantic schools. Concerned parents and teachers should be fighting for smaller schools in which the adults can help create more socially safe environments.

Of course smaller schools won't even begin to happen without a partnership between educators and parents. Parents are the taxpayers. They have to say no when the call comes for a huge new school. Educators know the research. They have seen study after study confirm the value of smaller class sizes and more familylike schools.

Side by Side, a charter school in Norwalk, Connecticut, is one such small school. They have rejected the idea that every school has children in serious social trouble at the bottom of the social pecking order. "They don't at our school," says one teacher, "and it's because of small class sizes in a small school, parents and faculty who make the school climate a priority, and students who agree that true respect and civility are worthy goals." Because of a partnership that works, that school does not have a bottom 10 percent that is left behind. Everyone knows you can't just put "no bullying" in a school's mission statement and make social cruelty disappear. You actually have to change.

Many educators believe in Utopia, and performance-oriented parents worry that the kinds of efforts I'm talking about in this chapter will take precious time away from academics. I totally disagree. Every minute you spend effectively helping children feel safer, more accepted, more included, and better able to build good friendships means that children will be able to pay better attention in class, enjoy being at school, and focus on their schoolwork instead of on the popularity wars. So it actually *adds* time, or at least productive time, to the academic school day. Even if it didn't, we still need to offer more to our children than educational factories with the equivalent of terrible working conditions. We need to offer them a place to really flourish—every one of them, not just the golden boys and girls.

Schools are founded on the essential belief that children can learn, study, and play together happily, that adults can teach, and that there is something of inestimable value in the exchange. Every September schools begin again with new children, reinvigorated veteran teachers, and idealistic new instructors whose aim is to make the world a better place. These institutions are, after all, an investment in the future.

Schools are utopian. That is, even when they don't reach the highest ideals they set for themselves, they keep striving for them. That's the attitude we need to take on social cruelty in all its forms.

I asked Don Grace, head of school at Chapel Hill–Chauncy Hall, to explain something about the idealism and dreaming that informs schools. His school, a day and boarding school in the Boston suburbs, educates 170 high school students, about half of whom have diagnosed learning differences. The school's motto is nothing if not utopian: "A school without labels. An education without limits."

Community rituals help the school maintain its sense of hope and optimism. "We do a whole-school art project at the beginning of the year," says Grace. "Everyone gets something to design or create. Faculty and staff and students all participate. One year we made silk hope banners. Each of us wrote a hope for the year, and the flags were strung together and hung in trees around campus, like Tibetan prayer flags. Last year everyone received a brick to design and paint on, and a mason on our grounds crew took them all and designed a patio. It's now part of the entryway into our assembly space and arts classes." Grace believes that activities such as these foster a value for the individual as well as a sense of belonging in community.

"Kids come here because we have a reputation for an acceptance of difference," he says. "We fly all flags. One of the most moving things for me is to attend our 'coffeehouses,' which are talent shows open to anyone who shows up. There's no audition. That gives the message that we are looking for a wide range of voices, not just the same few who always get the leads in the school plays. And everyone's contribution is welcomed, attended to, and applauded. Kids feel safe to take risks they might not have considered before."

At the school, which is diverse by race and national culture as well as by learning style, there is some self-segregation in the dining hall and in the dorms. "We don't try to push students away from these groups," says Grace. "But we also provide opportunities for mixing, such as a universal after-school program that unites everyone and a weeklong Winter Carnival that assigns students to mixed teams. Everyone is on a team, including faculty and administrators. Everyone comes into contact with more members of the community than usual."

Of course harsh realities intrude on utopian dreams. As I write this chapter on a late September afternoon, there is a news report on the radio about a school shooting in New Orleans. Two middle schoolers have been rushed, bleeding, to the hospital. They are in critical condition. The police say the shootings came in the aftermath of a fight. They don't know what it was about.

Clearly there is an enormous amount that we as a culture have to change. But even in my shock and sadness over this latest shooting, I believe that schools can commit themselves to educating children to be good people as well as good students. We must. We must resolve to pay attention to the emotional needs of children and adults in our learning communities. We must devise and implement systems to address conflict before it happens. We must remember that our schools serve a high civic purpose: to educate and produce good citizens. We must hold fast to our ethical standards and utopian ideals in the face of the inevitable daily losses, failures, and misunderstandings of group life.

Schools must cooperate with families in a central task of civilization: raising responsible children. Responsible children have a good enough emotional foundation to go to school every day and meet the moral demands of communal life. It isn't easy to create a caring school. It takes intelligence, political savvy, energy, money, and love. But it's possible. And isn't a caring school the one you want for your children?

Chapter Twelve

What Parents Can Do

Just recently an anxious mother said to me, only half in jest, "No child of mine leaves my house without a helmet, not for any reason." I laughed. I recognize the anxiety of being a parent. I recognize the need to protect one's children. My next-door neighbor is a doctor and has seen enough brain-injured young people on the operating table that she requires her twin son and daughter to set the safety standard for the neighborhood. Without exception, they wear helmets whenever they go skating or bicycling. And did I mention my own children? Despite their protests, and sometimes after a fight, my children wear helmets. I feel re-assured when I see them ride by with those colorful plastic shells on their sweet heads. I may still worry a little, but in general I realize that my children are safe and I'm doing a good job as a parent.

But what about their social lives? The traffic can whiz by awfully fast. What am I supposed to do? How can I protect my children from being hurt by friends or cliques? The problem is that there are no helmets to protect them from threats to their emotional safety. A child can learn to ride a bicycle safely, and if there is a mishap, that helmet will come between him and catastrophe. But when it comes to learning how to ride through the twists and turns of friendship and popularity, all children will fall down and get hurt from time to time. All children will show bad judgment at times. All children will experience meanness and betrayal and teasing. Sooner or later all children will reveal their nasty side and will hurt others. What is the parent's role in an environment where there are no helmets and collisions are inevitable?

First of all, we need to think of our children's social lives, and our role in them, in terms beyond those of protection or accidents. Perhaps it's better to think about children's friendships the way we do about their swimming. All children have a powerful natural capacity for swimming. You've seen the photos of babies underwater, holding their breath and paddling toward the surface. Most children are a few years older than that before they learn to swim, but they all have the skills. They just need places to swim and competent coaches or teachers. That's where we come in.

In their early years we are our children's swimming partners. We take them into the pool with us. We hold them tightly against us at the start, but later we spin and swirl them around, making noises like a motorboat. Two parents in a pool might toss a two-year-old back and forth a short distance between them, so that the youngster gets the feeling of motion and the experience of not being held at every moment. These are the basic ingredients of building up a child's confidence in the water. Finally children begin to swim and we stay close by, supportive, enthusiastic, and vigilant. Some children need more attention from us than others, of course, depending on their confidence level, our worry level, and their degree of cautiousness or bravery.

You know the rest of the story. By the time kids are seven or eight years old, we parents sit by the pool keeping an eye out for recklessness—"Hey, no running by the pool!"—yet for the most part children can protect themselves. Even if they get a nose full of water or come up gasping for air, even if they occasionally dunk one another, they are okay. As the years go by we parents pay less attention, standing by only for a scream for help. At a lake you let them swim further and further out. They are perfectly competent in the water now (indeed, my fifteen-year-old daughter recently reminded me that she is a faster swimmer than I am). A parent is necessary only for the rare crisis or to remind the children not to do anything stupid or excessively daring.

Why do things usually go so well with children in the water? Because you have done the underwater equivalent of the secure attachment I discussed back in Chapter 2. You provided a safe harbor for them to come back to, first letting them cling tightly to you, then watching from the edge of the pool, finally remaining unobtrusively nearby in case of emergencies. You have allowed both for close comfort and for daring adventure; you've provided a warm towel and a high diving board.

So children grow into swimmers. But because they are young, they may underestimate the dangers of the sea: the strength of the outgoing tide, the undertow, the rolling power of the surf. You have to keep an eye on them. As they grow into adolescence, they may experiment with sports you could not imagine yourself doing. They will go ocean kayaking or surfing. They may want to imitate the diving tricks or the dangerous stunts of older, more experienced swimmers. They will scare you at times, and you have to do your best not to overwhelm them with your anxiety. The parent's job is to be a lifeguard—to be aware and engaged without being anxious.

In this chapter I will offer parents suggestions for what they can do as they sit on the sidelines watching their children swim in the rough surf of popularity wars, social cruelty, and friendship betrayal. It is my hope that I can help anxious parents not to overreact. Most young children do not need their parents to manage their social lives. What they do need is for their parents to provide a steady, supportive environment for their experimentation: a pool with a lifeguard. The best lifeguards are relaxed and confident, but when they see a child struggling in the surf, they snap into action. In the same way, when a child is in real trouble socially, you must act.

Everything I know about helping you help your children manage their social lives can be summed up in a few sentences. I will expand on each point in the sections that follow. Here are ten points:

1. Don't worry so much. Remember that you gave your child a sociable start in life.
2. Recognize the crucial difference between friendship and popularity. Friendship is more important.
3. Support children's friendships.
4. Make your child's friends welcome in your home.
5. Be a good friendship role model and teacher.
6. Provide a wide range of friendship and group opportunities.
7. Make friends with the parents of your child's friends (and enemies).
8. Empathize with your child's social pain, but keep it in perspective.
9. Know where your child stands in the group. If your child is in trouble socially, step in to help. If your child is popular or accepted, help him or her be a positive moral leader. Don't act like a middle schooler yourself
10. Take the long view.

1. Don't Worry So Much

I wish sometimes that we parents could hear a booming voice from the sky announce in a tone that dispels all our worries: "Everything is going to turn out fine for your beloved children." Alas, we have to settle for the more mundane reassurances of psychology and human development. The fact is that most kids figure out friendships and group life pretty well. Most will get over the inevitable upsets and rejections and betrayals without terrible scars. But even those scars have a chance to heal as we grow up and find new opportunities for friendship, romantic love, and group acceptance.

In just about every chapter of this book I have introduced you to one or two parents who worry too much (myself included at times). It's always easier to recognize that trait in others! If you saw yourself in those portraits, I hope you can join me in laughing at ourselves a little for our excessive anxiety. We all get upset because we remember how painful those years can be and are horrified that our own children have to endure similar difficulties. But when I suggest that we should worry less, I do not mean that the pain our children suffer isn't real. It is indeed genuine pain, whether it results in tear-soaked pillows or in tragedy. It's just that our worry is usually out of proportion to the real danger. And when we do need to step in, it works best if we do so with relaxed confidence rather than panic.

We don't have to have had perfect childhoods ourselves to be effective with our children. A study at Duke University found that mothers who had lonely, painful childhood memories of peer interactions could still raise happy, socially competent children—as long as the mothers were nurturing and loving rather than anxious and fearful.

Because we are biased about our own children, it also helps to ask independent observers, such as teachers or the parents of our children's classmates, how they see our child. Anxious parents tend to forget how competent their children are and think they have to micromanage every situation. Your friends or your child's teacher may see strengths and resilience in them you don't see. Of course, as I'll discuss below, they may also give us unwelcome news about things we should be worrying about. Laissez-faire parents, meanwhile, might feel that everything is fine with their child's social life, while other adults see a different picture.

Luckily, children grow up. They mature. They become more capable of getting the big picture. They develop the skills that make friendship, especially good friendship, possible. And it happens naturally. One of the best perks of being a child therapist is that parents think you are awfully clever when their child shows dramatic improvement. Mostly what happened is that the child grew up. He reached a new developmental stage that let him share, control his aggressive impulses, or make a friend. And that's true of every child. We worry about each new challenge—going to preschool, starting kindergarten, attending birthday parties, dealing with cliques, dating (the list is endless, isn't it?). In fact, most of the time your sons and daughters are ready for each new challenge because that's how development works. My advice is to trust your child's creativity and resilience. The vast majority of children, as many as 85 percent of them, have what they need socially. Perhaps they do not have all they want, but they have a social life good enough to meet their needs. And most of the other 15 percent can get their needs met too if we notice early enough what they need and set out to provide it for them.

When parents are anxious about a child's friendships or place in the group, often it's because parental expectations are unrealistic. It's okay for a kindergartner not to have a best friend. It's okay for a ten-year-old boy to prefer to play Nintendo alone in his room instead of spending every minute outdoors playing football with friends. It has to be okay for a child not to be an alpha male or queen bee—otherwise almost everyone is doomed to misery. Set your sights a little lower and look to see if your child has the basics covered. Watch your child with a friend. Are they happy to see one another? Do they engage in reciprocal play? Do they take each other's feelings into account? Can they resolve conflict without help? Do they have more peaceful time than fighting time? If your child can do these things at least some of the time, you can relax.

Another set of unrealistic expectations comes from wanting children to behave in ways that don't fit their age or their temperament. Most two-year-olds are not going to share their toys happily, and that's that. It doesn't make them a menace to the community. Most kindergartners are not ready to make their own play dates and structure their social lives. They need adult help. A shy child is not going to make a new friend at every church supper or company picnic, but that doesn't make her socially incompetent. A highly energetic boy who talks nonstop is not going to win the popularity contest at a meeting of the chess club, but that doesn't mean he won't find friends. There is nothing wrong with wanting to spend time alone, or having one close friend, or having a dozen buddies, or hanging out all the time with siblings. All of those are fine ways to build a social life as long as they are *chosen by the child*. If the child is miserable with the way things are and feels stuck because he doesn't know how to make friends, resolve conflicts, or be part of a group, then by all means worry just enough to give him a hand and help him out of isolation.

No child—not even a shy or fearful one—heads into the deep waters of peer life without any social abilities. You taught your child to be a social creature in your early relationship with him or her. You kissed and hugged. You played together. You talked to her when you were changing her diaper; you laughed at her antics. You developed a profound attachment with your child. You and your spouse were her first friends, and you will continue to be close throughout her life. I don't know how many times I have heard girls and women say, "My mother is my friend" or even "My mom is my best friend." Many boys say it too. It's important to remember that you gave your child the gift of your friendship early in her life. More important than being your child's friend, though, is the way you taught them to *be* a friend. That is a gift that is completely portable, going with the child into every new interaction.

I'm not saying it's easy to remember those blissful moments of gazing into your infant's eyes when she comes home from fifth grade in tears because the girls started an "I hate Heather" club, or when you find a poem in your tenth grade son's backpack about death, hate, guns, and revenge. But try this experiment. No matter how old your child is now, try to remember that incredible sociability of infants and toddlers—the way they flirt, smile, pull at our heartstrings. Everything you see now has been built on that foundation. It's hard to see that happy little guy you raised inside your touchy fifteen-year-old. But does that little boy emerge when your son is laughing with a group or watching TV with a friend? If so, relax. If, however, you cannot spot *any* sign of your happy youngster in your older child, if he or she cannot take *any* pleasure in friends or in a group or is always isolated, then, as a psychologist, I am worried—and you should be too.

2. Recognize the Crucial Difference Between Friendship and Popularity—Friendship Is More Important

Most of us manage to live a decent life without owning a Porsche or wearing a Versace gown. We don't vacation in Palm Beach and we don't play polo with Tommy Lee Jones. We make our peace with the fact that we are not as beautiful as Nicole Kidman or as personable as Katie Couric or as handsome as Kevin Costner. We become accustomed to the reality that we don't make as much money as Bill Gates and will never hit a tennis ball with the strength of Venus Williams. Life is full of things that we are not, and yet most of us get up in the morning, do a day's work anyway, and take great pleasure in our friends and our families. It may, however, have taken us some time to resign ourselves to a life of ordinary human relationships and achievement. Remember those teenage daydreams of being a movie star or a professional athlete? Remember being embarrassed by your parents' averageness or by your sister's geekiness? Remember hating your looks, wishing for a different body, thinking you sounded stupid compared to an articulate classmate? Remember that guy who was just a regular kid in third grade and is now president of the senior class, captain of the football team, and boyfriend of the head cheerleader?

Children spend a lot of time comparing themselves to others and wishing that they were different. One of the paradoxes of parenting is that we want our children to dream big dreams, yet we also want them to settle for small satisfactions. We want them to aspire to greatness and yet like themselves the way they are. It isn't always easy for them—or us—to accept that they are not the top dogs.

Earlier in this book I quoted a fifth grade boy from California who said that in his classroom there were a king and a queen, a court, and the commoners. I asked him what he was and he said, "A commoner." Was he okay with that? "Yes," he replied. Another girl in the class, however, was not so resigned. She asked, with a trace of bitterness, "How does somebody get to be queen?" I sensed that she was hoping that a royal title was still in the works for her. I hope that by now you know that there are only a few kids who will ever be kings of their classrooms. But we all faced up to that fact before fifth grade, didn't we? We adjusted to it, didn't we? Well, maybe not completely. It can hurt all over again to realize that it is not in the cards for your child, either.

You cannot guarantee that your child will be popular, and it is not your job to make your child popular. In any case, it can't be done. Remember that only 15 percent of children turn out to be "popular" as measured by researchers. Even fewer are popular by the stricter standards of most middle schoolers. Inevitably the gossip and attention in school focus on these popular children. That makes the majority of children believe that only the popular children really have a great life. It induces kids to wish they were cool and many of them work pretty hard at it for a couple of years. Just as adults watch *Entertainment Tonight* and read *People,* adolescents focus on the glamorous few. That's human. We're all fascinated by the beautiful people. But it can make us feel inferior, and that can be a problem.

What our children learn in school, particularly in middle school, is that the beautiful people don't always treat others well. The popular children have gifts, including mature social skills, but they may not always use their power wisely. Alpha males and queen bees are subject to being dethroned, resented, and pushed too early into pseudomature behavior. So eventually, even though they may have yearned for popularity, most kids develop a skepticism about group status. They come to a greater appreciation of having a friend, someone loyal and reliable.

It is friendship that is going to pull your child through the tough times. Your job as a parent is to remember that one fact and hold on to it with conviction when your son or daughter has forgotten it. When your child is miserable because she has been excluded by the popular clique, you should remain confident that she is going to be all right because she has two close friends who stand by her.

Even though it's often popularity that gets all the attention, it is friendship that can provide most of what a child needs from his social life. According to researchers, of the eight essential elements a child receives from other children as he grows up, seven can be found in friendship. These are affection, intimacy, a reliable alliance, instrumental aid, nurturance, companionship, and an enhancement of self-worth. That's a pretty good list.

There is only one thing that a friend cannot provide and that is the sense of inclusion in a group. When that is missing in a child's life, parents, teachers, coaches, and other caring social leaders can create groups, such as church groups and close-knit homerooms, that will provide many children with a sense of inclusion. What parents cannot do—what no one can do—is create a friend for a child. But you can support budding friendships in many different ways.

If you were to go to your twelve-year-old and say, "Look, I want to help you have a good social life. I read a book about it and now I am going to support your friendships with other children," your child would conclude that you had gone nuts. Time and time again, middle school children tell me that their parents are no help whatsoever when it comes to their social lives. In fact, parents are an embarrassment. Anything they do is likely to make things worse.

Children believe this fervently, yet they are wrong. Well, half wrong. When parents go off half-cocked, angrily phoning another parent for calling their child a name, they can indeed make things worse for a child. But parents, and other adults, can also make significant positive contributions to a child's social happiness.

3. Support Children's Friendships

Parents can provide a great deal of encouragement, direction, modeling, and support for their children's friendships. Most of the time this support should be invisible, below a child's radar. Let me give you an example. If you had a twelve-year-old daughter and two boys, ages eight and two, and you had just moved to a new house, your daughter might be frightened to go down the street to scout out the neighborhood. That's understandable. However, every child within sight of your new home has watched your family's moving van unload. Every mother on the street has discussed the fact, gleaned from the real estate broker, that a family with three children is moving in. An eleven-year-old girl in the neighborhood whose best friend moved away last year has hopes that your daughter might become her friend. This is a moment filled with excitement and social expectation. It shouldn't be wasted. Your daughter is sitting in front of the TV (the first thing she unpacked) watching reruns of *Gilligan's Island* on Nickelodeon. You are worried that she will do this for the rest of August.

You're likely to say to your daughter, "Honey, why don't you go out and explore the neighborhood?" She's likely to say, "I'm tired." What she means is that she is scared and doesn't want to look like a geek. Or perhaps she'll tell you the simple truth, like the son of a friend of mine who moved to a new city last year. The mom suggested that her ninth grade son go across the street to introduce himself to the fourteen-year-old boy who lived there. "Mom," he said, "if you go over and introduce yourself, they'll know you're really desperate."

Let's get back to our twelve-year-old newcomer. A parent, sensing the girl's fear and not wanting to push too hard, might say: "Well, would you take your brother? He wants to go out and I don't want him going alone." Your eight-year-old son is dying to find a friend—he's more extroverted than his sister—and he will provide her with a cover. She won't look desperate for friends. Instead, she'll appear mature and competent. She has a job to do—she's baby-sitting her brother. If all goes well, each will find a friend. Often a little behind-the-scenes work or compassionate encouragement is all that's needed to get kids started.

What if your daughter is an only child? You might say, "Well, I'm going to walk around the neighborhood. Will you come with me?" If she refuses, you should go anyway. Then you can return and say, "I met Mrs. Parshegian and she has an eleven-year-old daughter who's going to be in sixth grade too. Her name is Maryann." Better yet, "The Parshegians invited us over for dinner on Saturday and I accepted. You'll meet Maryann then." The connection is made. All your daughter has to do is follow the path that you have created for her.

This may seem painfully obvious to you. But not all families support their children in this way. If you are so absorbed with the details of moving that you don't attend to your child's friendship needs, if you start unpacking boxes and don't come up for air for a week, your daughter might see a lot of *Gilligan's Island* and not meet anyone. Meanwhile, the kids in the neighborhood might already have formed the impression that your family is unfriendly. A social opportunity has been squandered. A study of twelve-year-old children who had moved to new towns found that kids made a social adjustment more quickly if their families socialized with other parents and their children in the new locale. Geographical proximity is the strongest factor in childhood friendships, but that advantage may be lost if a new family does not take the initiative.

Young children, in kindergarten or first grade, may be drawn to one another during the school day but not know how to transfer that friendship into out-of-school hours. Usually it is their mothers who ask the simple question "Would you like to have him over to our house?" If the child says yes, she finds the name and number of the other family and makes the phone call. Virtually all parents, unless they are incredibly hard pressed by their life circumstances, are able to support their child's beginning friendships in these ways.

4. Make Your Child's Friends Welcome in Your Home

When should parents stop encouraging their children's friendships? Never. If your child is going to have friends, he has to have permission from his family to be a host. If he can't be a host, he has to have your blessing to go to other children's houses and know that you approve. He has to feel that you want him to pursue friendships. He also needs a setting in which to cultivate friendships. That is true whether he is in first grade or in college. If you can provide a home like that, so much the better for your child. In your home your son or daughter may feel more secure and may be able to call upon you.

Here is what Ben told me about making friends when he started to attend a private school twenty minutes from his home, across a state line:

"I live in Kentucky and I go to school in Cincinnati. When you tell your friends, 'I live in Kentucky,' it's like a mental block. My parents were always willing to let me have time to develop friendships. It was especially bad in freshman and sophomore year in high school, before anyone drove. My parents were always willing to take me to my friends' houses. If I wanted to do something with a friend, they would take me."

"Did you always have good friends?" I asked Ben. His reply is a lovely illustration of how the opportunity for friendship presents itself.

"I switched schools in fifth grade. There was a little time there in the beginning when I didn't know anyone. This guy who is now one of my best friends called me up to play. My parents took me over to his house. Up till sophomore year he was my only best friend."

As a result of one phone call in fifth grade and his parents' willingness to drive, Ben had a best friend for five years. Of course, if things hadn't worked out on that first meeting, both Ben and the other boy would have moved on. The willingness to host on the part of one family and the willingness to drive on the part of the other created the environment for his best friendship.

Children are hard on furniture. They don't always wipe their feet before entering a home and they inevitably spill Coke and drop pizza cheese-side-down on the rug. I was in Atlanta recently speaking to parents about the subject of friendship and found myself asserting, "You cannot expect your child to feel comfortable bringing friends over to the house if you have a white-rug home."

After my speech, three mothers came up to the podium to confess that they did indeed have white carpets on their floors. What were they to do? I reassured them that what really worried me wasn't their decor but a white-rug attitude. I had a patient in therapy whose mother had had white rugs in the house. Whenever children came over she greeted them at the door with a lot of anxiety about their dirtying the rug. She required them to take their shoes off. Fair enough—many families insist on shoe removal—but this mother did it with a sense of nervousness about what the children might do to her house. Her attitude was extremely off-putting. All the kids who came over felt slightly uncomfortable, and my patient, sensing their discomfort, felt ashamed. So she stopped inviting friends over to her house because she couldn't resolve the parent-friend loyalty issue.

I believe that a child's first loyalty is always to his parents. That is true in all families; it is even true when, as an adolescent, he is acting as if he doesn't need or even like his family. If your fourteen-year-old daughter wants to bring a couple of new friends over to the house, your answer may influence the course of the friendship. If you say no, she may feel embarrassed, she may feel the tug of family loyalty, or she may feel that she has no safe place in which to build her relationships.

When my son, Will, was eight years old, he went to a sleep-over at his friend Matt's house. Only it wasn't Matt's old house, where he had slept many times. It was Matt's new house and Will did not feel secure there yet. At about 10:00 P.M. Will called home and asked to come back home to his own bed. My wife, Theresa, tried to persuade him to stay but he was adamant. So she asked to talk to Matt's mother. Ordinarily if a boy becomes fearful at his friend's house and needs to go home, it might be a problem for the relationship. The host boy might feel insulted, abandoned, or contemptuous and the nervous boy might feel ashamed. The two mothers took care of that. Theresa asked Matt's mother if she would be willing to have the boys come over to our house, even at that late hour. She graciously agreed. The sleep-over moved to a new and "safer" venue and there were no accusations or hurt feelings between the boys. The friendship was shielded from harm by the maternal Mafia, the protection racket that guards so many childhood friendships.

I make it a practice to remember to do three things when my children's friends are in my house: I try to say hello and make contact with them; I find a moment during the play date to tell each child directly that I enjoy his or her presence in the house; and I compliment the child on his or her behavior in front of the parent who picks the child up.

Frequently, when I am busy, the temptation is to say hi and walk on through the room without really acknowledging the presence of new children. And I admit I have done that on more than one occasion. Indeed, I am certain that this is a temptation for many parents. Whenever children are together it is difficult to walk into the middle of the group without feeling out of place or intrusive. The problem is that if you develop the habit of not ever greeting individuals in the group or not spending time with the children in your house, the distance between you and your guests grows wider than would ordinarily be required by their development. If a parent doesn't make a connection with his or her child's friends, the parent soon becomes a servant or a spy. But after you make the connection, leave them on their own. Depending on their age, supervise and join the play as much as necessary, but don't hover.

In my years as a psychotherapist I have heard many adult patients complain about not being able to bring friends home because their parents were unfriendly, drunk, or embarrassing. I have also heard stories about parents who did not allow their children any space or privacy at home when they had friends over or, worst of all, acted like kids themselves. I know of fathers who have supplied marijuana to sons and their friends. I have heard more than one woman patient complain about having a "Mrs. Robinson" sort of mother who acted seductively with the boys that she brought home. When I advise you to make your child's friends welcome, I don't want you to go overboard. Obviously there is a balance here that must be maintained between driving your children's friends off and trying to be excessively chummy.

I learned to compliment children on their behavior as guests in our house from a friend of mine. There is something lovely in having another child's mother say, "Susan was a great guest. We enjoyed having her." Complimenting a child honors the child, dignifies the child's visit, and makes him or her self-conscious of having been a guest all along. Many parents don't realize it, but complimenting a child also makes him or her aware that there is a process of evaluation going on in the host parent. That is to say, if a child is accustomed to hearing a compliment and doesn't receive it one time, then he or she will think about what made it a not-so-good visit.

Let me be perfectly clear: I don't believe it is necessary or dignified to suck up to your child's friends. However, if you truly enjoy the presence of another child in your house, you ought to tell him or her so. If you relate directly to your children's friends, you are augmenting the relationship between the kids and you are letting the visitor know that there is at least one safe environment for her in the world beyond her own home.

Remember that your children have no place else to take their friends. If they can't use your house as home base, then they may go where there is less supervision, where the group rules, where risk taking is more important than friendship building. That's especially problematic for children with fewer social skills and a lower social status in the group. They are vulnerable to being frightened, lonely, manipulated, or exploited. So make their friends welcome. If you can handle it, make their whole gang of friends welcome.

5. Be a Good Friendship Model and Teacher

Most of what your children learn about friendship won't have to be taught to them explicitly. They don't need to go to friendship school. They will follow their social instincts, they will read the cues of other children, they will model themselves after older kids, and they will watch you with your friends. Your son or daughter will model his or her friendship patterns on yours. However, there may be times when you can tell that your child simply does not understand what a dedicated, loyal friendship is about. In those moments you may need to define friendship.

The mother of a sixth grader told me a story about her son, Max. He had a dear friend who did not share her son's love of athletics or athletic ability. The friend, Eric, was an actor who had played roles in a number of community productions. Eric had come to many of Max's soccer games, but Max had not reciprocated by attending any of Eric's performances. It was Max's mother who perceived the inequity in the relationship. One Saturday after a soccer game Max asked his mother for permission to go to the house of a teammate. He felt totally free that night because Eric was busy with his play, so they weren't going to have their usual Saturday-night sleep-over.

"No, you can't go with the team," Max's mom said. "We have other plans tonight."

"Oh, Mom, what?"

"We're going to see Eric's play."

"But, I don't want to go. I'm not interested in a play."

"Oh, I know you're not interested in a play. We're going to support your friend."

"Mom, Eric never even asked me to come. He doesn't care."

The mother wisely didn't get into an argument with Max. She knew that Eric would never insist or even request that Max come, because that would violate a rule of cool for boys. Instead she simply said, "Max, Eric comes to many of your games and you've never seen him in any of his productions. You missed the one last Christmas and the one in May. I don't think it is fair for one friend to see the other play and his friend not to return the favor."

"But Mom . . ."

They went to the theater. Max was genuinely impressed with his friend's acting ability and with his maturity. Watching Eric take a bow gave Max new appreciation for his friend and he was lavish in his praise of Eric when he saw him backstage. "You were great, Eric. You were the best one out there. I never knew you were so good." And Eric didn't hide how happy he was that Max had come.

Later Max acknowledged to his mother that he appreciated her insisting that he see Eric in his play. He had not realized that Eric's interest in drama was equal to his in athletics or that supporting each other's interests was a crucial part of friendship.

6. Provide a Wide Range of Friendship and Group Opportunities

It's important for families to socialize across generations. That means getting together with other families, where some of the time is spent all together and the rest of the time the kids run off and the adults sit around talking. It also means family gatherings with three or even four generations together. This type of activity used to be commonplace, but nowadays life is increasingly segregated by age. I don't know of any research that's been done on this topic, but I have frequently observed that children whose families socialize across generations have a broader social range than young people whose families don't create such opportunities for them. It helps kids to develop a more sophisticated repertoire if they have to converse with people who are their grandparents' ages. You may notice that your children are instinctively more respectful when they are speaking to older people; they may also be more responsible when they have to tend children younger than themselves at a party.

Another benefit of inviting whole families over, instead of always inviting the kids over for play dates and getting baby-sitters for adult nights out, is that it gives shyer kids a chance to make good contacts with their peers. If a family comes over and the adults are talking endlessly about boring adult stuff, the kids are going to bond. Even if they didn't think they had anything in common, they will generally start with the one thing they do have in common: They are both kids and neither one wants to hang out with the adults. From there they will often go on to have a great time together. Parents can help this along by talking to the child beforehand about not spending the whole visit with their nose in a book or engrossed in a one-person computer game. Of course, many shy kids have one or two shy parents, so it also helps children to see their parents overcoming their shyness enough to invite people over.

Give your children practice at talking to people of many different ages. They will benefit from the experience and will remember such times. Indeed, I would venture to say that if you examine your pleasant childhood memories of parties, you will find that you recall occasions that included members of three generations far more vividly than you do the many parties composed just of your agemates. Even those famous early teen make-out parties are a case in point. If everybody else at a party is making out, drinking, or smoking cigarettes, then there is intense pressure to join in. But if one couple sneaks off to kiss behind the barn at a family reunion, or a couple of older boys skulk away to smoke cigarettes, there is more leeway for each person to experiment with these activities at their own pace or not at all.

What I have said about socializing across generations applies just as much, or more, to socializing across cultural or racial lines. As we saw in Chapter 10, children learn a great deal about empathy and the limitations of their own cultural assumptions when they talk with people from other countries or cultures. Recently I was talking about the lives of boys with eight high school students, five Americans and three Israelis. We were discussing why boys have difficulty making close friends and why they are so competitive with one another. The Israeli boys observed that their friendships were better than most American boys' friendships. Their contention forced the American boys to acknowledge that they envied the close friendships of the Israelis. It also caused them to look at one another and ask what prevented them from being closer. They had a conversation about trust, affection, and culture that none of them would have had in a group of boys who were all exactly alike. It forced them to

stretch in a way that developed their inner lives and their social repertoire. Socializing across these lines of difference isn't always comfortable, but sometimes it is this very discomfort that is transformed later
into a memorable experience.

Children who have attended one-room schools and children who
have attended schools in another culture can relate to almost anyone. Indeed, without any doubt the most socially skilled children, on average,
that I have ever met have been children who have attended an international school. But even if you are not intending to move abroad to
widen your child's social experience, you can expose them to a wider variety of people, primarily by broadening your own group of friends and
acquaintances.

7. Make Friends with the Parents of Your Child's Friends (and Enemies)

It is important to know the parents of your child's friends and to reach out
to the parents of your child's enemies as well. Don't wait until you are
hurt and furious to call those other parents. A phone call made in anger is
almost always a disaster. Without exception, such a call makes the other
child's parent defensive. Find an opportunity at back-to-school night, or
on the sidelines of the soccer field, to approach that parent. Even a short,
friendly conversation can make a difference.

One mother I know followed this advice beginning when her son
was very young. She sought out other parents at his preschool, organiz-
ing a group play date for two other moms and their children. The moms
ate shrimp salad and talked while the little ones played in the sprinkler
and sandbox. Over time this group expanded to include dads as well. Before long three sets of parents and some ten children were planing an annual October retreat to a simple family resort in West Virginia for a
weekend of hiking, board games, and family-style meals in the cafateria.
Over the years both the child group and the adult group retained their
friendships, although the cast of characters changed through a divorce
and remarriage, moves, and changes of schools. Through the inevitable
squabbles and changes of status that developed among the children, the
parents stayed friendly, providing a safe and nonjudgmental base for
their sometimes struggling children.

Twenty years after the first tentative play date these families are still spending an October weekend together every year. "Within the next five years, I hope we'll add another generation to this tradition as the kids get married and have kids themselves," my friend says.

8. Empathize with Your Child's Social Pain, but Keep It in Perspective

Children experience pain, and we empathetically experience it with them. When a toddler bumps his head, we say "ouch" at the same time he does. We *feel* it. We feel our children's social pain too—sometimes more than they do, sometimes too much. But empathy is good, isn't it? How can there be too much of it? How can it be possible that we feel the pain *more* than they do?

There are four reasons why we feel the pain more. First, children get over it sooner. They bounce back faster from insults and injuries, the same way they heal faster from a cut hand or a broken leg. Second, they are highly motivated to work things out and reconcile with their friends and their peer groups, as we saw in Chapter 7. Third, they deliberately hand over their pain to us so we can carry it for a while. They know we'll take it, the same way we hold out our hands for whatever they have stuck in their mouths when they are toddlers. Fourth, and most significantly, we suffer from excesses of empathy because we carry around all our own old memories of how we were treated as children and how we felt about it.

Children's moods change rapidly and they bounce back from social situations that might make an adult resentful. As I write I am watching my son, Will, and his friend, Jon, digging in the sand in our backyard. Less than an hour ago they were shouting bitterly at one another over whose turn it was to use the Kroc program on the computer and over who had played it longer. Now they are the best of friends again. The earlier incidents are forgotten.

Forgotten by them, that is. I am still thinking about it, confused momentarily by their shouting, "I hate you! I never want to play with you again!" I was all set to protect my son, or else to teach him a lesson about sharing and friendship, or to step in to rescue a friendship on the brink of disaster. But now there is nothing to do. All is well. Except I'm still all worked up.

I bet you know that feeling. When it happens, we can unwittingly undermine the friendship by imposing our adult standard of justice instead of the child's standard of forgive and forget. Imagine you have a daughter who has just started second grade. She comes home from school one day and says, "Mom, Kathy was mean to me today." You are likely to ask, "What happened, dear?" And then she will tell you some incident of real meanness. You will be sympathetic with her and angry with Kathy, and maybe you will tell your daughter that in your judgment Kathy did something that she shouldn't have done. You may not think to ask if there is any background to the story, such as something provocative your daughter might have done to Kathy. After all, we are wired to empathize first and foremost with our own children. Feeling loved and supported by you, your daughter will leave the kitchen and head outdoors. She will also let go of the incident with Kathy. But you may not be able to do so. Soon you will be pacing around the kitchen fuming and muttering, "I never did like Kathy all that much. And her mother is always trying to be my friend. What a phony!" You start to build up a head of steam on behalf of your daughter.

Your daughter, meanwhile, is outside probably thinking of how much fun she and Kathy are going to have tomorrow. Somehow you overlook the fact that she's running around in the sprinkler, enjoying herself immensely, because in your mind she has been traumatized. This is no accident. Stuck with a pile of tumultuous feelings about her friend, your daughter handed those feelings off to you. Now she can go out and play happily, while you are the one with the overload of feelings. In his book *Playful Parenting*, Larry Cohen calls this the game of emotional hot potato. We are sitting ducks for this game because we are hardwired to empathize with our child. We have to make sure we don't overreact because we were the last ones left with the potato: the anger at Kathy in this case.

Let's add a chapter to the story to see why this can be a problem. When your daughter gets home from school the next day, you are likely to ask her, "How were things in school today?" And she'll say, "Fine." Yet you might not be satisfied. You haven't forgotten that your child was in school with *that girl*. So you'll say, "Were things better with Kathy?" She might be startled, because she has forgotten that she was ever mad at Kathy, but she might notice your special interest in this topic and dredge up every little thing that Kathy—and every other kid—ever did wrong to her. She skips off again to play, but now you are really fuming. "Ha! That's two days in a row!" On the third day, as soon as you pick her up at school, you get right to the point: "Was Kathy mean to you today?"

By now your daughter realizes that you are very wrapped up in being her champion and she starts to spin things. Who doesn't love having an advocate? Making an enemy out of Kathy might be a small price to pay. Unconsciously she senses that you are in a ferocious frame of mind and need to be thrown some red meat, so she'll say, "Yeah, Kathy was mean to me again today." And you'll conclude, "Just as I thought."

I call a dialogue like this *interviewing for pain.* It is a destructive thing to do. At its worst, I have seen this parenting technique taken to extremes, with both parents sitting in front of a child with pencils and notebooks, asking for gory details of every mean word and every shove by each child in a kindergarten class. I think this happens not just because we want to protect our children, even from normal and inevitable conflicts, but because we feel so helpless. We see our child suffering, and we forget that all she needs is a listening ear or a shoulder to cry on. She doesn't need a plaintiff's attorney or a bodyguard. She just needs her parents to *be there*.

As a psychologist, I think it is very important to listen to children and believe what they say. However, I also know that children are the original spin doctors, conveying information in a way that puts themselves in the best light, which often means that they are portrayed as the victim and the other child is cast as the bully. But as we saw in Chapter 6, the actual situation is seldom so unambiguous. Parents, in turn, are prone to distort the information they receive from their kids, asking questions that further distort the truth. As someone who practices what is called narrative therapy, I believe that we live the story we tell ourselves—and others—about the life we're leading. The same principle applies to a child's social life. If you constantly interview your child for pain, your child may begin to hear a story of social suffering emerge from her own mouth. Soon she will begin to believe it and will see herself as a victim. I have seen too many children who see themselves as victims when in fact they are accepted members of a classroom.

Please understand that I am not advising you to disbelieve your children, nor am I saying that you should not be empathic. You have to pay attention and provide a lot of understanding. But try not to get personally involved in your child's social ups and downs. Don't interview for pain, don't nurture resentments, and don't hold on to ancient history. Kids don't. Why should you?

Listen to the wisdom of Raquel, age twelve, who told Catherine, "If you tell your parents something bad about one of your friends, they constantly remember that bad thing about them. I know if I tell my mom one thing that my friend did that was bad, she will always remember it. It's like, 'Oh, yeah, that girl. She was mean to you when you were in second grade.' "

"And in the meantime you've worked it out?" Catherine asked.

"Yes," said Raquel with a theatrical sigh. "All those good things and my mom will just concentrate on that bad thing."

There is a good reason why parents get so confused. Our children's social lives remind us of our own social lives as children and adolescents. We may mix up our own histories and our children's present lives. A son is rejected by a group of boys, and the father adds the boy's hurt to his own deeply buried feelings from similar situations thirty years before.

It is difficult if you have a child whose social style is different from your own. Many times a mother has come up to me after a talk I've given and said, "Dr. Thompson, I'm worried. My son doesn't have many friends. He doesn't get many invitations to parties and he rarely calls anyone else. He just plays with one friend and his brother." Whenever I hear such a question, I immediately ask two in return: "Were you a very social person growing up?" and "Is your husband a very social person?" The answer to the first question is almost invariably "Yes, I had lots of friends and I used to call kids all the time." The answer to the second question is usually "No, my husband doesn't have many friends." At that point the mother usually looks wistfully at me and says, "But I was hoping my son wouldn't turn out like my husband."

It is natural to use oneself as a point of comparison for a child's social life. But remember that there are a great variety of styles among children, some that mirror parents, some that don't. My daughter is vastly more social than my son; I am far more gregarious than my wife. I sometimes reassure my wife about our daughter, saying, "She doesn't seem *too* social to me; she's just very social," and she'll reassure me about our son: "He needs time alone to play with Legos and just relax after school. He was with people all day."

Don't you have those differences in your family? If your child plays alone a lot, that fact is not necessarily evidence of developmental trouble. It is only a problem if your child plays alone because he or she lacks social skills and cannot make the friends he or she wishes to make. You must assess your child's social functioning in comparison to his temperamental preferences and his level of happiness. Does he have the friends, or the alone time, that he needs? Then compare your child to the needs and styles of other children. How different is he from other children? Is he a real loner or just a boy who likes some down time? If you find no problem in those two areas, then being different from the mom's or dad's social style is not evidence of anything worrisome.

After all, children come into our lives to shatter our assumptions, push our buttons, and make us grow. Often they are wildly different from us in numerous ways. We simply cannot expect that our children will have the same social patterns that we followed growing up. The circumstances of their lives may be different than ours, times have changed, and there are somebody else's genes involved in this child. Every once in a while parents give birth to a temperamental replica of themselves, but usually we have to get over the universal, narcissistic wish to have a clone and come to grips with the fact that our children are truly unique. Some parents arrive at that place of wisdom more easily and with more grace than others. It is a help to our children when we get there relatively quickly, so that they don't have to beat us over the head with their differences.

9. Know Where Your Child Stands in the Group

One of the saddest aspects of American suburban life is how isolated our homes and our lives have become. When I drive through the suburbs I see that children no longer have real neighborhoods, and I doubt that the parents in the various houses know one another. We are all so busy these days, and Americans are so affluent in comparison to the way that we used to be, that many of us can afford to live in splendid isolation. Though there may be good reasons why parents may wish for space and privacy, it is important to remember that children rarely wish for this. What any child wants, from a social point of view, is a group of children playing right out in front of his or her house, and especially a group of kids whose parents all know one another.

Because most children don't have safe, kid-filled neighborhoods for free play anymore, lots of your child's friendship activities will happen during play dates. Play dates are a source of anxiety and difficulty for some parents, for various reasons. Some are tired out from all the driving and arranging and having friends over. Others are worried about whether their child is having the right kind of play dates with the right kind of child. Often play dates interfere with a child's time to just hang out or with a family's time together. I don't have any simple answers to these dilemmas.

The basic principle is to look closely at your child's happiness and your own. If your child is lonely, help her spend more time with peers and make sure to spend some time coaching her on being a good friend. If he is socially confident, let him take the lead, but not if it makes you into an exhausted chauffeur and entertainer. If your kids are less confident, help them think about whom they'd like to invite over. If they have a craving for peer contact, don't force them to spend every Sunday afternoon with Grandma and Grandpa (or let them bring a friend along). If they are happy to have some time away from their peers, hanging out at home without a scheduled activity, that's fine. If you are burned out from overscheduling, scale back and set aside regular time for quiet family times, like Friday nights with pizza and a video or pancakes on Sunday morning.

When I wrote about learning to swim at the beginning of this chapter, I didn't mean to give the impression that absolutely every child learns to swim easily. Some have a great deal of trouble mastering this skill or never learn it at all. They may avoid the water entirely or stay in the shallow end splashing around, but they won't dive or swim out to the middle. If your child has trouble learning how to swim, you make a special effort to help overcome the obstacles, or you let it slide, figuring that a kid can get by without knowing how to swim or will learn when he decides it's important to him. But friendships are a different story. They are absolutely necessary. We can't just let things slide if a child really has no friends or if the group turns against him.

Do you know where your child stands in his or her various groups, especially at school? Sixty percent of children are going to be in the popular or accepted categories at school; another 20 percent are classified as ambiguous but are not considered at risk. The 4 percent of neglected children who have made that one vital friend by the end of elementary school are considered to be out of harm's way. That leaves approximately 15 percent who are at risk. They may be lonely at best and mercilessly teased at worst. If your child is one of these kids, you have to face this painful fact and wade in to help before your child drowns.

Before I suggest what to do to help a socially troubled child, I want to say a few words about how to tell if a child is at risk or not. Complaints or lack of complaints are not necessarily the best guide. A child may be in serious distress but keep it hidden. Or a child might yelp loudly at every social scrape and bruise. We have to look deeper. Are they happy? Do they have any friends at all? Are they always left out or rejected? What does the teacher have to say? Hardest of all to face, is your child consistently cruel or mean to others? Those are the children at risk.

There are five things you can do if you suspect your child is in social trouble. First and foremost, you need to talk with your child's teacher. If you think that your child is on the margins of the class, ask the teacher if that is true. It is a painful question to ask and a tough question to answer. Be blunt. Explain your worry and lay out the facts as you see them. It may take this kind of bold appraisal before a teacher will say, "Yes, I'm sorry to say that your child doesn't have a friend in the class," or "Yes, he is teased an awful lot." Parents need to know that teachers are generally very kind, diplomatic, and supportive. It is difficult for them to be direct about a child's terrible social situation unless he is a bully who's causing problems for other children. If a child is a real victim, teachers sometimes hold themselves responsible for fixing the problem and feel defensive if they cannot.

If you are really going to help your child, you have to get past your own fear and the teacher's uneasiness. You can't blame the teacher for the child's social difficulties or demand that the teacher fix it. Instead you should form an alliance with the teacher. This will be a comfort to you both and produce a better result for your child. Listening to a teacher's perspective can be hard if the teacher has anything negative to say about our child. It is especially hard to listen to comments about how a child may be unwittingly contributing to his or her own rejection. It can sound like blaming the victim. But it may help find a solution to the problem, and that's the important thing.

Second, you need to assess whether your child lacks some social skills that other children possess. Is your son young for his age? Does your daughter crash into social situations, demanding this or that, and in the process does she put off other children? Is your child too anxious or too babyish? Is he or she a chronic tattletale? Your teacher has seen your child in action and can provide this diagnostic information, but she will provide it only if you ask for it. If your child does lack the social skills of others her age, then you have to consider whether she should be in a social skills group led by a guidance counselor at school. Many elementary schools and middle schools run such "friendship groups." They can help children to overcome their isolation and develop insight into their social difficulties. Any parent with a rejected or isolated child should also be in touch with school administrators. The principal needs to support a teacher who is trying to make classroom life safer for a rejected child. It might be necessary to organize the teachers into a team to monitor the child's social progress. The principal also needs to consider whether the school environment is socially hostile and whether there needs to be a system-wide response to teasing such as I described in Chapter 11.

Third, you must ask yourself whether your child's troubles are sufficiently serious to warrant some psychotherapy. There are children whose social problems are a symptom of an underlying emotional condition, such as excessive fears and anxiety. Many departments of child psychiatry at major city hospitals run social skills groups for children. Parents in small towns do not usually have medical center options, but there may be a psychologist or psychiatrist who runs such groups.

Fourth, you should consider family therapy. I have found that children with social problems often benefit more from family therapy than from individual therapy. There are several reasons for this. The child's social history may mirror the social problems of a parent. One or the other parent may not be very socially graceful. I once sat in on an interview between a school principal, a teacher, and an upset mother. The mother talked on and on, wringing her hands and expressing extreme anxiety. She interrupted us when we tried to address her daughter's issues and she digressed on many points, fragmenting the conversation. Finally, when I could feel that all of us were beginning to become angry with her, the mother herself exploded, making this admission about herself and her daughter: "Oh, I know why Joy has social problems. It's because I talk too much and I'm not all that good socially!"

We appreciated her honesty, and I thanked her for this insight, because, to be frank, she was absolutely right. It is hard to acknowledge when our own child lacks social skills, but it can be even tougher to admit that our child did not learn all she needed to learn at home. Family therapy can help the entire family to work on its social difficulties. Because it is family therapy, the "loser" label isn't attached to the child. The whole family accepts its part in the child's difficulties. Furthermore, in the context of family therapy, I have heard more socially skilled brothers and sisters—older or younger—make helpful observations to a sibling based on what they have seen in school or in the neighborhood. What might have been a put-down becomes a useful contribution. Indeed, I have heard siblings express tremendous compassion for a brother or sister's social difficulties.

Fifth and finally, if your child is isolated, you should keep up your connections with other parents. It is human nature to want to withdraw when your child has been hurt. However, it is essential that you maintain a network of relatives, cousins, and good people from church and the neighborhood to enhance your child's possibilities for friendship. Extended family members, in particular, are willing to reach out to a socially awkward child because he is a relative. Cousins are often willing to suspend the rules of cool to include a child who is not included at school. There is a feeling of acceptance in one's family that is both nourishing and confidence-building. While such acceptance is important for all children, it can be lifesaving for a child who is rejected at school. Whenever you can create an adult social environment that provides such safety, your child can build on that protection to expand his or her social repertoire.

Many families have vacationed in family camps, such as the Appalachian Mountain Club's Cold Water Camp or the YMCA's Sandy Island Camp in New Hampshire. They will tell you stories of being enveloped at these camps by a social safety net. They will describe some wonderful interactions that occurred between children and teenagers there. Recently I spoke with a woman who was headed back to Sandy Island for a reunion with her friends from that one-week family camp. Her memories of her time there were so rich and happy. Can I guarantee those kinds of memories for every child, including a rejected one? No, of course not, but I know that families can shore up their children's social worlds and exert a positive influence.

If your children are popular or accepted, I am delighted for them. They're going to have an easier childhood than some other kids. However, your work is not done. The daily newspaper provides numerous examples of well-known political or entertainment figures who behave extremely badly toward others. Such misbehavior begins early because such leaders were allowed, when they were young, to use their social influence in any way that they wanted. As we have seen through countless examples in this book, popular and accepted children wield a lot of power over the lives of other children.

Some of that power is pretty destructive, so parents have to take every opportunity to be moral teachers. Many potential bullies can be transformed into positive leaders who actually enhance the moral and social atmosphere of a school or a group of children. Children parade their social cruelty in front of adults all the time: gossip in the car pool ride, exclusion during neighborhood play, snickering at playmates, and rejecting other children. These moments are opportunities for parents. Look for openings in the action to say, "What are the rules of your game? Don't you think it would be fairer if . . . ?" Or if the gossip you overhear in the car sounds totally nasty to you, say, "I wonder whether the other girls in the class talk about you this way. What do you think they say about you?" Sometimes a well-placed question can help children who are absorbed in their nastiness see their own conversation through a moral lens.

Whenever I recommend this approach to mothers they say, "Yes, but it happens so much. If I address it every time I hear it, I'll turn into a nag." Fair enough. But it is my observation that the modern parent often sits and listens to horrible interactions between children and is immobilized by them, or reprimands children in ineffective ways. A parent might say: "That's not nice . . . couldn't you be a little nicer?" or "That's inappropriate" or "You're being mean." These are bloodless responses. To listen to children dissect one another in public and respond with weak words is not helpful. Wait for an opportunity, catch the malefactors in the act, and then label their behavior for what it is: "That's cruel." If it continues, you may have to stop the car and declare, "I have to ask you to stop talking about Isabel that way. It is unbearably cruel and I cannot tolerate it." Your child and your child's classmates should know that you do not condone their horrible treatment of one another and will not collude silently with it. (Stopping the car always gets the attention of children. In our rush-rush-rush society, bringing things to a halt to make a moral point is extremely effective.)

Beyond addressing your child's individual acts of cruelty, you should look for opportunities to turn your child into a social leader. Brownies, Girl Scouts, Boy Scouts, Indian Guides, National Outdoor Leadership Schools, church and synagogue youth groups, and almost any type of community service opportunity are extraordinarily helpful to popular children. These opportunities allow them to turn their attractive traits into concrete acts of generosity toward others. Good leaders show respect toward other people; good leaders use win-win strategies. It is not enough for children to be smart or to be able to reflect on moral problems. Children need to be put into situations where they can practice moral acts—and that is as true of the socially gifted as it is of kids who veer toward the antisocial. We have to give our naturally popular children the moral guidance to make them into true leaders.

We are all tempted at some time or another to regress to middle school and join in our child's popularity wars and friendship battles. Don't do it. Don't let your own social ambitions get out of hand. Whenever parents at a school get together and talk about a "nightmare of a girl" who almost destroyed a whole class through her negative power, they almost invariably start talking about the girl's mother's social ambitions as well. The mother is seen by the other mothers as supporting her daughter's meanness, exclusivity, and power grabbing. You should not attack the popular children and accuse them of being hateful.

When children get overwrought about their social lives, it is tempting for parents, especially fathers, to tease them about it. Don't do it. The pain is real, even if it seems out of proportion to the situation. Teasing just makes the child feel more alone, which actually makes them even more desperate to be liked and accepted by the group. So be compassionate instead of putting a child down. If you want to lose the trust and respect of your eighth grade daughter, there is no faster way to do that than to comment sarcastically about her social struggles. Please don't tease your children about their social problems. No good can come of it.

The vast majority of mothers would never think of mocking their children about their social difficulties. But many of them unwittingly reproduce their child's troubles on the adult level. Mothers talk about a school "situation" and soon begin to gossip about other children and their parents. I know that I have said you need to be aware of your child's social position. I know too that it is often difficult to draw a clear line between the exchange of information and gossip. But there is a line, and it has to do with motivation.

I know a mother of an extremely bright, arrogant, socially inept boy. She waited anxiously for fifth grade to come because that was when the school system in New York State began to offer enriched activities for "gifted and talented" children. Once the choices were made, not only did she feel triumphant that her son was selected for the program, she couldn't stop talking about which other children had (and had not) been picked. She even announced to another mother that she wanted her son to play only with other gifted kids.

When parents start entertaining themselves with stories of what "he did" and "she did," when they get together to plot revenge on the adult level to retaliate for things that have been done to their children, when parents start to exclude other parents because of incidents that have occurred among their children, it is fair to say that they are gossiping in many different forms. When you are gossiping, plotting, and excluding, you are right back in middle school yourself. Don't go back there. You should only have to endure middle school once in your life!

10. Take the Long View

Whether you are the parent of an active toddler whose face lights up at the sight of a day care classmate, a fourth grader who has tearfully broken up with her best friend (again), or a nineteen-year-old who has just told you that he wants to hike the Appalachian Trail on his own, your child's social world permeates your consciousness. And you tend to live in the moment. You wonder if your toddler is normal or precocious; you worry that your fourth grader is too emotional, too volatile, for social succes; you hope that your son will find companions on the road. In the midst of the rough-and-tumble of daily parenting, it's easy to forget that your toddler's sunny temperament may predict a lifetime of happy relationships or that your fourth grader is doing what every fourth grader does. As you watch your son head off into the woods alone, you may not be thinking about his long history of leadership among his peers and his gift for connecting with new people. I hope this book has encouraged you to see your children's social lives from a broader perspective. I hope you understand more about the social forces at work in and around our children. I hope I have reassured you that you are doing a good job as a parent and that your wisdom, compassion, and love will pay off throughout your child's life.

Of course, part of taking the long view involves letting our children go.

Even though I have spent the last year writing and lecturing about the importance of celebrating children's friendships, I still feel twinges of loss when my children choose to be with their friends instead of with me. This is especially true as my daughter heads into high school. After a recent soccer game she played in a nearby town, I had planned, without telling her, to take her out for a special dinner afterward. When I announced this, she burst into angry tears. "I wanted to go on the bus with my friends. Why do you have to spoil everything?"

Once again I had underestimated the power of the group and the hold it has on virtually every child. In this case it was a benevolent hold, a team bonding that I wanted to encourage and support, even though I knew I'd miss her. She went with her friends, and I drove home alone thinking of how bittersweet it can be to celebrate and support our children's friendships as they grow more independent from us and more dependent on their peers. (Lest you think I always give in, there are certainly other times when family gatherings, events, and plans come first, despite the horrified outrage: "But Dad, I can't go to your stupid thing. *Everybody* is going to the mall tonight!")

There will be times when any child, especially a teenager, will extrapolate from the pain of the present moment to his or her entire future. A child who is suffering socially may feel that it is never going to get better, that he or she will always be excluded and alone. At such times it is important that you neither overreact nor underreact. Don't leap into the pool and start to drown alongside your child. It is also essential that you notice when he's in trouble, and act.

I hope this book has given you some guidance about how to recognize when a situation is serious and requires your intervention. I also hope it has reassured you about what is normal so that you can relax the rest of the time—at least a little.

The vast majority of children cope with the rigors of their social lives with humor, resilience, and wisdom. It is a great privilege for us parents to watch our children learn to connect with and love the other people with whom they will share their journey through life. Let's enjoy it.

Notes

Chapter 1

Page 8: The observations about the importance of friendship are based on research contained in a comprehensive review entitled *The Company They Keep: Friendship in Childhood and Adolescence*, edited by W. M. Bukowski, A. F. Newcomb, and W. W. Hartup (Cambridge University Press, 1996). It is the best single volume available reviewing the research on friendship.

Chapter 2

Page 15: Perhaps the best discussion of attachment for the nonprofessional audience is found in John Bowlby, *A Secure Base* (Basic Books, 1988).

Page 16: Alicia Lieberman, *The Emotional Life of the Toddler* (Macmillan, 1993).

Page 16: K. Kerns, "Individual Difference in Friendship Quality," in W. M. Bukowski, A. F. Newcomb, and W. W. Hartup, eds., *The Company They Keep: Friendship in Childhood and Adolescence* (Cambridge University Press, 1996).

Page 16: Stanley Greenspan, *Playground Politics* (Perseus Books, 1994).

Page 17: The critical role of early attachment and its impact on later friendship is reviewed by F. E. About and M. J. Mendelson in "Determinants of Friendship Selection and Quality: Developmental Perspectives," in W. M. Bukowski, A. F. Newcomb, and W. W. Hartup, eds., *The Company They*

Keep: Friendship in Childhood and Adolescence (Cambridge University Press, 1996).

Page 17: Judith Rich Harris, *The Nurture Assumption* (Free Press, 1998).

Page 18: Internal representation of others as good or bad is discussed by Ruth Verschueren and A. Marcoen, "Representations of Self and Socioemotional Competence in Kindergartners: Differential and Combined Effects of Attachment to Mother and Father," *Child Development* 70, 1 (1999).

Page 18: Unmet attachment needs are discussed by John Bowlby in *A Secure Base*.

Page 24: Edward M. Hallowell, *Connect* (Pantheon, 1999).

Page 24: Carollee Howes, *Continuity in Children's Relations with Peers* (Blackwell, 1998).

Page 25: L. Alan Sroufe, "Attachment and the Roots of Competence," *Human Nature* 1 (1978), 50–59.

Page 26: A. Thomas and S. Chess, *Temperament* (Brunner/Mazel, 1977).

Chapter 3

Page 32: The early developmental stages of friendship are discussed by C. Howes in "The Earliest Friends," in W. M. Bukowski, A. F. Newcomb, and W. W. Hartup, eds., *The Company They Keep: Friendship in Childhood and Adolescence* (Cambridge University Press, 1996). Later stages of friendship are discussed by W. W. Hartup in "Behavior Manifestations of Children's Friendships," in T. Berndt and G. Ladd, eds., *Peer Relationships in Childhood* (Wiley and Sons, 1989).

Page 33: D. F. Hay, J. Castle, L. Davies, H. Demetriou, and C. A. Stimson, "Prosocial Action in Very Early Childhood," *Journal of Child Psychology and Psychiatry* 40, 6 (1999), 905–16.

Page 34: Park's research on the length of children's friendships is reviewed by Carollee Howes in "The Earliest Friendships" p. 66ff.

Page 42: Quote from Carollee Howes, "The Earliest Friendships."

Page 44: Berndt and Ladd. Hartup discusses the "play plateau" in "Behavioral Manifestations of Children's Friendships."

Page 52: Mark McConville, *Adolescence* (Jossey-Bass, 1995).

Page 54: Berndt and Ladd.

Chapter 4

Page 61: The centrality of friendship in children's lives is explored in Harry Stack Sullivan's classic *The Interpersonal Theory of Psychiatry* (W. W. Norton, 1953).

Page 62: Reciprocity is discussed by T. Berndt and W. W. Hartup, "The Effects of Friendship Quality and Social Development," in W. M. Bukowski, A. F. Newcomb, and W. W. Hartup, eds., *The Company They Keep* (Cambridge University Press 1996).

Page 66: Hartup has emphasized the importance of the quality, as opposed to the quantity, of friendship in many different articles. He reviews the research in "Cooperation, Close Relationships, and Cognitive Development," in W. M. Bukowski, A. F. Newcomb, and W. W. Hartup, eds., *The Company They Keep: Friendship in Childhood and Adolescence* (Cambridge University Press, 1996).

Page 67: Bukowski, Newcomb, and Hartup.

Chapter 5

Page 77: Rudyard Kipling, from an Ashley Montague discussion in *The Humanization of Man* (World, 1962).

Page 79: For an entertaining introduction to social psychology and the famous early experiments, read R. Cialdini, *Influence: The Psychology of Persuasion* (William Morrow, 1993).

Page 80: Solomon Asch's classic "Studies of Independence and Conformity: A Minority of One Against a Unanimous Majority" appeared originally in *Psychological Monographs* 70 (1956). It is also featured in his definitive text *Social Psychology* (Wiley, 1983).

Page 82: S. Hauser, *Adolescents and Their Families* (Macmillan, 1991).

Page 83: Pioneering teacher Jane Elliott's "Blue Eyes/Brown Eyes" experiment is discussed in Margot S. Strom, *Facing History and Ourselves: Holocaust and Human Behavior* (Facing History and Ourselves National Foundation, 1982).

Page 86: Frans de Waal, *Good Natured: The Origins of Right and Wrong in Humans and Other Animals* (Harvard University Press, 1996).

Page 87: J. Goodall, *The Chimpanzees of Gombe: Patterns of Behavior* (Harvard University Press, 1986).

Page 91: P. G. Zimbardo, "The Pathology of Imprisonment," *Society* 9, 6 (1972).

Page 92: Kurt Lewis, *The Other Side of Psychology* (St. Martin's Press, 1995).

Page 98: Personal communication with Dan Kindlon. Dr. Kindlon says that it is impossible to know exactly how many adolescents engage in delinquent or antisocial acts in adolescence, because they are not all honest in surveys, but he believes that an extremely high percentage of boys do so, and many girls as well.

Page 98: Frans de Waal, *Peacemaking Among Primates* (Harvard University Press, 1989).

Chapter 6

Page 104: P. H. Hawley and T. D. Little, "On Winning Some and Losing Some: A Social Relations Approach to Social Dominance in Toddlers," *Merrill-Palmer Quarterly* 45, 2 (1999): 185–214.

Page 105: This useful term was coined by psychologist Irving L. Janis in *Victims of Groupthink* (Houghton Mifflin, 1972).

Page 107: This passage comes from Phillip Gwynne's young-adult novel *Deadly, Unna?* (Penguin, 1999).

Page 110: J. D. Coie and G. K. Koeppel, "Adapting Interventions to the Problems of Aggressive and Disruptive Rejected Children," in S. R. Asher and J. D. Coie, eds., *Peer Rejection in Childhood* (Cambridge University Press, 1990).

Page 110: K. Dodge, J. D. Coie, G. S. Pettitt, and J. M. Price, "Peer Status and Aggression in Boys' Groups: Developmental and Contextual Analyses," *Child Development* 61 (1990): 1289–1309.

Page 111: S. R. Asher and J. D. Coie, eds., *Peer Rejection in Childhood* (Cambridge University Press, 1990).

Page 122: Educational psychologist A. D. Pellegrini's discussion of rough-and-tumble play appears in A. D. Pellegrini and P. L. Smith, "Physical Activity Play," *Child Development* 69 (1998) pp. 577–598.

Page 122: D. Olweus, "Bullying in School," in R. Huesmann, ed., *Aggressive Behavior* (Plenum, 1994).

Page 125: D. Kindlon and M. G. Thompson, *Raising Cain: Protecting the Emotional Life of Boys* (Ballantine, 1998).

Page 130: A 1999 study by Nadine C. Hoover, Ph.D., and Norman J. Pollard, Ed.D., published by Alfred University in New York in 2000 estimated that 79 percent of National Collegiate Athletic Association athletes had been subjected to hazing during the 1998–1999 school year, with one in five involved in "unacceptable and potentially illegal" activities. Students were "kidnapped, beaten, or tied up and abandoned," the study reported. And half were required to take part in drinking contests or other hazing related to alcohol. Alfred researchers found that hazing activities prevailed in every part of the country, across sports, across divisions, across size of schools, and across gender.

Page 130: The information on the Marquesas Islands comes from Martini, (paper presented at the annual meeting of the Association for Social Anthropology in Oceania, 1994).

Page 131: The aftermath of the University of Vermont's hockey team hazing scandal was discussed in Joe LaPointe, "Trying to Skate Past a Hazing Scandal, *New York Times,* September 21, 2000.

Chapter 7

Page 142: Frans de Waal, *Peacemaking Among Primates* (Harvard University Press, 1989).

Page 156: Ibid.

Chapter 8

Page 160: E. Maccoby, *The Two Sexes* (Harvard University Press, 1998).

Page 161: L. Cohen, *Playful Parenting: A Bold New Way to Nurture Close Connections, Solve Behavior Problems and Encourage Children's Confidence* (Ballantine, 2001).

Page 161: B. Thorne, *Gender Play: Girls and Boys in School* (Rutgers University Press, 1994).

Page 161: L. Cohen, "Hunters and Gatherers in the Classroom," *Independent School* 57 (1997) pp. 28–36.

Page 167: S. Thompson, *Going All the Way* (Hill and Wang, 1995).

Page 167: S. Gilbert, *The Difference Between Girls and Boys* (HarperCollins, 2000).

Page 169: D. Eder's notion of the cycle of popularity is discussed in "Distinguishing Friendship from Acceptance," in W. M. Bukowski, A. F. Newcomb, and W. W. Hartup, eds., *The Company They Keep: Friendship in Childhood and Adolescence* (Cambridge University Press, 1996).

Page 173: C. Beal, *Boys and Girls: The Development of Gender Roles* (McGraw-Hill, 1994).

Page 177: Stephen S. Hall, "The Smart Set," *New York Times Magazine,* June 4, 2000.

Page 178: D. Eder with C. Evans and P. Parker, *School Talk: Gender and Adolescent Culture* (Rutgers University Press, 1995).

Chapter 9

Page 185: N. Darling and B. Dowdy, "Boys More Vulnerable than Girls When Dating Starts," *Journal of Youth and Adolescence* vol. 28 no. 4 (1999).

Page 191: Since 1964 the nonprofit Sexuality Information and Education Council of the United States (SIECUS) has collected and disseminated information and promoted comprehensive education about sexual behavior among young people. Their research can be accessed at www.siecus.org.

Page 192: B. Laursen, "Closeness and Conflict in Adolescent Peer Relationships," in W. M. Bukowski, A. F. Newcomb, and W. W. Hartup, eds., *The Company They Keep: Friendship in Childhood and Adolescence* (Cambridge University Press, 1996).

Chapter 10

Page 201: M. L. Hoffman, *Empathy and Moral Development: Implications for Caring and Justice* (Cambridge University Press, 2000).

Page 202: R. C. Rist, *Desegregated Schools* (Academic Press, 1979).

Page 203: J. G. Deegan, *Children's Friendships in Culturally Diverse Classrooms* (Falmer, 1996).

Page 203: The mission of the Gay Lesbian Straight Educators Network (GLSEN), a national nonprofit research and advocacy group, is to ensure that each member of every school community is valued and respected, regardless of sexual orientation or gender identity. GLSEN material can be accessed at www.glsen.org.

Chapter 11

Page 216: T. Lickona, *Educating for Character* (Bantam, 1991).

Page 216: K. Hays, *Practicing Virtues: Moral Traditions at Quaker and Military Boarding Schools* (University of California Press, 1994).

Page 217: C. Stern-LaRosa and E. H. Bettmann, *Hate Hurts: How Children Learn and Unlearn Prejudice* (Scholastic, 2000).

Page 219: The Council to Combat Teen Cruelty (CCTC) is a comprehensive training program for middle and high school students. For more information go to www.combatcruelty.org.

Page 220: Open Circle's social competency program is based at the Stone Center at Wellesley College. For more information, go to www.wellesely.edu/OpenCircle.

Page 221: V. G. Paley, *You Can't Say You Can't Play* (Harvard University Press, 1992).

Page 222: V. G. Paley, *The Kindness of Children* (Harvard University Press, 1999).

Page 223: C. Garrity et al., *Bullyproofing Your School: A Comprehensive Approach for Elementary Schools* (Sopris West, 1994). The Bullyproofing Your School curriculum, developed in Canada, is intended to address the needs of victims as well as bullies. There are five parts to the program: staff training, student instruction, victim support, intervention with bullies, and working with parents.

Page 226: D. Olweus, "Bullying in School," in R. Huesmann, ed., *Aggressive Behavior* (Plenum, 1994).

Page 228: PeaceBuilders is a community-based violence prevention program conducted in the schools. For more information go to www.peacebuilders. com.

Page 233: B. D. Tatum, *Why Are All the Black Kids Sitting Together in the Cafeteria?* (Basic Books, 1997).

Chapter 12

Page 238: M. Putallaz, P. Costanzo, and T. Klein, "Parental Childhood Social Experiences and Their Effects on Children's Relationships," in S. Duck, ed., *Learning About Relationships* (Sage, 1993).

Page 253: L. Cohen, *Playful Parenting: A Bold New Way to Nurture Close Connections, Solve Behavior Problems and Encourage Children's Confidence* (Ballantine, 2001).

Bibliography

Aboud, F. E., and M. J. Mendelson. "Determinants of Friendship Selection and Quality: Developmental Perspectives." In W. M. Bukowski, A. F. Newcomb, and W. W. Hartup, eds., *The Company They Keep: Friendship in Childhood and Adolescence*. Cambridge University Press, 1996.

Adler, P. A., S. J. Kless, and P. Adler. "Socialization to Gender Roles: Popularity Among Elementary School Boys and Girls." *Sociology of Education* 65 (1992): 169–87.

Agassi, M. *Hands Are Not for Hitting*. Free Spirit, 2000.

Apter, T., and R. Josselson. *Best Friends: The Pleasures and Perils of Girls' and Women's Friendships*. Crown, 1998.

Asch, S. "Effects of Group Pressure on the Modification and Distortion." In E. E. Maccoby, T. M. Newcomb, and E. L. Hartley, eds., *Readings in Social Psychology*. Holt, Rinehart and Winston, 1958.

Asher, S. R. "Recent Advances in the Study of Peer Rejection." In S. R. Asher and J. D. Coie, eds., *Peer Rejection in Childhood*. Cambridge University Press, 1990.

Asher, S. R., and J. D. Coie, eds. *Peer Rejection in Childhood*. Cambridge University Press, 1990.

Asher, S. R., J. G. Parker, and D. L. Walker. "Distinguishing Friendship from Acceptance: Implications for Intervention and Assessment." In W. M. Bukowski, A. F. Newcomb, and W. W. Hartup, eds., *The Company They Keep: Friendship in Childhood and Adolescence*. Cambridge University Press, 1996.

Bagwell, C. L., A. F. Newcomb, and W. M. Bukowski. "Preadolescent Friendship and Peer Rejection as Predictors of Adult Adjustment." *Child Development* 69, 1 (1998): 140–53.

Bagwell, C., J. D. Underwood, R. A. Terry, and J. E. Lochman. "Peer Clique Participation and Social Status in Preadolescence." *Merrill-Palmer Quarterly* 46, 2 (2000): 280–305.

Bank, B. "Effects of National, School, and Gender Cultures on Friendships Among Adolescents in Australia and the United States." *Youth and Society* 25, 4 (1994): 435–56.

Beane, A. L. *The Bully Free Classroom.* Free Spirit, 1999.

Berliner, B. *Adolescence, School Transitions and Prevention: A Research-Based Primer.* Western Regional Center for Drug-Free Schools and Communities, 1993.

Berndt, T. J. "Contributions of Peer Relationships to Children's Development." In T. Berndt and G. Ladd, eds., *Peer Relationships in Child Development.* John Wiley and Sons, 1989.

Berndt, T. J. "Exploring the Effects of Friendship Quality on Social Development." In W. M. Bukowski, A. F. Newcomb, and W. W. Hartup, eds., *The Company They Keep: Friendship in Childhood and Adolescence.* Cambridge University Press, 1996.

Biever, J. L., K. McKenzie, M. Wales-North, and R. Gonzalez. "Stories and Solutions in Psychotherapy with Adolescents." *Adolescence* 30, 118 (1995): 491–99.

Bishop, J. A. "Peer Acceptance and Friendship: An Investigation." *Journal of Early Adolescence* 15, 4 (1995): 476–89.

Bishop, K., and K. Jubala. "By June, Given Shared Experiences, Integrated Classes, and Equal Opportunities, Jaime Will Have a Friend." *Exceptional Children,* 36–40, 1994.

Blum, D. *Sex on the Brain.* Viking, 1997.

Booth, C. L., K. H. Rubin, and L. Rose-Krasnor. "Perceptions of Emotional Support from Mother and Friend in Middle Childhood: Links with Social-Emotional Adaptation and Preschool Attachment Security." *Child Development* 69, 2 (1998): 427–42.

Boulton, M. J. "Concurrent and Longitudinal Relations Between Children's Playground Behavior and Social Preference, Victimization and Bullying." *Child Development* 70, 4 (1999): 944–54.

Bowlby, J. *A Secure Base.* Basic Books, 1988.

Bremdgen, M., T. D. Little, and L. Krappmann. "Rejected Children and Their Friends: A Shared Evaluation of Friendship Quality." *Merrill-Palmer Quarterly* 46, 1 (2000): 45–70.

Brown, B. B. "The Role of Peer Groups in Adolescents' Adjustment to Secondary School." In T. Berndt and G. Ladd, eds., *Peer Relationships in Child Development.* John Wiley and Sons, 1989.

Buhrmester, D. "Need Fulfillment, Interpersonal Competence, and the Developmental Contexts of Early Adolescent Friendship." In W. M. Bukowski, A. F. Newcomb, and W. W. Hartup, eds., *The Company They Keep: Friendship in Childhood and Adolescence.* Cambridge University Press, 1996.

Bukowski, W. M., and B. Hoza. "Popularity and Friendship: Issues in Theory, Measurement and Outcome." In T. Berndt and G. Ladd, eds., *Peer Relationships in Child Development*. John Wiley and Sons, 1989.

Bukowski, W. M., B. Hoza, and M. Boivin. "Popularity, Friendship and Emotional Adjustment During Early Adolescence." In B. Laursen, ed., *Close Friendships in Adolescence*. New Directions in Child Development, no. 60. Jossey-Bass, 1993.

Bukowski, W. M., Newcomb, A. F., and Hartup, W. W., eds. *The Company They Keep: Friendship in Childhood and Adolescence*. Cambridge University Press, 1996.

Bukowski, W. M., and L. K. Sippola. "Friendship and Morality: (How) Are They Related?" In W. M. Bukowski, A. F. Newcomb, and W. W. Hartup, eds., *The Company They Keep: Friendship in Childhood and Adolescence*. Cambridge University Press, 1996.

Bullock, J. R. "Lonely Children." *Young Children* 48 (1993): 53–57.

Burks, V. S., K. A. Dodge, and J. M. Price. "Internal Representational Models of Peers: Implications for the Development of Problematic Behavior." *Developmental Psychology* 35, 3 (1999): 802–10.

Busselli, C. A., and N. File. "Building Trust in Friends." *Young Children* 44, 3 (1989): 70–75.

Caissy, G. A. *Early Adolescence: Understanding the 10 to 15 Year Old.* Insight Books, 1994.

Campbell, J. D. "Soothing the Sting of Rejection." *Learning* 19 (1990): 58–61.

Chen, X., D. Li, Z. Li, B. Li, and M. Liu. "Sociable and Prosocial Dimensions of Social Competence in Chinese Children: Common and Unique Contributions to Social, Academic, and Psychological Adjustment." *Developmental Psychology* 36, 3 (2000): 302–14.

Clausen, J. S. "Adolescent Competence and the Shaping of the Life Course." *American Journal of Sociology* 96, 4 (1991): 805–42.

Cobham, V. E., M. R. Dadds, and S. H. Spence. "Anxious Children and Their Parents: What Do They Expect?" *Journal of Clinical Child Psychology* 28, 2 (1999): 220–31.

Cohen, L. "Hunters and Gatherers in the Classroom." *Independent School* 57 (1997): 28–36.

Cohen, L. *Playful Parenting: A Bold New Way to Nurture Close Connections, Solve Behavior Problems and Encourage Children's Confidence.* Ballantine, 2001.

Coie, J. D., and G. K. Koeppl. "Adapting Intervention to the Problems of Aggressive and Disruptive Rejected Children." In S. R. Asher and J. D. Coie, eds., *Peer Rejection in Childhood*. Cambridge University Press, 1990.

Coie, J. D., and G. K. Krehbiel. "Effects of Academic Tutoring on the Social Status of Low-achieving, Socially Rejected Children." *Child Development* 55 (1981): 1465–78.

Cowie, H., et al. *Cooperation in the Multi-Ethnic Classroom: The Impact of Cooperative Group Work on Social Relationships in Middle Schools.* Fulton, 1994.

Crum, T., J. Warner, and C. Steerman. *The New Conflict Cookbook—A Parent/Teacher Guide for Helping Young People Deal with Anger and Conflict.* AIKI Works, 2000.

Damon, W., and E. Phelps. "Strategic Uses of Peer Learning in Children's Education." In T. Berndt and G. Ladd, eds., *Peer Relationships in Child Development.* John Wiley and Sons, 1989.

de Waal, Frans. *Peacemaking Among Primates.* Harvard University Press, 1989.

de Waal, Frans. *Good Natured: The Origins of Right and Wrong in Humans and Other Animals.* Harvard University Press, 1996.

Deegan, J. *Children's Friendships in Culturally Diverse Classrooms.* Falmer, 1996.

Degirmencioglu, S., et al. "Stability of Adolescent Social Networks Over the School Year." Paper presented at the 60th Biennial Meeting of the Society for Research in Child Development, New Orleans, 1993.

Dodge, K. A., J. D. Coie, G. S. Pettit, and J. M. Price. "Peer Status and Aggression in Boys' Groups: Developmental and Contextual Analyses." *Child Development* 61 (1990): 1289–1309.

Dodge, K. A., G. S. Pettit, and J. E. Bates. "Socialization Mediators of the Relation between Socioeconomic Status and Child Conduct Problems." *Child Development* 65 (1994): 649–65.

Dodge, K. A., and J. M. Price. "On the Relation Between Social Information Processing and Socially Competent Behavior in Early School-Aged Children." *Child Development* 65 (1994): 1385–97.

Doyle, A. B., and D. Markiewicz. "Parents' Interpersonal Relationships and Children's Friendships." In W. M. Bukowski, A. F. Newcomb, and W. W. Hartup, eds., *The Company They Keep: Friendship in Childhood and Adolescence.* Cambridge University Press, 1996.

Eder, D. "The Cycle of Popularity: Interpersonal Relations Among Female Adolescents." *Sociology of Education* 58 (1985): 154–65.

Eder, D., with C. Evans and P. Parker. *School Talk: Gender and Adolescent Culture.* Rutgers University Press, 1995.

Eder, D., and D. Kinney. "The Effect of Middle School Extra-Curricular Activities on Adolescents' Popularity and Peer Status." *Youth and Society* 26, 3 (1995): 298–324.

Eisenberg, N., P. A. Miller, R. Shell, S. McNalley, and C. Shea. "Prosocial Development in Adolescence: A Longitudinal Study." *Developmental Psychology* 27, 5 (1991): 849–57.

Eliade, M. *Rites and Symbols of Initiation.* Translated by W. Trask. Harvill, 1958.

Epstein, J. L. "The Selection of Friends: Changes Across the Grades and in Different School Environments." In T. Berndt and G. Ladd, eds., *Peer Relationships in Child Development*. John Wiley and Sons, 1989.

Evans, M. D. "A Single-Gender Learning Strategy." *Principal* 73 (1993): 52–53.

Fabes, R. A., N. Eisenberg, S. Jones, M. Smith, I. Guthrie, R. Poulin, S. Shepard, and J. Friedman. "Regulation, Emotionality, and Preschoolers' Socially Competent Peer Interactions." *Child Development* 70, 2 (1999): 432–42.

Fasick, F. A. "On the 'Intervention' of Adolescence." *Journal of Early Adolescence* 14, 1 (1994): 6–23.

Feiring, C. "Concepts of Romance in 15-Year-Old Adolescents." *Journal of Research on Adolescence* 6, 2 (1996): 181–200.

Field, T. "American Adolescents Touch Each Other Less and Are More Aggressive Toward Their Peers as Compared with French Adolescents." *Adolescence* 34, 136 (1991): 753–58.

Freeman, J. *Gifted Children Growing Up*. Cassell, 1991.

Friedman, A. J. Todd, and P. W. Kariuki. "Cooperative and Competitive Behavior of Urban and Rural Children in Kenya." *Journal of Cross-Cultural Psychology* 26, 4 (1995): 374–83.

Furman, W. "The Measurement of Friendship Perceptions: Conceptual and Methodological Issues." In W. M. Bukowski, A. F. Newcomb, and W. W. Hartup, eds., *The Company They Keep: Friendship in Childhood and Adolescence*. Cambridge University Press, 1996.

Furman, W., and L. A. Gavin. "Peers' Influence on Adjustment and Development: A View from the Intervention Literature." In T. Berndt and G. Ladd, eds., *Peer Relationships in Child Development*. John Wiley and Sons, 1989.

Galotti, K. M., S. F. Kozberg, and D. Appleman. "Younger and Older Adolescents' Thinking and Commitments." *Journal of Experimental Child Psychology* 50 (1990): 324–39.

Garrity, C., et al. *A Guide to Bully-Proofing*. Sopris West, 1994.

Garrod, A., L. Smulyan, S. Powers, and R. Kilkenny. *Adolescent Portraits*. Allyn and Bacon, 1998.

George, T. P., and D. P. Hartmann. "Friendship Networks of Unpopular, Average, and Popular Children." *Child Development* 67 (1996): 2301–16.

Gerler, E. R., Jr., "The Challenge of Self-Discovery in Early Adolescence." In E. R. Gerler Jr., et al., *The Challenge of Counseling in Middle Schools*. Caps, 1990.

Gilbert, S. *The Difference Between Boys and Girls*. HarperCollins, 2000.

Goldstein, A., R. Sprafkin, N. Gersham, and P. Klein, eds., *Skillstreaming the Adolescent: A Structural Learning Approach to Teaching Prosocial Skills*. Research Press, 1980.

Goodall, J. "The Chimpanzees of Gombe: Patterns of Behavior." Harvard University Press, 1986.

Gore Camerer, M. C. *A Parent's Guide to Coping with Adolescent Friendships: The Three Musketeer Phenomenon.* Thomas, 1996.

Greenbaum, S. "What Can We Do About Schoolyard Bullying." *Principal* 67 (1997): 21–24.

Greenspan, S. *The Growth of the Mind.* Addison-Wesley, 1997.

Greenspan, S., with J. Salmon. *Playground Politics.* Addison-Wesley, 1994.

Gross, M. U. M. "The Pursuit of Excellence or the Search for Intimacy? The Forced-Choice Dilemma of Gifted Youth." *Roeper Review* 11, 4 (1989): 189–94.

Guralnick, M. J. "Family and Child Influences on the Peer-Related Social Competence of Young Children with Developmental Delays." *Mental Retardation and Developmental Disabilities Research Reviews* 5 (1999): 21–29.

Hallowell, Edward M. *Connect: 12 Vital Ties That Open Your Heart, Lengthen Your Life, and Deepen Your Soul.* Pantheon, 1999.

Hanna, N. A., and T. J. Berndt. "Relations Between Friendship, Group Acceptance, and Evaluations of Summer Camp." *Journal of Early Adolescence* 15, 4 (1995): 456–75.

Harris, Judith Rich. *The Nurture Assumption. Why Children Turn Out the Way They Do: Parents Matter Less Than You Think and Peers Matter More.* Free Press, 1998.

Hartup, W. W. "Behavioral Manifestations of Children's Friendships." In T. Berndt and G. Ladd, eds., *Peer Relationships in Child Development.* John Wiley and Sons, 1989.

Hartup, W. W. "Adolescents and Their Friends." In B. Laursen, ed., *Close Friendships in Adolescence.* New Directions in Child Development, no. 60. Jossey-Bass, 1993.

Hartup, W. W. "Cooperation, Close Relationships, and Cognitive Development." In W. M. Bukowski, A. F. Newcomb, and W. W. Hartup, eds., *The Company They Keep: Friendship in Childhood and Adolescence.* Cambridge University Press, 1996.

Hartup, W. W. "The Company They Keep, Friendships and Their Developmental Significance." *Child Development* 67 (1996): 1–13.

Hawley, P. H., and T. D. Little. "On Winning Some and Losing Some: A Social Relations Approach to Social Dominance in Toddlers." *Merrill-Palmer Quarterly* 45, 2 (1999): 185–214.

Hay, D. F., J. Castle, and L. Davies. "Toddlers' Use of Force Against Familiar Peers: A Precursor of Serious Aggression?" *Child Development* 71, 2 (2000): 457–67.

Hay, D. F., J. Castle, L. Davies, H. Demetriou, and C. A. Stimson. "Prosocial Action in Very Early Childhood." *Journal of Child Psychology and Psychiatry* 40, 6 (1999): 905–16.

Hodges, E. V. E., M. Boivin, F. Vitaro, and W. M. Bukowski. "The Power of

Friendship: Protection Against an Escalating Cycle of Peer Victimization." *Developmental Psychology* 35, 1 (1999): 94–101.

Howes, C. "The Earliest Friendships." In W. M. Bukowski, A. F. Newcomb, and W. W. Hartup, eds., *The Company They Keep: Friendship in Childhood and Adolescence*. Cambridge University Press, 1996.

Howes, C. *Continuity in Children's Relations with Peers*. Blackwell, 1998.

Jones, G. P., and M. H. Dembo. "Age and Sex Role Differences in Intimate Friendships During Childhood and Adolescence." *Merrill-Palmer Quarterly* 35, 4 (1989): 445–62.

Jules, V. "Interaction Dynamics of Cooperative Learning Groups in Trinidad's Secondary Schools." *Adolescence* 26, 104 (1991): 931–49.

Kahen, V. J. "Parent-Child Interaction and Children's Peer Relationships: The Differential Contributions of Mothers and Fathers to Children's Dyadic Peer Interactions." Paper presented at the 60th Biennial Meeting of the Society for Research in Child Development, New Orleans, 1993.

Kalkoske, M. S. "Sex Differences in Moral Orientation: Results from an Examination of Concurrent Correlates." Paper presented at the 60th Biennial Meeting of the Society for Research in Child Development, New Orleans, 1993.

Kalof, L. "Sex, Power and Dependency: The Politics of Adolescent Sexuality." *Journal of Youth and Adolescence* 24 (1995): 229–49.

Keise, C. *Sugar and Spice? Bullying in Single-Sex Schools*. Trentham Books, 1992.

Keller, M. "The Development of Moral Responsibility in Friendship." Paper presented at the 1991 Biennial Meeting of the Society for Research in Child Development, Seattle, 1991.

Kemple, K., H. Speranza, and N. Hazen. "Cohesive Discourse and Peer Acceptance: Longitudinal Relations in the Preschool Years." *Merrill-Palmer Quarterly* 38, 3 (1992): 364–81.

Kennedy, J. H. "Determinants of Peer Social Status: Contributions of Physical Appearance, Reputation, and Behavior." *Journal of Youth and Adolescence* 19, 3 (1990): 233–44.

Kerns, K. A. "Individual Differences in Friendship Quality: Links to Child-Mother Attachment." In W. M. Bukowski, A. F. Newcomb, and W. W. Hartup, eds., *The Company They Keep: Friendship in Childhood and Adolescence*. Cambridge University Press, 1996.

Kerr, M., and H. Stattin. "What Parents Know, How They Know It, and Several Forms of Adolescent Adjustment: Further Support for a Reinterpretation of Monitoring." *Developmental Psychology* 36, 3 (2000): 366–80.

Kindlon, D., and M. Thompson *Raising Cain: Protecting the Emotional Life of Boys*. Ballantine, 1999.

Kinney, D. "From Nerds to Normals: The Recovery of Identify Among Adolescents from Middle School to High School." *Sociology of Education* 66 (1993): 21–40.

Kochenderfer, B. J., and G. W. Ladd. "Peer Victimization: Manifestations and Relations to School Adjustment in Kindergarten." *Journal of School Psychology* 34, 3 (1996): 267–83.

Krappmann, L. "Amicitia, Drujba, Shin-yu, Philia, Freundschaft, Friendship: On the Cultural Diversity of a Human Relationship." In W. M. Bukowski, A. F. Newcomb, and W. W. Hartup, eds., *The Company They Keep: Friendship in Childhood and Adolescence*. Cambridge University Press, 1996.

Kupersmidt, J., et al. "Childhood Aggression and Peer Relations in the Context of Family and Neighborhood Factors," *Child Development* 66, 2 (1995): 360–79.

Ladd, G. "Toward a Further Understanding of Peer Relationships and Their Contributions to Child Development." In T. Berndt and G. Ladd, eds., *Peer Relationships in Child Development*. John Wiley and Sons, 1989.

Ladd, G. W., and B. J. Kochenderfer. "Linkages Between Friendship and Adjustment During Early School Transitions." In W. M. Bukowski, A. F. Newcomb, and W. W. Hartup, eds., *The Company They Keep: Friendship in Childhood and Adolescence*. Cambridge University Press, 1996.

Lamb, M. E., and A. Nash. "Infant-Mother Attachment, Sociability, and Peer Competence." In T. Berndt and G. Ladd, eds., *Peer Relationships in Child Development*. John Wiley and Sons, 1989.

Larson, R., and M. H. Richards. "Introduction: The Changing Life Space of Early Adolescence." *Journal of Youth and Adolescence* 18, 6 (1989): 501–9.

Laursen, B. "Closeness and Conflict in Adolescent Peer Relationships: Interdependence with Friends and Romantic Partners." In W. M. Bukowski, A. F. Newcomb, and W. W. Hartup, eds., *The Company They Keep: Friendship in Childhood and Adolescence*. Cambridge University Press, 1996.

Leeming, F. C., W. Dwyer, and D. Oliver, eds. *Issues in Adolescent Sexuality*. Allyn and Bacon, 1996.

Levitt, M. J., N. Guacci-Franco, and J. L. Levitt. "Convoys of Social Support in Childhood and Early Adolescence: Structure and Function." *Developmental Psychology* 29, 5 (1993): 811–18.

Lewis, M., and C. Feiring. "Early Predictors of Childhood Friendships." In T. Berndt and G. Ladd, eds., *Peer Relationships in Child Development*. John Wiley and Sons, 1989.

Lieberman, A. *The Emotional Life of the Toddler.* Macmillan, 1993.

Lieberman, M., A. Doyle, and D. Markiewicz. "Developmental Patterns in Security of Attachment to Mother and Father in Late Childhood and Early Adolescence: Associations with Peer Relations." *Child Development* 70, 1 (1999): 202–13.

Lochman, J. E., J. D. Coie, M. K. Underwood, and R. Terry. "Effectiveness of a Social Relations Intervention Program for Aggressive and Nonaggressive, Rejected Children, *Journal of Consulting and Clinical Psychology* 61, 6 (1993): 1053–58.

Maccoby, E. E. "Gender and Relationships." *American Psychologist* 45, 4 (1990): 513–20.

MacKinnon-Lewis, C., D. Rabiner, and R. Starnes. "Predicting Boys' Social Acceptance and Aggression: The Role of Mother-Child Interactions and Boys' Beliefs About Peers." *Developmental Psychology* 35, 3 (1999): 632–39.

Maran, H. E. *Why Doesn't Anybody Like Me? A Guide to Raising Socially Confident Kids.* William Morrow, 1998.

Matthews, M. W. "Addressing Issues of Peer Rejection in Child-Centered Classrooms." *Early Childhood Education Journal* 24, 2 (1996): 93–97.

McConville, M. *Adolescence: Psychotherapy and the Emergent Self.* Jossey-Bass Publishers, 1995.

Merten, D. "Visibility and Vulnerability: Responses to Rejection by Nonaggressive Junior High School Boys." *Journal of Early Adolescence* 16, 1 (1996): 5–26.

Moller, L. C., S. Hymel, and K. H. Rubin. "Sex Typing in Play and Popularity in Middle Childhood." *Sex Roles* 26, 7/8 (1992): 331–53.

Moss, E., D. Rousseau, P. Parent. D. St-Laurent, and J. Saintonge. "Correlates of Attachment at School Age: Maternal Reported Stress, Mother-Child Interaction, and Behavior Problems." *Child Development* 69, 5 (1998): 1390–1405.

Murphy, K., and B. Schneider. "Coaching Socially Rejected Early Adolescents Regarding Behaviors Used by Peers to Infer Linking: A Dyad-Specific Intervention." *Journal of Early Adolescence* 14, 1 (1994): 83–95.

Newcomb, A. F., and C. L. Bagwell. "The Developmental Significance of Children's Friendship Relations." In W. M. Bukowski, A. F. Newcomb, and W. W. Hartup, eds., *The Company They Keep: Friendship in Childhood and Adolescence.* Cambridge University Press, 1996.

Newcomb, A. F., W. M. Bukowski, and L. Patee. "Children's Peer Relations: A Meta-Analytic Review of Popular, Rejected, Neglected, Controversial and Average Sociometric Status." *Psychological Bulletin* 113, 1 (1993): 99–128.

Oliver, R. L., T. A. Young, and S. M. LaSalle. "Early Lessons in Bullying and Victimization: The Help and Hindrance of Children's Literature." *The School Counselor* 42 (1994): 137–43.

Olweus, D. *Bullying at School: What We Know and What We Can Do.* Blackwell, 1993.

Paley, V. G. *You Can't Say You Can't Play.* Harvard University Press, 1992.

Parke, R., and G. Ladd, eds. *Family-Peer Relations: Modes of Linkage.* Erlbaum, 1992.

Parker, J. G., and S. R. Asher. "Friendship and Friendship Quality in Middle Childhood: Links with Peer Group Acceptance and Feelings of Loneliness and Social Dissatisfaction." *Developmental Psychology* 29, 4 (1993): 611–21.

Parker, J. G., and J. M. Gottman. "Social and Emotional Development in a Relational Context: Friendship Interaction from Early Childhood to Adolescence." In T. Berndt and G. Ladd, eds., *Peer Relationships in Child Development*. John Wiley and Sons, 1989.

Patterson, C. J., J. B. Kupersmidt, and P. C. Griesler. "Children's Perceptions of Self and of Relationships with Others as a Function of Sociometric Status." *Child Development* 61 (1990): 1335–49.

Pepler, D. J., W. M. Craig, and W. L. Roberts. "Observations of Aggressive and Non-aggressive Children on the School Playground." *Merrill-Palmer Quarterly* 44, 1 (1988): 55–76.

Peters, W. *A Class Divided: Then and Now.* Yale University Press, 1987.

Petit, G. S., M. A. Clawson, K. A. Dodge, and J. E. Bates. "Stability and Change in Peer-Rejected Status: The Role of Child Behavior, Parenting, and Family Ecology." *Merrill-Palmer Quarterly* 42, 2 (1996): 267–94.

Ponton, L. *The Sex Lives of Teenagers: Revealing the Secret World of Adolescent Boys and Girls*. Dutton, 2000.

Pope, A. W., and K. L. Bierman. "Predicting Adolescent Peer Problems and Antisocial Activities: The Relative Roles of Aggression and Dysregulation." *Developmental Psychology* 35, 2 (1999): 335–46.

Poulin, F., T. Dishion, and E. Haas. "The Peer Influence Paradox: Friendship Quality and Deviance Training Within Male Adolescent Friendships." *Merrill-Palmer Quarterly* 24, 1 (1999): 42–61.

Price, J. M. "Friendships of Maltreated Children and Adolescents: Contexts for Expressing and Modifying Relationship History." In W. M. Bukowski, A. F. Newcomb, and W. W. Hartup, eds., *The Company They Keep: Friendship in Childhood and Adolescence*. Cambridge University Press, 1996.

Price, J. M., and K. A. Dodge. "Peers' Contributions to Children's Social Maladjustment: Description and Intervention." In T. Berndt and G. Ladd, eds., *Peer Relationships in Child Development*. John Wiley and Sons, 1989.

Quicke, J., and C. Winter. "Best Friends: A Case Study of Girls' Reactions to an Intervention Designed to Foster Collaborative Group Work." *Gender and Education* 7, 3 (1995): 259–81.

Quinn, M. M., A. Jannasch-Pennell, and B. B. Rutherford Jr. "Using Peers as Social Skills Training Agents for Students with Antisocial Behavior." *Preventing School Failure* 39, 4 (1995): 26–31.

Ramsey, P. G. *Making Friends in School: Promoting Peer Relationships in Early Childhood*. Teachers College Press, 1991.

Roberts, W. B., Jr., and D. H. Coursol. "Strategies for Intervention with Childhood and Adolescent Victims of Bullying, Teasing, and Intimidation in School Settings." *Elementary School Guidance and Counseling* 30 (1996): 204–12.

Rodkin, P. C., T. W. Farmer, R. Pearl, and R. Van Acker. "Heterogeneity of

Popular Boys: Antisocial and Pro-social Configurations." *Developmental Psychology* 36, 1 (2000): 14–24.

Roland, E., and E. Munthe, eds. *Bullies: An International Perspective.* Fulton, 1989.

Rowe, D. C. "Families and Peers: Another Look at the Nature-Nurture Question." In T. Berndt and G. Ladd, eds., *Peer Relationships in Child Development.* John Wiley and Sons, 1989.

Sandstrom, M. J., and J. D. Cole. "A Developmental Perspective on Peer Rejection: Mechanisms of Stability and Change." *Child Development* 70, 4 (1999): 955–66.

Scarr, S. "Developmental Theories for the 1990s: Developmental and Individual Differences." *Child Development* 63 (1992): 1–19.

Schmitz, C. C., and J. Galbraith. "Cognitive and Affective Characteristics." In *Managing the Social and Emotional Needs of the Gifted: A Teacher's Survival Guide.* Free Spirit, 1985.

Selman, R. L., and L. Hickey Schultz. "Children's Strategies for Interpersonal Negotiation with Peers: An Interpretive/Empirical Approach to the Study of Social Development." In T. Berndt and G. Ladd, eds., *Peer Relationships in Child Development.* John Wiley and Sons, 1989.

Shakeshaft, C., et al. "Peer Harassment in Schools." *Journal for a Just and Caring Education* 1, 1 (1995): 30–44.

Shantz, C. U., and C. J. Hobart. "Social Conflict and Development: Peers and Siblings." In T. Berndt and G. Ladd, eds., *Peer Relationships in Child Development.* John Wiley and Sons, 1989.

Sherif, M., O. J. Harvey, B. J. White, W. R. Hood, and C. Sherif. *Intergroup Conflict and Cooperation: The Robbers Cave Experiment.* University Book Exchange, 1961.

Shulman, M., and E. Mekler. *Bringing Up a Moral Child.* Addison-Wesley, 1985.

Shulman, S. "Close Friendships in Early and Middle Adolescence: Typology and Friendship Reasoning." In B. Laursen, ed., *Close Friendships in Adolescence.* New Directions in Child Development, no. 60. Jossey-Bass, 1993.

Shulman, S., and W. A. Collins, eds. *Romantic Relationships in Adolescence: Developmental Perspective.* New Directions for Child Development Series, no. 78. Jossey-Bass, 1997.

Skoe, E. E. "Care-Based Moral Reasoning in Male and Female Children." Paper presented at the 60th Biennial Meeting of the Society for Research in Child Development, New Orleans, 1993.

Spradling, V. Y., et al. "Conflict Between Friends During Early Adolescence: Sources, Strategies and Outcomes." Paper presented at the 97th Annual Meeting of the American Psychological Association, New Orleans, 1989.

Steele, H., M. Steele, C. Croft, and P. Fonagy. "Infant-Mother Attachment at One Year Predicts Children's Understanding of Mixed Emotions at Six Years." *Social Development* 8, 2 (1999): 161–76.

Stern-LaRosa, C., and E. H. Bettmann. *Hate Hurts: How Children Learn and Unlearn Prejudice.* Scholastic, 2000.

Suitor, J., and H. Heavis. "Football, Fast Cars, and Cheerleading: Adolescent Gender Norms, 1978–1989." *Adolescence* 30 (1995): 265–72.

Sullivan, H. S. *The Interpersonal Theory of Psychiatry.* W. W. Norton, 1953.

Sutton, J., P. K. Smith, and J. Swettenham. "Bullying and 'Theory of Mind': A Critique of the 'Social Skills Deficit' View of Anti-Social Behaviour." *Social Development* 8, 1 (1999): 117–27.

Swiatek, M. A. "An Empirical Investigation of the Social Coping Strategies Used by Gifted Adolescents." *Gifted Child Quarterly* 39, 3 (1995): 154–61.

Tatar, M. "Parental Views of Popularity and Stress Among Adolescents." *Journal of Adolescence* 18 (1995): 679–86.

Thomas, A., and S. Chess. *Temperament and Development.* Brunner/Mazel, 1997.

Thompson, S. *Going All the Way.* Hill and Wang, 1995.

Thorne, B. *Gender Play: Girls and Boys in School.* Rutgers University Press, 1994.

Turner, P. B. "Sensitivity to Verbally and Physically Harassing Behaviors and Reported Incidents in Junior High/Middle School Students." Master's thesis, Fort Hays State University College of Education, 1995.

Verschueren, K., and A. Marcoen. "Representation of Self and Socioemotional Competence in Kindergartners: Differential and Combined Effects of Attachment to Mother and to Father." *Child Development* 70, 1 (1999): 183–201.

Vitaro, F., R. E. Tremblay, and C. Gagnon. "Peer Rejection from Kindergarten to Grade 2: Outcomes, Correlates, and Prediction." *Merrill-Palmer Quarterly* 38, 3 (1992): 382–400.

Wentzer, K. R., and C. A. Erdley. "Strategies for Making Friends: Relations to Social Behavior and Peer Acceptance in Early Adolescence." *Developmental Psychology* 29, 5 (1993): 819–26.

Weston, D. C., and M. S. Weston. *Playful Parenting: Turning the Dilemma of Discipline into Fun and Games.* Putnam, 1993.

Winnicott, D. W. *Through Paediatrics to Psycho-Analysis.* Basic Books, 1975.

Young, S. K., N. A. Fox, and C. Zahn-Waxler. "The Relations Between Temperament and Empathy in 2-Year-Olds." *Developmental Psychology* 35, 5 (1999): 1189–97.

Youniss, J., and J. Smollar. "Adolescents' Interpersonal Relationships in Social Context." In T. Berndt and G. Ladd, eds., *Peer Relationships in Child Development.* John Wiley and Sons, 1989.

Zarbatany, L., M. Van Brunschot, K. Meadows, and S. Pepper. "Effects of

Friendship and Gender on Peer Group Entry." *Child Development* 67 (1996): 2287–300.

Zimbardo, P. G. "The Pathology of Imprisonment." *Society* 9, 6 (1972): 4–8.

Zisman, P., and V. Wilson. "Table Hopping in the Cafeteria: An Exploration of 'Racial' Integration in Early Adolescent Social Groups." *Anthropology and Education Quarterly* 23 (1992): 199–220.

Index

© J. D. Sloan

Michael Thompson, Ph.D., is a psychologist specializing in children and families, a lecturer, a consultant, and a former seventh-grade teacher. He conducts workshops on social cruelty, childrens' friendships, and boys' development across the United States. He is the author of *Speaking of Boys* and coauthor of the *New York Times* bestseller *Raising Cain*. The father of a daughter and a son, he and his wife live in Arlington, Massachusetts.

Catherine O'Neill Grace is the author of numerous nonfiction books for children and the former editor of *Independent School* magazine. For fifteen years she wrote a column in the *Washington Post* for young readers about health and psychology. She and her husband live in Waltham, Massachusetts.

Lawrence J. Cohen, Ph.D., is a psychologist and the author of *Playful Parenting*. He is also a columnist for the *Boston Globe*. He lives in Brookline, Massachusetts, with his wife and daughter.